Definitive
XSLT
and
XPath

ISBN 0-13-065196-6

90000

9 780130 651969

The Charles F. Goldfarb
Definitive XML Series

Megginson
Structuring XML Documents

McGrath
XML by Example: Building E-commerce Applications

Floyd
Building Web Sites with XML

Morgenthal and la Forge
Enterprise Application Integration with XML and Java

McGrath
XML Processing with Python

Cleaveland
Program Generators with XML and Java

Holman
Definitive XSLT and XPath

Walmsley
Definitive XML Schema

Garshol
Definitive XML Application Development

Goldfarb and Prescod
Charles F. Goldfarb's XML Handbook Fourth Edition

Titles in this series are produced using XML, SGML, and/or XSL. XSL-FO documents are rendered into PDF by the XEP Rendering Engine from RenderX: www.renderx.com

About the Series Author
Charles F. Goldfarb is the father of XML technology. He invented SGML, the Standard Generalized Markup Language on which both XML and HTML are based. You can find him on the Web at: www.xmlbooks.com

About the Series Logo
The rebus is an ancient literary tradition, dating from 16th century Picardy, and is especially appropriate to a series involving fine distinctions between markup and text, metadata and data. The logo is a rebus incorporating the series name within a stylized XML comment declaration.

Definitive
XSLT
and
XPath

G. Ken Holman

Prentice Hall PTR, Upper Saddle River, NJ 07458
www.phptr.com

A Cataloging-in-Publication Data record for this book can be obtained from the Library of Congress.

Editorial/Production Supervisor: *Faye Gemmellaro*
Acquisitions Editor: *Mark L. Taub*
Editorial Assistant: *Sarah Hand*
Marketing Manager: *Bryan Gambrel*
Manufacturing Manager: *Maura Zaldivar*
Cover Design: *Anthony Gemmellaro*
Cover Design Director: *Jerry Votta*
Book Design: *Dmitry Kirsanov*

Excerpts from World Wide Web Consortium documents are included in accordance with the W3C® IPR Document Notice, http://www.w3.org/Consortium/Legal/copyright-documents.html. Copyright © 1994–2001 World Wide Web Consortium (Massachusetts Institute of Technology, Institut National de Recherche en Informatique et en Automatique, Keio University). All Rights Reserved.

Opinions expressed in this book are those of the Author and are not necessarily those of the Publisher or Series Editor.

Series logo by Dmitry Kirsanov and Charles F. Goldfarb, copyright © 2002 Charles F. Goldfarb.

Prentice Hall books are widely used by corporations and government agencies for training, marketing, and resale.

The publisher offers discounts on this book when ordered in bulk quantities. For more information, contact: Corporate Sales Department, Phone: 800–382–3419; Fax: 201–236–7141; Email: corpsales@prenhall.com; or write: Prentice Hall PTR, Corp. Sales Dept., One Lake Street, Upper Saddle River, NJ 07458.

Printed in the United States of America

10 9 8 7 6 5 4 3 2 1

ISBN 0–13–065196–6

Pearson Education LTD.
Pearson Education Australia PTY, Limited
Pearson Education Singapore, Pte. Ltd.
Pearson Education North Asia Ltd.
Pearson Education Canada, Ltd.
Pearson Educación de Mexico, S.A. de C.V.
Pearson Education—Japan
Pearson Education Malaysia, Pte. Ltd.

Overview

Contents

Contents

Contents

Foreword

In just four years, XML has become the universal data interchange format. Thanks to its ability to represent data in any imaginable structure, along with associated metadata, it has been particularly embraced for application integration.

Legacy data can now be represented in an XML document for interchange. The receiving system can then transform that document into one whose structure it understands.

The operative word here is *transform*, and XSLT and XPath are the key technologies that enable transformation:

- XML Path Language (XPath) lets you locate single or multiple pieces of the data and metadata of an XML document.
- Extensible Stylesheet Language Transformations (XSLT) lets you specify how the XPath-located portions of a source document can be transformed into a result document.

The concept — and the reality as well — is extremely powerful. There is very little that can't be specified in this way. But the power comes at a price that presents a unique challenge to a teacher of XSLT, who must discuss five different things at once:

1: the source XML document,
2: the source XPath data model created by parsing it,
3: the XSLT stylesheet containing the XPath location expressions and transformation instructions,
4: the XPath data model that results from executing the stylesheet, and
5: the result document that can be written out from the result XPath data model.

It's also a challenge for a Series Editor needing to develop a book on the subject! It's always difficult to find real experts who can communicate well, but an XSLT book presents additional challenges in both content and presentation.

The content problem is that normal prose writing, which utilizes lots of pronouns and connectors, tends to obscure structure and blur vital distinctions. Unfortunately, some of those distinctions — such as between documents and their XPath data models — can make the difference between really learning XSLT or just learning to "copy and customize" code samples from a book.

Lists, on the other hand, like the ones I've been using, tend to emphasize structure and clarify the relationships between things.

The solution to the content problem was to enlist G. Ken Holman to write the book, for several reasons:

1: He knows the subject as few do. Ken chairs the OASIS XSLT/XPath Conformance Committee and was a member of the W3C group that developed XML.
2: No one has taught the subject more. For his consulting firm, Crane Softwrights, Ken teaches XSLT and XPath personally throughout the world and on Web-casts, and indirectly though licensing his training course, "Practical Transformation Using XSLT and XPath."

3: Ken has developed a unique list-based style for writing about XSLT and XPath that eliminates the problems that normal prose can introduce. *Web Techniques* said "Holman's outline style is surprisingly easy to read. I'd like to see other authors adopt his approach."

XML may let you separate content from presentation, but it takes both to communicate effectively. The solution here was the noted Web designer, Dmitry Kirsanov. After reading the book, he created a book design that fully supports Ken's writing.

The result was *Definitive XSLT and XPath*. It will help you really understand — and master — the power of transforming XML.

Charles F. Goldfarb
Saratoga, CA
December 2001

Acknowledgements

It is an amazing group of people in the W3C XSL Working Group that developed the XSLT Recommendation. Their names are listed at the end of the Recommendation in an informative annex. Of note, I would like to thank James Clark for his many years of generous contribution of ideas, rationale, and working program source code to the markup community. He is the editor of the XSLT 1.0 Recommendation, and co-editor with Steve DeRose of the XPath 1.0 Recommendation. I'm not sure where our community would be today without the work James has contributed over the years.

As I describe in the colophon of this book, the content has been developed over two and a half years of delivering instructor-led tutorials and lectures on XSLT and XPath from before they became finalized Recommendations. I very much appreciate the continuing feedback from students who take the time after their class to help me understand what did and did not work for them regarding how I express the content. Others have volunteered their help and, in particular, I thank Stan Swaren and Dave Pawson for their assistance editing early drafts of the prose version of the introductory chapters they had the chance to review.

The many people participating in the early days of the Mulberry Technologies XSL mail list gave excellent insights through the questions they asked. They helped me understand what needs to be explained from the draft and final Recommendations. I also appreciate the unsolicited assistance from Makoto Murata who supplied a modified script of one I created from ideas posted on the list.

The meticulous editing and the published appearance of the final content of this book was effected by Dmitry Kirsanov, a very talented individual who well understands nuances of markup, of the editing process, and of the impact of publishing choices on the reader. I very much appreciate what I have learned from Dmitry during this effort, and I am more than pleased with his results. Many thanks to his wife Alina for writing the XSLFO stylesheets to bring his vision of my material to fruition.

Thanks also to Roman Kagarlitsky and the team at RenderX for the generous use of their XEP tool to render the book to PostScript according to the XSLFO stylesheets.

This is my first foray into commercial paper-based book publishing, as my prior self-directed publishing accomplishments have been entirely electronic. I thank Charles Goldfarb for his encouragement and guidance during my work, for believing that I could come up with a result worthy of his excellent series, and for choosing Dmitry to bring the end result to life. I also appreciate the assistance of Mark Taub and Faye Gemmellaro for their management of the project at Prentice Hall PTR.

G. Ken Holman
Kars, Ontario, Canada
July 2001

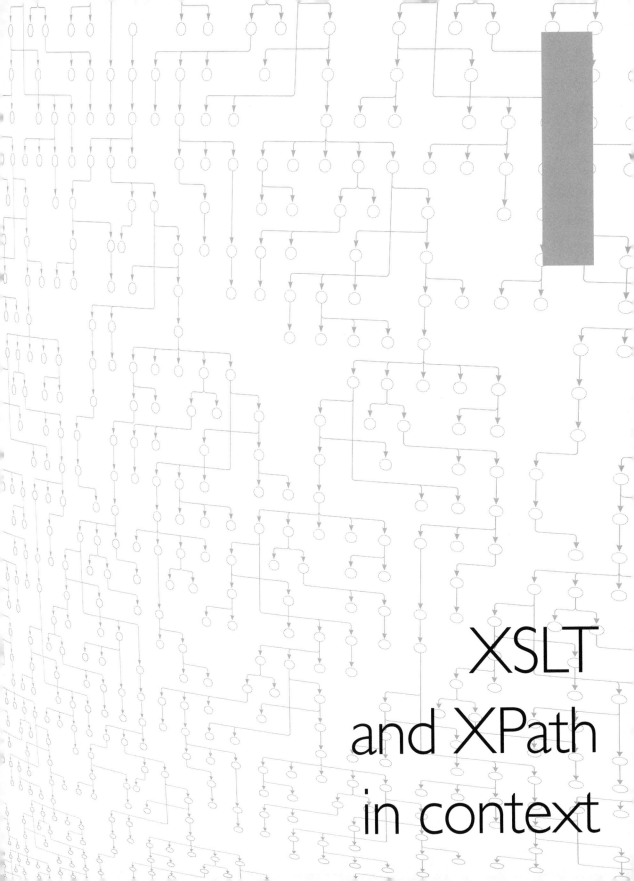

XSLT
and XPath
in context

XSLT and XPath in context

The first step to using XSLT and XPath with confidence is to understand the context of the two W3C Recommendations — Extensible Stylesheet Language Transformations and XML Path Language — within the growing family of Recommendations related to the Extensible Markup Language (XML). Later we will look at detailed examples, but first let's focus on XSLT and XPath in the context of a few of the Recommendations in the XML family and examine how these two Recommendations work together to address separate and distinct functionality required when working with structured information technologies.

Extensible Markup Language (XML). For years, applications and vendors have imposed their constraints on the way we can represent our information. Our data has been created, maintained, stored and archived according to the rules enforced by others. The advent of the Extensible Markup Language (XML) moves the control of our information out of the hands of others and into our *own* by providing two basic facilities.

XML describes rules for structuring our information using embedded markup of our own choice. We can take control of our information representation by creating and using a vocabulary we design of elements and attributes that makes sense for the way we do our business and use our data.

In addition, XML describes a language for formally declaring the vocabularies we use. This allows our tools to constrain the creation of an instance of our information, and allows our users to validate a properly created instance of information against our set of constraints.

Note: An XML "document" is just an instance of well-formed XML. The two terms "document" and "instance" could be used interchangeably, but this book uses the term "instance" to help readers remember that XML isn't just for publication-oriented documents or documentation. With XML we describe a related set of information in a tree-like hierarchical fashion, and gain the benefits of having done so, whether the information captures an invoice-related transaction between computers, or the content of a user manual to be rendered on paper.

XML Path Language (XPath). XPath is both a data model for XML instances and a string syntax for building addresses to the information found in that data model. We use this syntax to specify the locations of information structures or data found in an XML instance when processing that information using XSLT. XPath allows us, from any location in the information, to address any other location or content of the information.

Extensible Stylesheet Language Family (XSLT/XSL). Two vocabularies specified in separate W3C Recommendations provide for the two distinct styling processes of transforming and rendering XML instances.

The Extensible Stylesheet Language Transformations (XSLT) is a templating language used to express how a processor creates a transformed result from an instance of XML information.

The Extensible Stylesheet Language (XSL/XSLFO) is a pagination markup language describing a rendering vocabulary capturing the semantics of formatting information in a paged format for different media. Sometimes this Recommendation is referred to colloquially the as Extensible Stylesheet Language Formatting Objects (XSLFO).

XSLT is normatively referenced by XSL and, historically, used to be defined together in a single W3C Recommendation. While XSLT is primarily for the kinds of transformation required for using XSL, it can also be used for arbitrary transformation requirements.

Namespaces. We use XML namespaces to distinguish information when mixing multiple vocabularies in a single instance. Without namespaces our processes would find the information ambiguous when identical names have been chosen by the modelers of the vocabularies we use.

Stylesheet Association. We declare our choice of an associated stylesheet for an XML instance by embedding the construct described in the Stylesheet Association Recommendation. Recipients and applications can choose to respect or ignore this choice, but the declaration indicates that we have tied some process (typically rendering) to our data, which specifies how to consume or work with our information.

1.1 The XML family of Recommendations

Now let's look at the objectives of these selected Recommendations.

1.1.1 Extensible Markup Language (XML)

Historically, the ways we have expressed, created, stored and transmitted our electronic information have been constrained and controlled by the vendors we choose and the applications we run. Alternatively, we now can express our data in a structured fashion oriented around our perspective of the nature of the information itself rather than the nature of an application's choice of how to represent our information. With Extensible Markup Language (XML), we describe our information using embedded markup of elements, attributes and other constructs in a tree-like structure:

* `http://www.w3.org/TR/REC-xml`

Structuring information

Contrasted to a file format where information identification relies on some proprietary hidden format, predetermined ordering, or some kind of explicit labeling, the tree-like hierarchical structure used in XML infers relationships between information items by the scope of the item (from the start of the item to the end of the item) encompassing other items.

Though trees shape a number of areas of XML, both physically (entities such as files or other resources) and logically (markup), they are not the only means by which relationships are specified. For example, a quantum of information can arbitrarily point or refer to other information elsewhere through use of unique identifiers.

Two basic objectives of representing information hierarchically are satisfied by the XML Recommendation. It provides —

- the concept of well-formedness with a syntax for markup languages;
  - XML defines the concept of well-formedness. Well-formedness dictates the syntax used for markup languages within the content of an instance of information. This is the syntax of using angle brackets ("<" and ">") and the ampersand ("&") to demarcate and identify constituent components of information within a file, a resource or a bound data stream. Users of the Hypertext Markup Language (HTML) will recognize the use of these characters for marking the vocabulary described by the designers of the World Wide Web for web documents;
  - well-formedness applies to both the physical and logical hierarchies present in an XML document. The physical hierarchy being the nesting of physical resources of XML syntax through external general entity referencing, and the logical hierarchy being the nesting of XML markup within each given physical resource;
- a language for specifying how a system can constrain the allowed logical hierarchy of information structures;
  - XML defines the concept of validity with a syntax for a meta-markup language used to specify vocabularies. A Document Type Definition (DTD) describes both the structural schema mandating the user-defined constraints on well-formed information, as well as supplemental data that augments the information set of an XML instance of the vocabulary. The semantics of the constructs in a vocabulary, the meanings behind why the constructs exist, are documented in a DTD using comments or documented elsewhere typically using prose;
  - the HTML vocabulary is formalized through such a DTD, thus declaring the allowed or expected relationships between components of a hypertext document.

The semantics of HTML have been documented describing the expected implemented by user agents interpreting the vocabulary. Presentation conventions for the HTML vocabulary have been prescribed by the W3C just for that vocabulary.

Since there are no formalized semantic description facilities in XML, any XML that is used is not tied to any one particular concept or application. The only purpose of XML is to unambiguously identify and deliver constituent components of data. Therefore, there are no inherent meanings or semantics of any kind associated with element types defined in a document model. As such, there are no defined controls for implying any rendering semantics.

Some new users of XML who have a background in a markup language such as HTML often assume a magical association of semantics with element types of the same names they have been exposed to in their prior work. In a web page, they can safely assume that the construct p will be interpreted as a paragraph or em as emphasized text. However, this interpretation is solely the purview of the designers of HTML and user agents attempting to conform to the World Wide Web Consortium (W3C)-published semantics. Utilizing this vocabulary in arbitrary XML structures, or defining XML constructs that are coincidentally named the same as HTML constructs, in no way automatically ascribes the HTML semantics or presentation conventions. Applications using XML processors to access XML information must be instructed how to interpret and implement the desired semantics.

Note: It is a common misconception that merely the identification of a vocabulary and a component of that vocabulary magically confers the semantics of what the markup is guaranteed to "mean." In fact, the precise definition of the semantics of a stream of XML is exactly whatever any program wants it to mean: the way information is processed defines the semantics of that information. Nothing prevents one from "improperly" processing an purchase order XML stream using invoice information processing logic, the process will assume the semantics are in the information supplied by the user. Until formalisms are created in our XML community for the expression of semantic information, the onus is on the user to ensure semantically "correct" information is supplied to the "proper" processing algorithms.

A formalized document model (the explicit declarations of the individual models of the content components, also known as the document grammar) is but one component used to help describe the semantics of the information found in an instance. While well-formed instances do not have a formal document model, often the names of the constructs used within the instances give hints to the associated semantics. We users of XML do (or should!) capture the semantics of a given vocabulary in prose, whether or not the document model is formalized. This prose can be captured in the formal document model using XML comments to maintain the information with the formal declarations.

Physical hierarchy.   A single collection of information (the XML instance) may be expressed by referencing multiple physical resources (the XML entities) and is not constrained to only being a single document entity. This practice promotes ease of maintenance of subsets of the information.

The main document entity references each external resource using an external parsed general entity construct (see Figure 1–1).

When writing stylesheets, this physical hierarchy need not be known by the stylesheet writer. One can exploit the location of given XML entities in the hierarchy when looking for other unrelated XML entities, but the explicit knowledge of the entities' locations in the user's system is considered not material to the stylesheet writer.

Logical hierarchy.   Every XML instance has a logical hierarchy that is distinct from the physical hierarchy. This nested tree of structures, expressed in a user-defined granularity, is comprised of elements, attributes, text and other XML constructs. Every document entity in the physical hierarchy has a well-formed logical hierarchy.

Figure 1–1   Physical hierarchy of external general entities

Files:

```
adir/a.xml
adir/c.xml
bdir/b.xml
bdir/e.xml
bdir/ddir/d.xml
```

```
<!ENTITY b SYSTEM "../bdir/b.xml">
<!ENTITY c SYSTEM "c.xml">
<!ENTITY d SYSTEM "ddir/d.xml">
<!ENTITY e SYSTEM "e.xml">
```

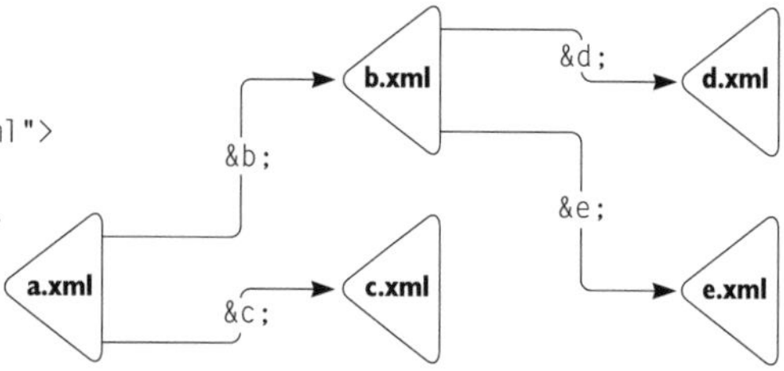

Consider the following well-formed XML instance `purc.xml`:

Example 1–1   A well-formed XML purchase order instance

```
Line 1  <?xml version="1.0"?>
    2   <purchase id="p001">
    3     <customer db="cust123"/>
    4     <product db="prod345">
    5       <amount>23.45</amount>
    6     </product>
    7   </purchase>
```

Observe the content nesting (whitespace has been added only for illustrative purposes). The instance follows the rules for XML markup and the hierarchical model is implicit by the nesting of elements. Pay particular attention to the markup on line 3 for the empty element of type `customer`, with the attribute named `db`. It will be used later in examples throughout this chapter. The customer element is a child of the document element, whose type is `purchase`.

There is an implicit document model for an instance of well-formed XML defined by the mere presence of nested elements found in the information. There is no need to declare this model because the syntax rules governing well-formedness guarantee the information to be seen properly as a hierarchy. As with all hierarchies, there are family-tree-like relationships of parent, child, and sibling constructs relative to each construct found.

Consider the kind of information in the above purchase order and how the nesting of constructs arranges the logical hierarchy (Figure 1–2).

Although the presence of an explicit formal document model with element content model definitions is useful to an XML processor or to a system working with XML instances, those definitions have no impact on the implicit element structure model. This point holds true whether the model is expressed in a DTD or in some other language for defining structural and content schemata. Additional information that supplements the information set of the instance can be expressed in certain attribute declarations, but these have no impact on the element structure model.

Therefore, when writing stylesheets, the content models expressed in any supplied document model declarations are considered not material to the stylesheet writer.

Consider the following valid XML instance `purcdtd.xml`:

Example 1–2   A valid XML purchase order instance

```
Line 1  <?xml version="1.0"?>
     2  <!DOCTYPE purchase [
     3  <!ELEMENT purchase ( customer, product+ )>
     4  <!ATTLIST purchase id ID #REQUIRED>
     5  <!ELEMENT customer EMPTY>
     6  <!ATTLIST customer db CDATA #REQUIRED>
     7  <!ELEMENT product  ( amount )>
     8  <!ATTLIST product  db CDATA #REQUIRED>
     9  <!ELEMENT amount   ( #PCDATA )>
    10  ]>
    11  <purchase id="p001">
    12    <customer db="cust123"/>
    13    <product db="prod345">
    14      <amount>23.45</amount>
    15    </product>
    16  </purchase>
```

See how the information content is no different from the previous example, but in this case an explicit document model using XML 1.0 DTD syntax is included (it could have been included by reference to a separate resource). A processor can confirm that the information represented in XML is well formed. In addition, because the document model exposes the structure and other properties of the document

Figure 1–2   Logical hierarchy of information

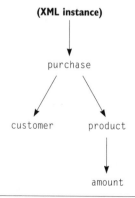

type, a validating processor can validate the information against the model.

Looking at the same `customer` element as before (now on line 12), the document model indicates on line 6 that the `db` attribute is, indeed, required: if the attribute is absent the XML processor can report structural model constraint violation even if the element is otherwise well-formed.

The document model can also provide additional information to supplement the information set of a well-formed XML instance. This supplement is not evident without a document model and is only conveyed in the DTD declarations associated with the instance. An example of such information is on line 4 where the `id` attribute for `purchase` is declared to be of XML type `ID`. Useful for `ID`/`IDREF` processing, `ID`-typed attributes confer element identification uniqueness in an instance. The DTD can also supply defaulted attribute values for attributes that are not specified in the start tags of elements. Supplying attribute information does not affect the well-formed nature of an XML instance.

All content model information found in the declarations associated with an XML instance is not required by the kind of stylesheet processing that is focused on the implicit logical model of the instance. Such processing relies entirely on the model exhibited by the presence of markup in the instance and ignores any model-related declarations in the DTD. In effect, what the logical model could contain does not affect what the actual logical model does contain.

The XML 1.0 Recommendation only describes the behavior required of an XML processor acting on an XML stream, and how it must identify constituent data that is to be provided to an application using the processor. How the processor delivers the content to the application is also not defined in the XML Recommendation. Two examples of approaches to application development using XML are the tree-oriented paradigm using the Document Object Model (DOM) and the stream-oriented paradigm using the Simple API for XML (SAX).

There are no rendition or transformation rules or constructs defined in XML. Even the `xml:space` attribute allowing for the differentiation of whitespace found in a document is not an aspect of rendering but of information description. The author or modeler of an instance is indicating with this reserved attribute (termed "special" in XML 1.0) the nature of the information and how the whitespace found in the information is to be either preserved or handled by a processor in a default fashion.

1.1.2   XML Path Language (XPath)

Assuming that we have structured our information using XML, how are we going to talk about (address) what is inside our documents? Locating information in an XML document is critical to both transforming it and to associating or relating it to other information. When we write stylesheets and use linking languages, we can address components of our information for a processor by our use of the XML Path Language, also called XPath:

- `http://www.w3.org/TR/xpath`

1.1.2.1   *Addressing structured information*

The W3C working group responsible for stylesheets collaborated with the W3C working group responsible for the next generation of hyperlinking to produce XPath as a common base for addressing requirements shared by their respective Recommendations. Both groups extend the core XPath facilities to meet the needs they have in each of their domains: the stylesheet group uses XPath as the core of expressions in XSLT; the linking group uses XPath as the core of expressions in the XPointer Recommendation.

In order to address components you have to know the addressing scheme with which the components are arranged. The basis of addressing XML documents is an abstract data model of interlinked nodes arranged hierarchically echoing the tree-shape of the nested elements in an instance. Nodes of different types make up this hierarchy, each node representing the parsed result of a syntactic structure found in the characters of the XML instance.

This abstraction insulates addressing from the multiple syntactic forms of given XML constructs, allowing us to focus on the information itself and not the actual markup used to represent the information.

Note: We see XML documents as a stream or string of characters that follow the rules of the XML 1.0 Recommendation. Stylesheets do not regard instances in this fashion, and we have to change the way we think of our XML documents in order to successfully work with our information. We need to think of the organization of our information represented by the markup, rather than thinking about the markup itself. This leap of understanding ranks high on the list of key aspects of stylesheet writing I needed to internalize before successfully using this technology.

Using nodes in XPath is very similar to using nodes in the Document Object Model (DOM), though there is a different granularity used by the DOM. In both cases the nodes are presented as a complete tree representing the entire input. For in-memory implementations of both XPath and DOM, this presents a serious capacities question to users of very large XML instances: can your system accommodate the burden of how much memory the node tree requires?

We are given tools to work in the framework provided by the abstraction: a set of data types used to represent values found in the generalization, and a set of functions we use to manipulate and examine those values. The data types include strings, numbers, boolean values and sets of nodes of our information. The functions allow us to cast these values into other data type representations and to return massaged information according to our needs.

1.1.2.2   *Addressing identifies a hierarchical position or positions*

XPath defines common semantics and syntax for addressing XML-expressed information, and bases these primarily on the hierarchical position of components in the tree. This ordering is referred to as document order in XPath, while in other contexts this is often termed either parse order or depth-first order. Alternatively, we can access an arbitrary location in the tree based on points in the tree having unique identifiers.

We convey XPath addresses in a simple and compact non-XML syntax. Remembering we cannot have rich hierarchical markup in attributes, this flat syntax allows us to use an XPath expression as the value of an attribute as in the following examples:

Example 1–3   A simple XPath expression in a `select` attribute

`select="answer"`

The above attribute value expresses all child element nodes named "`answer`" of the current node of the tree in processor's focus.

Example 1–4   An XPath expression in a `match` attribute

`match="question|answer"`

The above attribute value expresses a test of an element being in the union of the element types named "`question`" and "`answer`".

The XPath syntax looks a lot like addressing subdirectories in a file system or as part of a Universal Resource Identifier (URI). Multiple steps in a location path are separated by either one or two oblique "`/`" characters. Filters can be specified to further refine the nature of the components of our information being addressed.

Example 1–5   A multiple step XPath expression in a `select` attribute

`select="question[3]/answer[1]"`

The above example selects only the first "`answer`" element child of the third "`question`" element child of the element in focus.

Example 1–6   A more complex XPath expression in a `select` attribute

`select="id('start')//question[@answer='y']"`

The above example uses an XPath address identifying some descendants of the element in the instance that has the unique identifier with the value "`start`". Those identified are the question elements whose answer attribute is the string equal to the lower-case letter "`y`". The value returned is the set of nodes representing the elements meeting the conditions expressed by the address. The address is used in a `select` attribute, thus the XSLT processor is selecting all of the addressed elements for some kind of processing.

1.1.2.3   *XPath is not a query language*

It is important to remember that addressing information is only one aspect of querying information. Other aspects include a query algebra and query operators that massage intermediate results into a final result. While a few operators and functions are available in XSLT to use values identified in documents, these are oriented to string processing, not to complex operations required by some applications.

1.1.3 Styling structured information

1.1.3.1 *Styling is* transforming *and* formatting *information*

Styling is the rendering of information into a form suitable for consumption by a target audience. Because the audience can change for a given set of information, we often need to apply different styling for that information to obtain dissimilar renderings to meet the needs of each audience. Perhaps some information needs to be rearranged to make more sense for the reader. Perhaps some information needs to be highlighted differently to bring focus to key content.

It is important when we think about styling information to remember that two distinct processes are involved, not just one. First, we must transform the information from the organization used when it was created into the organization needed for consumption. Second, when rendering we must express the aspects of the appearance of the reorganized information, whatever the target medium.

Consider the flow of information as a streaming process where information is created upstream and processed or consumed downstream. Upstream, in the early stages, we should be expressing the information abstractly, thus preventing any early binding of concrete or final-form concepts. Midstream, or even downstream, we can exploit the information as long as it remains flexible and abstract. Late binding of the information to a final form can be based on the target use of the final product; by delaying this binding until late in the process, we preserve the original information for exploitation for other purposes along the way.

It is a common but misdirected practice to model information based on how you plan to use it downstream. It does not matter if your target is a presentation-oriented structure, for example, or a structure that is appropriate for another markup-based system. Modeling practice should focus on both the business reasons and inherent relationships existing in the semantics behind the information being described (as such the vocabularies are then content-oriented). For example, emphasized text is often confused with a particular format in which it is rendered. Where we could model information using a b element type for eventual rendering in a bold face, we would be better off modeling the information using an emph element type. In this way we capture the reason for marking up information (that it is emphasized from surrounding information), and we do not lock the downstream targets into only using a bold face for rendering.

Many times the midstream or downstream processes need only rearrange, re-label or synthesize the information for a target purpose and never apply any semantics of style for rendering purposes. Transformation tasks stand alone in such cases, meeting the processing needs without introducing rendering issues.

One caveat regarding modeling content-oriented information is that there are applications where the content-orientation is, indeed, presentation-oriented. Consider book publishing where the abstract content is based on presentational semantics. This is meaningful because there is no abstraction beyond the appearance or presentation of the content.

Consider the customer information in Example 1–1. A web user agent doesn't know how to render an element named <customer>. The HTML vocabulary used to render the customer information could be as follows:

Example 1–7   HTML rendering semantics markup for example

```
Line 1   <p>From: <i>(Customer Reference) <b>cust123</b></i>
     2   </p>
```

The rendering result would then be as in Figure 1–3, with the rendering user agent interpreting the markup for italics and boldface presentation semantics.

The figure illustrates these two distinct styling steps: *transforming* the instance of the XML vocabulary into a new instance according to a vocabulary of rendering semantics; and *formatting* the instance of the rendering vocabulary in the user agent.

Two W3C Recommendations

To meet these two distinct processes in a detached (yet related) fashion, the W3C Working Group responsible for the Extensible Stylesheet Language (XSL) split the original drafts of their work into two separate Recommendations: one for transforming information and the other for rendering information.

The XSL Transformations (XSLT) Recommendation describes a vocabulary recognized by an XSLT processor to transform information from an organization in the source file into a different organization suitable for continued downstream processing.

The Extensible Stylesheet Language (XSL) Recommendation describes a vocabulary recognized by a rendering agent to reify abstract expressions of format into a particular medium of presentation. XSL normatively includes XSLT and historically both Recommendations were expressed in a single document.

Both XSLT and XSL are endorsed by members of WSSSL, an association of researchers and developers passionate about the application of markup technologies in today's information technology infrastructure.

1.1.4 Extensible Stylesheet Language (XSL)

XSL describes formatting and flow semantics for paginated presentation that can be expressed using an XML vocabulary of elements and attributes:

- `http://www.w3.org/TR/WD-xsl`

Figure 1–3   HTML rendering for example

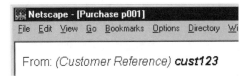

1.1.4.1   *Formatting and flow semantics vocabulary*

This hierarchical vocabulary captures formatting semantics for rendering textual and graphic information in different media in a paginated form. A rendering agent is responsible for interpreting an instance of the vocabulary for a given medium to reify a final result.

This is no different in concept and architecture than using HTML and Cascading Stylesheets (CSS) as a hierarchical vocabulary and formatting properties for rendering a set of information in a web browser. Such user agents are not pagination-oriented and effectively have an infinite page length. Indeed, the printed paged output from a browser of an HTML page is often less than satisfactory.

In essence, we are transforming our XML documents into a final display form by transforming instances of our XML vocabularies into instances of a particular rendering vocabulary that expresses the formatting semantics of our desired result. Our choice of vocabulary must be able to express the nature of the formatting we want accomplished. We can choose to transform our information to a combination of HTML and CSS for web browsers and can choose an alternate transformation of XSL for paginated display (be that paginated to a screen, to paper, or perhaps even aurally using sound).

1.1.4.2   *Target of transformation*

When using the XSL vocabulary as the rendering language, the objective for a stylesheet writer is to convert an XML instance of some arbitrary XML vocabulary into an instance of the formatting semantics vocabulary. The result of transformation cannot contain any user-defined vocabulary construct (e.g.: an "address", "customer identifier", or "purchase order number" construct) because the rendering agent would not know what to do with constructs labeled with these foreign, unknown identifiers.

Consider again the two examples: HTML for rendering on a single page infinite length in a web browser window, and XSL for rendering on multiple separated pages on a screen, on paper or audibly. In both cases, the rendering agents only understand the vocabulary expressing their respective formatting semantics and wouldn't know what to do with alien element types defined by the user.

Just as with HTML, a stylesheet writer utilizing XSL for rendering must transform each and every user construct into a rendering construct to direct the rendering agent to produce the desired result. By learning and understanding the semantics behind the constructs of XSL formatting, the stylesheet writer can create an instance of the formatting vocabulary expressing the desired layout of the final result (e.g. area geometry, spacing, font metrics, etc.), with each piece of information in the result coming from either the source data or the stylesheet itself.

Consider once more the customer information in Example 1–1. An XSL rendering agent doesn't know how to render a marked up construct named `<customer>`. The XSL vocabulary used to render the customer information could be as follows:

Example 1–8   XSL rendering semantics markup for example

```
Line 1   <fo:block space-before.optimum="20pt" font-size="20pt">From:
     2   <fo:inline font-style="italic">(Customer Reference)
     3   <fo:inline font-weight="bold">cust123</fo:inline>
     4   </fo:inline>
     5   </fo:block>
```

The rendering result when using the Portable Document Format (PDF) would then be as in Figure 1–4, with an intermediate PDF generation step interpreting the XSL markup for italics and boldface presentation semantics.

The figure again illustrates the two distinctive styling steps: *transforming* the instance of the XML vocabulary into a new instance according to a vocabulary of rendering semantics; and *formatting* the instance of the rendering vocabulary in the user agent.

Figure 1–4   XSL rendering for example

The rendering semantics of much of the XSL vocabulary are device independent, so we can use one set of constructs regardless of the rendering medium. It is the rendering agent's responsibility to interpret these constructs accordingly. In this way, the XSL semantics can be interpreted for print, display, aural or other presentations. There are, indeed, some specialized semantics we can use to influence rendering on particular media, though these are just icing on the cake.

We will look more at the features of the XSL vocabulary in Appendix B, focusing only on general issues we must be mindful of when transforming our information to send to a rendering agent.

1.1.5 Extensible Stylesheet Language Transformations (XSLT)

We all have needs to transform our structured information when it is not appropriately ordered for a purpose other than how it is created. The XSLT 1.0 Recommendation describes a transformation instruction vocabulary of constructs that can be expressed in an XML model of elements and attributes:

- `http://www.w3.org/TR/xslt`

1.1.5.1 *Transformation by example*

We can characterize XSLT from other techniques for transmuting our information by regarding it simply as "Transformation by Example," differentiating many other techniques as "Transformation by Program Logic." This perspective focuses on the distinction that our obligation is not to tell an XSLT processor how to effect the changes we need, rather, we tell an XSLT processor what we want as an end result, and it is the processor's responsibility to do the dirty work.

The XSLT Recommendation gives us, in effect, a templating language. It is a vocabulary for specifying templates that represent "examples of the result." Based on how we instruct the XSLT processor to access the source of the data being transformed, the processor will incrementally build the result by adding the filled-in templates.

We write our stylesheets, or "transformation specifications," primarily with declarative constructs though we can employ imperative techniques (also known as procedural techniques) if and when needed. We assert the desired behavior of the XSLT processor based on conditions found in our source. We supply examples of how each component of our result is formulated and indicate the conditions of the source that trigger which component is next added to our result. Alternatively we can selectively add components to the result on demand.

Note: Many programmers unfairly deride XSLT as not being a good programming language, when in fact it is a templating language and not a programming language at all. The idea of declaratively supplying templates of the result and the matching conditions of source tree nodes to the templates is a very different paradigm than imperative programming. I find by far the most disparaging and vociferous attacks against XSLT are from programmers unable or awkwardly trying to follow an algorithm-based imperative approach to the problem instead of the assertion-based declarative approach inherent in the language design.

XSLT is not a panacea, and there will be many algorithmic situations (particularly in character-level text manipulation) where XSLT is not the appropriate tool to use. Node tree rearrangement, and in particular mixed content processing, can be handled far more easily declaratively in XSLT than in many imperative approaches. This templating approach is ideal for the rearrangement of information for use with XSL formatting semantics. Critics will continue to claim XSLT a "bad" programming language until they stop using it as the incorrect pigeonhole for certain classes of problems.

Where XSLT is similar to other transmutation approaches is that we deal with our information as trees of abstract nodes. We don't deal with the raw markup of our source data. Unlike these other approaches, however, the primary memory management and information manipulation (node traversal and node creation) is handled by the XSLT processor not by the stylesheet writer. This is a significant difference between XSLT and a transformation programming language or interface like the Document Object Model (DOM), where the programmer is responsible for handling the low-level manipulation of information constructs.

Our objective as stylesheet writers is to supply the XSLT processor with enough "templates of the result" that the processor can build the result we desire when triggered by information in our source. Our data file becomes a hierarchy of nodes in our source tree. Our templates become a hierarchy of nodes in our stylesheet tree. The processor is doing the work building the result node tree from nodes in our stylesheet and source trees. We don't have to be programmers manipulating the node trees or serializing the result node tree into our result file. It isn't our responsibility to worry about the angle brackets and ampersands that may be needed in the result markup.

Consider once again the customer information in our example purchase order at Example 1–1. An example of the HTML vocabulary supplied to the XSLT processor to produce the markup in Example 1–7 would be:

Example 1–9   Example XSLT template rule for the HTML vocabulary

```
Line 1   <xsl:template match="customer">
     2     <p><xsl:text>From: </xsl:text>
     3       <i><xsl:text>(Customer Reference) </xsl:text>
     4         <b><xsl:value-of select="@db"/></b></i></p>
     5   </xsl:template>
```

An example of XSL vocabulary supplied to the XSLT processor to produce the markup in Example 1–8 would be:

Example 1–10   Example XSLT template rule for the XSL vocabulary

```
Line 1   <xsl:template match="customer">
     2     <fo:block space-before.optimum="20pt" font-size="20pt">
     3       <xsl:text>From: </xsl:text>
     4       <fo:inline font-style="italic">
     5         <xsl:text>(Customer Reference) </xsl:text>
     6         <fo:inline font-weight="bold">
     7           <xsl:value-of select="@db"/>
     8         </fo:inline></fo:inline></fo:block>
     9   </xsl:template>
```

Comparing both examples above, our practice as stylesheet writers is not different in any way. The templates are different in that they express different vocabularies for the elements and attributes in the result tree of nodes, but our methodology is not different. Each template is the example of the desired result for the given `<customer>` element as expressed in each of two different presentation vocabularies.

Comparing the style shown above in both examples to imperative programming techniques, one can see the XSLT stylesheet writer is not responsible for low-level node manipulation or markup generation. By declaring the nodes to be used in the result tree, one is describing the construction through the use of examples. These templates represent the information we want in the result tree that the processor must effect however it needs to in order that the information in the example be correctly included in the result. The processor only takes what is given as an example and is free to use whatever syntactic constructs it wishes that the downstream processor interpreting the result will use to understand the same information being represented in the template.

XSLT includes constructs which we use to identify and iterate over structures found in the source information. The information being transformed can be traversed in any order needed and as many times as required to produce the desired result. We can visit source information numerous times if the result of transformation requires that information to be present numerous times.

We users of XSLT also don't have the burden of implementing numerous practical algorithms required to present information. XSLT specifies a number of algorithms that are implemented within the processor itself, and have enabled us to engage these algorithms declaratively. High-level functions such as sorting and counting are available to us on demand when we need them. Low-level functions such as memory-management, node manipulation and garbage collection are all integral to the XSLT processor.

This declarative nature of the stylesheet markup makes XSLT so very much more accessible to non-programmers than the imperative nature of procedurally-oriented transformation languages. Writing a stylesheet is as simple as using markup to declare the behavior of the XSLT processor, much like HTML is used to declare the behavior of the web browser to paint information on the screen.

Not all examples of result are fixed monolithic sequences of markup, however, so XSLT includes the ability to conditionally include portions of a template based on testable conditions expressed by the stylesheet writer. Other constructs allow templates to be fragmented and added to the result on demand based on stylesheet logic. Templates can be parameterized to be used in different contexts by being added utilizing different parameter values.

In this way the XSLT accommodates the programmer as well as the non-programmer in that there is sufficient expressiveness in the declarative constructs that they can be used in an imperative fashion. XSLT is (in programming theory) "Turing complete," thus any arbitrarily complex algorithm could (theoretically) be implemented using the constructs available. While there will always be a trade-off between extending the processor to implement something internally and writing an elaborate stylesheet to implement something portably, there is sufficient expressive power to implement some algorithmic business rules and semantic processing in the XSLT constructs.

In short, straightforward and common requirements can be satisfied in a straightforward fashion, while unconventional requirements can be satisfied to an extent as well with some programming-styled effort.

Note: Theory aside, the necessarily verbose XSLT syntax dictated by its declarative nature and use of XML markup makes the coding of some complex algorithms a bit awkward. I have implemented some very complex traversals and content generation with successful results, but with code that could be difficult to maintain (my own valiant, if not always satisfactory, documentation practices notwithstanding).

Users of XSLT often need to maintain large transformation specifications, and many need to tap prior accomplishments when writing stylesheets so they have included a number of constructs supporting the management, maintenance and exploitation of existing stylesheets. Organizations can build libraries of stylesheet components for sharing among their colleagues. Stylesheet writers can tweak the results of a transformation by writing shell specifications that include or import other stylesheets known to solve problems they are addressing. Stylesheet fragments can be written for particular vocabulary fragments; these fragments can subsequently be used in concert, as part of an organization's strategy for common information description in numerous markup models.

I.I.5.2   Not *intended for general purpose XML transformations*

It is important to remember that XSLT is *primarily for transforming XML vocabularies to the XSL formatting vocabulary*. This doesn't preclude us from using XSLT for other transformation requirements, but it does influence the design of the language and it does constrain some of the functionality from being truly general purpose.

For this reason, the specification *cannot* claim XSLT is a general purpose transformation language. However, it is still powerful enough for *all* downstream processing transformation needs within the assumptions of use of the transformation results. XSLT stylesheets are often called XSLT transformation scripts because they can be used in many areas not at all related to stylesheet rendering. Consider an electronic commerce environment where transformation is not used for presentation purposes. In this case, the XSLT processor may transform a source instance, which is based on a particular vocabulary, and deliver the results to a legacy application that expects a different vocabulary as input. In other words, we can use XSLT in a non-rendering situation when it doesn't matter what markup is utilized to represent the content; when only the parsed result of the markup is material.

An example of using such a legacy vocabulary for the XSLT processor would be:

Example 1–11   Example XSLT template rule for a legacy vocabulary

```
Line 1   <xsl:template match ="customer">
     2     <buyer><xsl:value-of select="@db"/></buyer>
     3   </xsl:template>
```

The transformation would then produce the following result acceptable to the legacy application:

Example 1–12   Example legacy vocabulary for customer information

```
<buyer>cust123</buyer>
```

XSLT assumes that results of transformation will be processed by a rendering agent or some other application employing an XML processor as the means to access the information in the result. The information being delivered represents the serialized result of working with the information in XML instance, and if supplied the XML document model definition of information set augmentation, expressed as a tree of nodes. The actual markup within either the source XML instance or within the XSLT stylesheet is, therefore, not considered material to the application and therefore need not be preserved during transformation. All that counts is the result of having processed the output will find the underlying content the input markup represents in the source and stylesheet.

By focusing on this processed result for downstream applications, there is little or no control in an XSLT stylesheet over the actual XML markup constructs found within the input documents, or for the actual XML markup constructs utilized in the resulting output document. This prevents a stylesheet from being aware of such constructs or controlling how such constructs are used. Any transformation requirement that includes "original markup syntax preservation" would not be suited for XSLT transformations.

Note: Is not being able to support "original markup syntax preservation" really a problem? That depends how you regard the original markup syntax used in an XML instance. XML allows you to use various markup techniques to meet identical information representation requirements. If you treat this as merely syntactic sugar for human involvement in the markup process, then it will not be important how information is specifically marked up once it is out of the hands of the human involved. If, however, you are working with transformations where such issues are more than just a sugar coating, and it is necessary to utilize particular constructs based on particular requirements of how the result "looks" in syntactic form, then XSLT will not provide the kind of control you will need.

Therefore, in comparison to imperative languages and interfaces offering the programmer tight control over the markup of the result of transformation, XSLT cannot be considered as general purpose because of the lack of control over the markup. Two examples are that when using XSLT one cannot specify the order of attributes in the start tag of the serialized result tree, nor can one specify the technique by which sensitive markup characters present in #PCDATA content are escaped.

However, if the result of the XSLT transformation is going to be processed by some other processor delivering the information to a browser or application or some other process, the markup of the result is immaterial as long as it is well formed. The process is, indeed, absolutely general purpose in this situation.

1.1.5.3   *Document model and vocabulary independent*

While checking source documents for validity can be very useful for diagnostic purposes, all of the hierarchical relationships of content are based on what is found inside of the instance, not what is found in the document model. The behavior of the stylesheet is specified against the presence of markup in an instance as the *implicit* model, not against the allowed markup prescribed by any *explicit* model. Because of this, an XSLT stylesheet is independent of any Document Type Definition (DTD) content models or other explicit schema that may have been used to constrain the instance at other stages. This is very handy when working with well-formed XML that doesn't have an explicit document model.

If an explicit document model is supplied, certain information such as attribute types and defaulted values enhance the information found in the input documents (the instance's "information set"). Without this supplemental information, the processor can still perform stylesheet processing as long as the absence of the information does not influence the desired results.

Without a reliance on the document model for the instance, we can design a single stylesheet that can process instances of different models. When the models are very similar, much of the stylesheet operates the same way each time and the rest of the stylesheet only processes that which it finds in the source files.

It may be obvious but should be stated for completeness that a given source file can be processed with multiple stylesheets for different purposes. This means, though, that it is possible to successfully process a source file with a stylesheet designed for an entirely different vocabulary. The results will probably be totally inappropriate, but there is nothing inherent to an instance that ties it to a single stylesheet or a set of stylesheets. Stylesheet designers might well consider how their stylesheets could validate input; perhaps issuing error messages when unexpected content arrives. However, this is a matter of practice and not a constraint.

1.1.5.4 *XML source and stylesheet*

The input files to an XSLT processor are one stylesheet file (possibly made up of more than one stylesheet fragment) and one or more input files. The initial input is a single source file. All stylesheet fragments are assimilated before this first source file is processed. The XSLT processor may then access other source files according to the first file's XML content, or at any time under stylesheet control.

All of the inputs must be well-formed (but not necessarily valid) XML documents. This precludes using an HTML file following non-XML markup conventions, but does not rule out processing an Extensible Hypertext Markup Language (XHTML) file as an input. Many users of existing HTML files that are not XML compliant will need to manipulate or transform them; all that is needed to use XSLT for this is a preprocess to convert existing Standard Generalized Markup Language (SGML) markup conventions into XML markup conventions.

XHTML can be created from HTML using a handy free tool on the W3C site: `http://www.w3.org/People/Raggett/tidy/`. This tool corrects whatever improperly coded HTML it can and flags any that it cannot correct. When the output is configured to follow XML markup conventions, the resulting file can be used as an input to the XSLT processor.

Users of other SGML vocabularies and instances may find the SX tool `http://www.jclark.com/sp/sx.htm` in James Clark's SP package `http://www.jclark.com/sp` useful for conversion of SGML instances to XML markup conventions.

1.1.5.5 *Validation unnecessary (but convenient)*

That an XSLT processor need not incorporate a validating XML processor to do its job does not minimize the importance of source validation when developing a stylesheet. Often when working incrementally to develop a stylesheet by working on the test source file and stylesheet algorithm, time can be lost by inadvertently introducing well-formed but invalid source content. Because there is no validation in the XSLT processor, all well-formed source will be processed without errors, producing a result based on the data found. The first reaction of the stylesheet writer is often that a problem has been introduced in the stylesheet logic, when in fact the stylesheet works fine for the intended source data. The real problem is that the source data being used isn't as intended.

Note: Personally, I run a separate post-process source file validation after running the source file through a given stylesheet. While I am examining the results of stylesheet processing, the post process determines whether or not the well-formed file validates against the model to which I'm designing the stylesheet. When anomalies are seen I can check the validation for the possible source of a problem before diagnosing the stylesheet itself.

1.1.5.6   *Multiple source files possible*

The first source file fed to the XSLT processor defines the first abstract tree of nodes the stylesheet uses.

The stylesheet may access arbitrary other source files, or even itself as a source file, to supplement the information found in the primary file. The names of these supplementary resources can be hardwired into the stylesheet, passed to the stylesheet as a parameter, or the stylesheet can find them in the source files.

A separate node tree represents every resource accessed as a source file, each with its own scope of unique node identifiers and global values. When a given resource is identified more than once as a source file, the XSLT processor creates only a single representation for that resource. In this way a stylesheet is guaranteed to work unambiguously with source information.

1.1.5.7   *Stylesheet supplements source*

A given transformation result does not necessarily obtain all of its information from the source files. It is often (almost always) necessary to supplement the source with boilerplate or other hardwired information. The stylesheet can add any arbitrary information to the result tree as it builds the result tree from information found in the source trees.

A stylesheet can be the synthesis of the primary file and any number of supplemental files that are included or imported by the main file. This provides powerful mechanisms for sharing and exploiting fragments of stylesheets in different scenarios.

The stylesheet is processed entirely before processing begins on the source file. This allows the stylesheet to be compiled in certain environments, since there is nothing in the source file that can possibly impact on the definition of the transformation as expressed in the stylesheet. This restriction means, however, that one cannot control the construction of the stylesheet by detecting conditions in the source file.

1.1.5.8   *Extensible language design supplements processing*

The "X" in XSLT stands for "Extensible" for a reason: built-in standardized facilities are available for accessing non-standard functionality requested by a stylesheet writer that may or may not be available in the XSLT processor interpreting the stylesheet. A conforming processor may or may not support such extensions and is only obliged to accommodate error and fallback processing in such a way that a stylesheet writer can reconcile the behavior if needed.

An XSLT processor can implement extension instructions, functions, serialization conventions and sorting schemes that provide functionality beyond what is defined in XSLT, all accessed through standardized facilities. The processor must accept a stylesheet attempting to invoke the non-standard functionality, but this is easily accommodated by adhering to the standardized language facilities.

A stylesheet writer must not rely on any extension facilities if the XSLT processor being used for the stylesheet is not known or is outside of the stylesheet writer's control. If an end-user base utilizes different brands of XSLT processors, and the stylesheet needs to be portable across all processors, only the standardized facilities can be used.

Standardized presence-testing and fallback facilities can be used by the stylesheet writer to accommodate the ability of a processor to act on extension facilities used in the stylesheet.

1.1.5.9   *Abstract structure result*

In the same way our stylesheets are insulated from the markup of our source files, our stylesheets are insulated from the markup of our result.

We do not focus on the markup of the file to be produced by the XSLT processor; rather, we create a result tree of abstract nodes, which is similar to the tree of abstract nodes of our input information. Our examples of transformation (converted to nodes from our stylesheet) are added to the result hierarchy as nodes, not as markup. Our objective as XSLT transformation writers is to create a result node tree that may or may not be serialized externally as markup syntax.

The XSLT processor is not obliged to externalize the result tree if the processor is integral to some process interpreting the result tree for other purposes. For example, an XSL rendering agent may embed an XSLT processor for interpreting the inputs to produce the intermediate hierarchy of XSL rendering vocabulary to be reified in a given medium. In such cases, serializing the intermediate tree in markup is not material to the process of rendering (though having the option to serialize the hierarchy is a useful diagnostic tool).

The stylesheet writer has little or no control over the constructs chosen by the XSLT processor for serializing the result tree. There are some behaviors the stylesheet can request of the processor, though the processor is not obliged to respect the requests. The stylesheet can request a particular output method be used for the serialization and, if supported, the processor guarantees the final result complies with the lexical requirements of that method.

Note: It is possible to coerce the XSLT processor to violate the markup rules through certain stylesheet controls that I personally avoid using at all costs. For every XML and HTML instance construct (not including the document model markup constructs) there are proper XSLT methodologies to follow, though not always as compact as coercing the processor.

The abstract nature of the node trees representing the input source and stylesheet instances and the hands-off nature of serializing the abstract result node tree are the primary reasons that source tree original markup syntax preservation cannot be supported.

The design of the language does, however, support the serialization of the result tree in such a way as not to require the XSLT processor to maintain the result tree in the abstract form. For example, the processor can instantly serialize the start of an element as soon as any of the content of the element is defined. There is no need to maintain, nor is there any ability in the stylesheet to add to, the start of an element once the stylesheet begins supplying the element's content.

The XSLT 1.0 Recommendation defines three output methods for lexically reifying the abstract result tree as serialized syntax: XML markup conventions, HTML markup conventions, and simple text conventions. An XSLT processor can be extended to support custom serialization methods for specialized needs.

1.1.5.10   *Result-tree-oriented objective*

This result abstraction impacts how we design our stylesheets. We have to always remember that the result of transformation is created in result parse order, thus allowing the XSLT processor to immediately serialize the result without maintaining the result for later purposes.

The examples of transformation that we include in our stylesheet already represent examples of the nodes that we want added to the result tree, but we must ensure these examples are triggered to be added to the result tree in result parse order, otherwise we will not get the desired result.

We can peruse and traverse our source files in any predictable order we need to produce the result, but we can only produce the result tree once and then only in result tree parse order. It is often difficult to change traditional perspectives of transformation that focus on the source tree, yet we must look at XSLT transformations focused on the result tree.

The predictable orders we traverse the source trees are not restricted to only source tree parse order (also called document order). Information in the source trees can be ignored or selectively processed. The order of the result tree dictates the order in which we must access our source trees.

Note: I personally found this required orientation difficult to internalize, having been focused on the creation of my source information long before addressing issues of transforming the sources to different results. Understanding this orientation is key to quickly producing results using XSLT.

It is not, however, an XSLT processor implementation constraint to serially produce the result tree. This is an important distinction in the language design that supports parallelism. An XSLT processor supporting parallelism can simultaneously produce portions of the result tree provided only that the end result is created as if it were produced serially.

1.1.6 Namespaces

To successfully use and distinguish element types in our instances as being from given vocabularies, the Namespaces in XML Recommendation gives us means to preface our element type names to make them unique. The Recommendation and the following widely-read discussion document describe the precepts for using this technique:

- `http://www.w3.org/TR/REC-xml-names`
- `http://www.megginson.com/docs/namespaces/namespace-questions.html`

New practices are being developed where namespaces may be used for resource discovery, though this is not an aspect of the original definition in any way. It is a widespread misconception that resource discovery or resource placement is part of the original definition, that users must somehow find or place some kind of document model or schema or some other structure through the use of namespaces, though this is not in any way described by the Recommendation.

1.1.6.1 *Vocabulary distinction*

It would be unreasonable to mandate that all document models have mutually unique element type names. We design our document models with our own business requirements and our own naming conventions; so do other users. A W3C working group developing vocabularies has its own conventions and requirements; so do other committees. An XML-based application knowing that an instance is using element types from only a single vocabulary can easily distinguish all elements by the name, since each element type is declared in the model by its name.

But what happens when we need to create an XML instance that contains element types and attributes from more than one vocabulary? If all such constructs are uniquely named then we could guess the vocabulary for a given construct by its name. But if the same name is used in more than one vocabulary, we need a technique to avoid ambiguity. Using cryptically compressed or unmanageably elongated element type names to guarantee uniqueness would make XML difficult to use and would only delay the problem to the point that these weakened naming conventions would still eventually result in vocabulary collisions.

Note: Enter the dreaded namespaces: a Recommendation undeserving of its sullied reputation. This is a powerful, yet very simple technique for disambiguating element type names in vocabularies. Perhaps the reputation spread from those unfamiliar with the requirements being satisfied. Perhaps concerns were spread by those who made assumptions about the values used in namespace declarations. As unjustified as it is, evoking namespaces unnecessarily (and unfortunately) strikes fear in many people. It is my goal to help the reader understand that not only are namespaces easy to define and easy to use, but that they are easy to understand and are not nearly as complex as others have believed.

The Namespaces in XML Recommendation describes a technique for exploiting the established uniqueness of Uniform Resource Identifier (URI) values under the purview of the Internet Engineering Task Force (IETF). We users of the Internet accept the authority of the registrar of Internet domain names to allot unique values to organizations, and it is in our best interest to not arrogate or usurp values allotted to others as our own. We can, therefore, assume a published URI value belongs to the owner of the domain used as the basis of the value. The value is not a Uniform Resource Locator (URL), which is a URI that identifies an actual addressed location on the Internet; rather, the URI is being used merely as a unique string value.

To set the stage for how these URI values are used, consider an example of two vocabularies that could easily be used together in an XML instance: the Scalable Vector Graphics (SVG) vocabulary and the Mathematical Markup Language (MathML). In SVG the set element type is used to scope a value for reference by descendent elements. In MathML the <set> element type defines a set in the mathematical sense of a collection.

Remembering that names in XML follow rigid lexical constraints, we pick out of thin air a prefix we use to distinguish each element type from each respective vocabulary. The prefix we choose is *not* mandated by any organization or any authority; in our instances we get to choose any prefix we wish. We should, however, make the prefix meaningful or we will obfuscate our information, so let's choose in this example to distinguish the two element types as `<svg:set>` and `<math:set>`. Note that making the prefix short is a common convention supporting human legibility, and using the colon ":" separating the prefix from the rest of the name is prescribed by the Namespaces in XML Recommendation. Since namespaces were developed after the release of the XML 1.0 Recommendation, this naming technique satisfies the constraints that are imposed.

While we are talking about names, let's not forget that some Recommendations utilize the XML name lexical construct for other purposes, such as naming facilities that may be available to a processor. We get to use this namespace prefix we've chosen on these names to guarantee uniqueness, just as we have done on the names used to indicate element types.

1.1.6.2   *URI value association*

But having the prefix is not enough because we haven't yet guaranteed global identity or singularity by a short string of name characters; to do so we must associate the prefix with a globally unique URI before we use that prefix. Note that we are unable to use a URI directly as a prefix because the lexical constraints on a URI are looser than those of an XML name; the invalid XML name characters in a URI would cause an XML processor to balk.

We assert the association between a namespace prefix and a namespace URI by using a namespace declaration attribute as in the following examples:

- `xmlns:svg="http://www.w3.org/2000/svg-20000629"`
- `xmlns:math="http://www.w3.org/1998/Math/MathML"`

Other examples of valid namespace declarations that use other protocols to dictate different lexical rules for the string values are:

- `xmlns:ex="urn:isbn:1-894049:example"`
- `xmlns:ex2="ftp://ftp.CraneSoftwrights.com/ns/example2"`

As noted earlier, the prefix we choose is arbitrary and can be any lexically valid XML name. The prefix may be discarded by the namespace-aware processor, and is immaterial to the application using the names; it is only a syntactic shortcut to get at the associated URI. The associated URI supplants the prefix in the internal representation of the name value and the application can distinguish the names by the new composite name that would have been illegal in XML markup. There is no convention for documenting a namespace-qualified name using its associated URI, but one way to perceive the uniqueness is to consider our example as it might be internally represented by an application:

- `<{http://www.w3.org/2000/svg-20000629}set>`
- `<{http://www.w3.org/1998/Math/MathML}set>`

The specification of a URI instead of a URL means that the namespace-aware processor will never look at the URI as a URL to accomplish its work. There never need be any resource available at the URI used in a namespace declaration. The URI is just a string and its value is used only as a string and the fact that there may or may not be any resource at the URL identified by the URI is immaterial to namespace processing. The URI does not identify the location of a schema, or a DTD or any file whatsoever when used by a namespace aware processor.

Note: Perhaps some of the confusion regarding namespaces is rooted in the overloading of the namespace URI by some Recommendations. These Recommendations require that the URI represent a URL where a particular resource is located, fetched, and utilized to some purpose. This behavior is outside the scope of namespaces and is mandated solely by the Recommendations that require it.

Practice has, however, indicated an end-user-friendly convention regarding the URI used in namespace declarations. The W3C has placed a documentation file at every URL represented by a namespace URI. Requesting the resource at the URL returns an HTML document discussing the namespace being referenced, perhaps a few pointer documents to specifications or user help information, and any other piece of helpful information deemed suitable for the public consumption. This convention should help clear up many misperceptions about the URI being used to obtain some kind of machine-readable resource or schema, though it will not dispel the misperception that there needs to be some resource of some kind at the URL represented by a namespace URI.

So now a namespace-aware XML processor can unambiguously distinguish an element's type as being from a particular vocabulary by knowing the URI associated with the vocabulary. Our choice of prefix is arbitrary and of no relevance, but at least satisfies uniqueness in non-namespace-aware XML processors. The URI we have associated with the prefix used in a namespace-qualified XML name (also called a QName) informs the aware processor of the identity of the name. Our choice of prefix is used and can then discarded by the processor, while the URI persists and is the basis of namespace-aware processing. We have achieved uniqueness and identity in our element type names and other XML names in a succinct legible fashion without violating the lexical naming rules of XML.

One last comment regarding URI strings addresses a common question "if one isn't required to go to the web to get a resource at the address specified, why use a web address at all?" Certainly, seeing the `http:` protocol identifier at the start of a URI string gives the impression one must somehow dereference some information. However, the protocol identifier performs two functions, only one of which is indicating how to communicate information over the Internet. The other function of the protocol identifier is the governance of the lexical constraints over the rest of the string that makes up the address portion of the URI for that protocol. The use of `http:` indicates the first portion of the remainder of the string is a domain name, thus ensuring uniqueness between registered users of different domain names. Uniqueness for the remainder of the string is then the responsibility of the registered domain name users.

1.1.6.3   *Namespaces in XSLT and XSL*

Namespaces identify different constructs for the processors interpreting XSL formatting specifications and XSLT stylesheets.

An XSL rendering agent responsible for interpreting an XSL formatting specification will recognize those constructs identified with the `http://www.w3.org/1999/XSL/Format` namespace. Note that the year value used in this URI value is not used as a version indictor; rather, the W3C convention for assigning namespace URI values incorporates the year the value was assigned to the working group.

An XSLT processor responsible for interpreting an XSLT stylesheet recognizes instructions and named system properties using the `http://www.w3.org/1999/XSL/Transform` namespace. An XSLT processor will not recognize using an archaic value for working draft specifications of XSLT.

XSLT use namespace-qualified names to identify extensions that implement non-standardized facilities. A number of kinds of extensions can be defined in XSLT including functions, instructions, serialization methods, sort methods and system properties. We will review the use of extension namespaces in each of these areas where the standardized facilities themselves are described.

The XT XSLT processor written by James Clark is an example of a processor implementing extension facilities. XT uses the `http://www.jclark.com/xt` namespace to identify the extension constructs it implements. Remembering that this is a URI and not a URL, you will not find any kind of resource or file when using this value as a URL.

We also use our own namespaces in an XSLT stylesheet for two other purposes. We need to specify the namespaces of the elements and attributes of our result if the process interpreting the result relies on the vocabulary to be identified. Furthermore, our own non-default namespaces distinguish internal XSLT objects we include in our stylesheets. Each of these will be detailed later where such constructs are described.

1.1.7   Stylesheet association

When we wish to associate with our information one or more preferred or suitable stylesheet resources geared to process that information, the W3C Stylesheet Association Recommendation describes the syntax and semantics for a construct we can add to our XML documents:

- `http://www.w3.org/TR/xml-stylesheet`

1.1.7.1   *Relating documents to stylesheets*

XML information in its authored form is often not organized in an appropriate ordering for consumption. A stylesheet association processing instruction is used at the start of an XML document to indicate to the recipient which stylesheet resources are to be used when reading the contents of that document.

The recipient is not obliged to use the resources referenced and can choose to examine the XML using any stylesheet or transformation process they desire by ignoring the preferences stated within. Some XML applications ignore the stylesheet association instruction entirely, while others choose to steadfastly respect the instruction without giving any control to the recipient. A flexible application will let the recipient choose how they wish to view the content of the document.

This specification adopts the same semantics of the `<LINK>` construct defined in the HTML 4.0 Recommendation:

- `<LINK REL="stylesheet">`
- `<LINK REL="alternate stylesheet">`

1.1.7.2   *Ancillary markup*

A processing instruction is ancillary to the XML document model constraining the creation and validation of an instance. Therefore, we do not have to model the presence of this construct when we design our document model. Any instance can have any number of stylesheet associations added into the document during or after creation, or even removed, without impacting on the XML content itself.

An application respecting this construct will process the document content with the stylesheet before delivering the content to the application logic. Two cases of this are the use of a stylesheet for rendering to a browser canvas and the use of a transformation script at the front end of an e-commerce application.

The following two examples illustrate stylesheet associations that, respectively, reference an XSL resource and a Cascading Stylesheet (CSS) resource:

Example 1–13   Associating an XSL stylesheet in IE5 with an unregistered MIME type

```
<?xml-stylesheet href="fancy.xsl" type="text/xsl"?>
```

Example 1–14   Associating a CSS stylesheet

```
<?xml-stylesheet href="normal.css" type="text/css"?>
```

The following example naming the association for later reference and indicating that it is not the primary stylesheet resource is less typical, but is allowed for in the specification:

Example 1–15   Alternative stylesheet association

```
Line 1   <?xml-stylesheet alternate="yes" title="small"
     2                   href="small.xsl" type="text/xslt+xml"?>
```

A URL that does not include a reference to another resource, but rather is defined exclusively by a local named reference, specifies a stylesheet resource that is located inside the XML document being processed, as in the following example:

Example 1–16   Associating an internal stylesheet

```
<?xml-stylesheet href="#style1" type="text/xslt+xml"?>
```

Additional schemes for linking stylesheets and other processing scripts to XML documents are expected to be defined in future XSLT specifications.

Note: Embedding stylesheet association information in an XML document and using the XML processing instruction to do so are both considered stopgap measures by the W3C. This Recommendation cautions readers that no precedents are set by employing these makeshift techniques and that urgency dictated their choice. Indeed, there is some question as to the appropriateness of tying processing to data so tightly, and we will see what considered approaches become available to us in the future.

An important issue about type= values for associating XSLT is that IE5 only recognizes type="text/xsl" yet this is not a registered MIME type. IETF RFC–3023 proposes type="text/xslt+xml" for XSLT and an appendix to the RFC document details the choice of this convention over other possible candidates for MIME types.

1.2 Transformation data flows

Here we look at the interactions between some of the Recommendations we focus on by examining how our information flows through processes engaging or supporting the technologies.

1.2.1 Transformation from XML to XML

As we will see when looking at the data model, the normative behavior of XSLT is to transform an XML source into an abstract hierarchical result. We can request that result to be serialized into an XML file, thus we achieve XML results from XML sources (see Figure 1–5).

An XSLT stylesheet can be applied to more than one XML document, each stylesheet producing a possibly (usually) different result. Nothing in XSLT inherently ties the stylesheet to a single instance, though the stylesheet writer can employ techniques to abort processing based on processing undesirable input.

Figure 1–5   Transformation from XML to XML

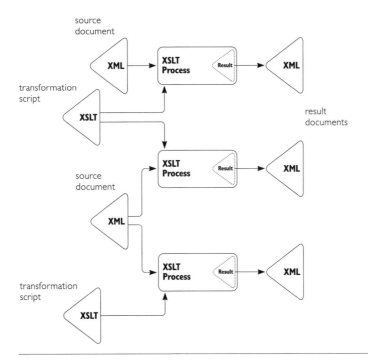

An XML document can have more than one XSLT stylesheet applied, each stylesheet producing a possible (usually) different result. Even when stylesheet association indicates an author's preference for a stylesheet to use for processing, tools should provide the facility to override the preference with the reader's preference for a stylesheet. Nothing in XML prevents more than a single stylesheet to be applied.

Note: In all cases in this chapter the depictions show the normative result of the XSLT processor's as the dotted triangle attached to the process rectangle. This serves to remind the reader that the serialization of the result into an XML file is a separate task, one that is the responsibility of the XSLT processor and not the stylesheet writer.

In all diagrams, the left-pointing triangle represents a hierarchically-marked up document such as an XML or HTML document. This convention stems from considering the apex of the hierarchy at the left, with the sub-elements nesting within each other towards the lowest leaves of the hierarchy at the right of the triangle.

Processes are depicted in rectangles, while arbitrary data files of some binary or text form are depicted in parallelograms. Other symbols representing screen display, print and auditory output are drawn with (hopefully) obvious shapes.

1.2.2 Transformation from XML to XSL formatting semantics

When the result tree is specified to utilize the XSL formatting vocabulary, the normative behavior of an XSL processor incorporating an XSLT processor is to interpret the result tree. This interpretation reifies the semantics expressed in the constructs of the result tree to some medium, be it pixels on a screen, dots on paper, sound through a synthesis device, or another medium that makes sense for presentation (see Figure 1–6).

Without employing extension techniques or supplemental documentation, the stylesheets used in this scenario contain *only* the transformation vocabulary and the resulting formatting vocabulary. There are no other element types from other vocabularies in the result, including from the source vocabulary. For example, rendering processors would not inherently know what to do with an element of type custnbr representing a customer number; it is the stylesheet writer's responsibility to transform the information into information recognized by the rendering agent.

There is no obligation for the rendering processor to serialize the result tree created during transformation. The feature of serializing the result tree to XML markup is, however, quite useful as a diagnostic tool, revealing to us what we really asked to be rendered instead of what we thought we were asking to be rendered when we saw incorrect results. There may also be performance considerations of taking the reified result tree in XML markup and rendering it in other media without incurring the overhead of performing the transformation repeatedly.

Appendix B introduces the concepts and vocabulary of XSL that capture common rendering semantics independent of the rendering medium.

1.2.3 Transformation from XML to non-XML

An XSLT processor may choose to recognize the stylesheet writer's desire to serialize a non-XML representation of the result tree as it's shown on Figure 1–7.

The XSLT Recommendation documents two non-XML tree serialization methods that can be requested by the stylesheet writer. When the processor offers serialization, it is *only* obliged to reify the result

---

Figure 1–6   Transformation from XML to XSL Formatting Semantics

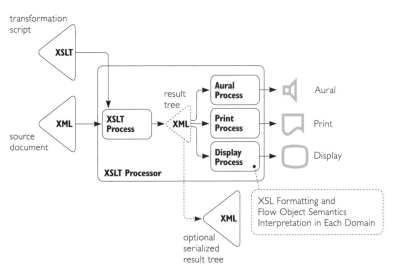

---

using XML markup and structural rules, and *may* support producing output following either HTML markup and structural rules or simple text.

1.2.3.1 *HTML markup and structural conventions*

Internet web browsers are specific examples of the generic HTML user agent. User agents are typically designed for instances of HTML following the parent of XML: the Standard Generalized Markup Language (SGML) markup conventions. Certain aspects of the HTML document model also dictate structural shortcuts available when working with SGML.

While some more recently developed user agents will accept XML markup conventions output from an XSLT processor, older user agents will not. Some of these user agents will not accept XML markup conventions for empty elements, while some require SGML minimization techniques to compress certain attribute specifications. More user agents will accept Extensible Hypertext Markup Language (XHTML) instances than XML instances, but XHTML has additional constraints beyond just the XML markup conventions. Therefore, just using the HTML vocabulary with the XML markup constraints is not sufficient to produce true XHTML output.

Additionally, user agents recognize a number of general entity references as built-in characters supporting accented letters, the non-breaking space, and other characters from public entity sets defined or used by HTML. An XSLT processor recognizes the use of these

Figure 1–7   Transformation from XML to Aware Non-XML

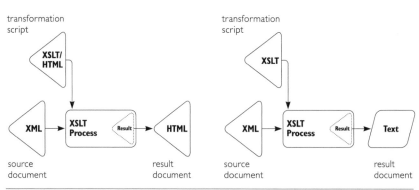

characters in the result tree and serializes them using the assumed built-in general entities.

1.2.3.2   *Text lexical conventions*

An XSLT processor can be asked to serialize only the `#PCDATA` content of the entire result tree, resulting in a file of simple text without employing any markup techniques. All text is represented by the characters' individual values, even those characters sensitive to XML interpretation.

Note: I use the text method often for synthesizing MSDOS batch files. By walking through my XML source I generate commands to act on resources identified therein, thus producing an executable batch file tailored to the information.

1.2.3.3   *Arbitrary binary and custom lexical conventions*

Many of our legacy systems or existing applications expect information to follow custom lexical conventions according to arbitrary rules. Often, this format is raw binary not following textual lexical patterns. We are usually obliged to write custom programs and transformation applications to convert our XML information to these non-standardized formats due to the binary or non-structured natures.

XSLT can play a role even here where the target format is neither structured, nor text, nor in any format accommodated in the design of the Recommendation. We do have a responsibility to fill in a critical piece of the formula described below, but we can leverage this single effort in the equation to allow us and our colleagues to continue to use W3C Recommendations with our XML data.

Not using XSLT to produce custom output.   Consider first the scenario without using XSLT where we must write individual XML-aware applications to accommodate our information vocabularies. For each of our vocabularies we need *separate* programs to convert to the common custom format required by the application. This incurs programming resources to accommodate any and every change to our vocabularies in order to meet the new inputs to satisfy the same custom output (see Figure 1–8).

Using XSLT to produce custom output. If, however, we focus on the custom output instead of focusing on our vocabulary inputs, we can leverage a single investment in programming across all of our vocabularies. Moreover, by being independent of the vocabulary used in the source, we can accommodate any of our or others' vocabularies we may have to deal with in the future.

The approach involves us creating our own custom markup language based on a critical analysis of the target custom format to distill the semantics of how information is represented in the resulting file. These semantics can be expressed using an XML vocabulary whose elements and attributes engage the features and functions of the resulting format. We must not be thinking of our source XML vocabularies, rather, our focus is entirely on the semantics of what exactly makes up our target custom format. Let's refer to this custom format's XML vocabulary we divine from our analysis as the Custom Vocabulary Markup Language (CVML).

Using our programming resources we can then write a single transformation application responsible for interpreting XML instances of CVML to produce a file following the custom format. This transformation application could be written using the Document Object Model (DOM) as a basis for tree-oriented access to the information. Alternatively, a SAX-based application can interpret the instances to produce the outputs if the nature of CVML lends itself to that orientation. The key is that regardless of how instances of CVML are created, the interpretation of CVML markup to produce an output file never changes. Our *one* CVML Instance Interpreter application can produce *any* custom format output file expressible in the CVML semantics.

Figure 1–8 Accommodating multiple inputs with different XML vocabularies

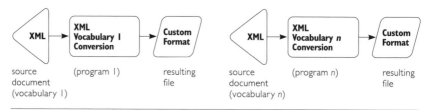

Getting back to our own or others' XML vocabularies, we have now reduced the problem to XML instance transformation. Our objective is simplified to produce XML instances of CVML from instances of our many input XML vocabularies. This is a classical XSLT situation and we need only write XSLT stylesheets combining the XSLT instructions with CVML as the result vocabulary. Our investment in XSLT for our colleagues is leveraged by the CVML Instance Interpreter so that they can now take their XML and use stylesheets to produce the binary or custom lexical format (see Figure 1–9).

This approach separates the awareness of the lexical and syntactic requirements of the custom output format from the numerous stylesheets we write for all of our possible input XML vocabularies. Our colleagues use XSLT just as they would with HTML or XSL as a result vocabulary. They leverage the single investment in producing the custom format by using the CVML Interpreter to serialize the results of their transformations to produce the files designed for other applications. This, in turn, leverages the investment in learning and using XSLT in the organization.

Remembering the "X" in XSLT represents the word "extensible" and result tree serialization is one of the areas where we can extend an XSLT processor's functionality, this allows us to implement non-standard vendor-specific or application-specific output serialization methods and engage these facilities in a standard manner. As with all extension mechanisms in XSLT, the trigger is the use of an XML

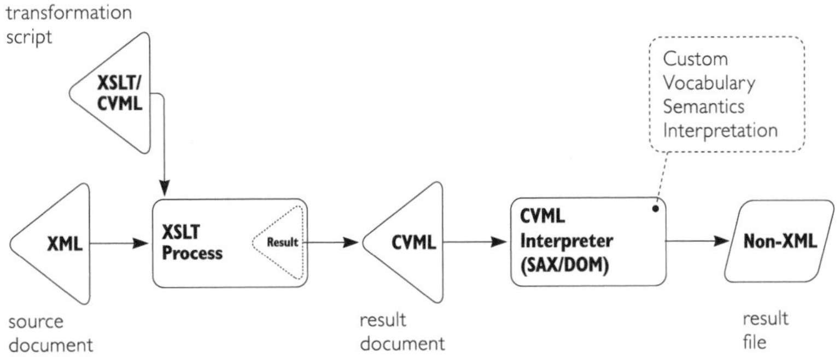

Figure 1–9 Transformation from XML to an arbitrary format

namespace recognized by the XSLT processor implementing the extension:

Example 1–17 Using namespaces to specify an extension serialization method

Line 1 `xmlns:prefix="processor-recognized-URI"`
2 `<xsl:output method="prefix:serialization-method-name"/>`

Comment The namespace declaration attribute on line 1 must be somewhere in the element or the ancestry of the instruction on line 2.

Using the same semantics described for the outboard CVML Interpreter program depicted in Figure 1–9, this translation facility can be incorporated into the XSLT processor itself as an inboard extension. The code itself may be directly portable based on the nature of how the outboard program is written. Such an extended processor would directly emit the custom format without reifying the intermediate structure (though this would be convenient for diagnostic purposes) as it is shown in Figure 1–10.

The XT XSLT processor implements an extension serialization method named NXML for "non-XML" (documented in detail in Section D.1.5):

Example 1–18 Using the XT namespace to specify the NXML extension serialization method

Line 1 `xmlns:prefix="http://www.jclark.com/xt"`
2 `<xsl:output method="prefix:nxml"/>`

Comment The namespace declaration attribute on line 1 must be somewhere in the element or the ancestry of the instruction on line 2.

Figure 1–10 Built-in Transformation from XML to Arbitrary Non-XML

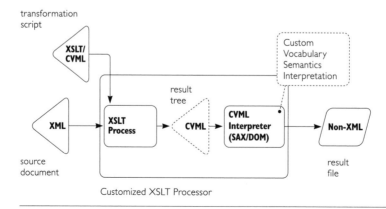

1.2.4 XSLT as an application front-end

Using XSLT opens up the opportunity to use a processor as a front-end to any application that can be modified to access the result tree. The intermediate result tree of CVML is not serialized externally; rather, it is fed directly to the application and the application interprets the internal representation of the content that would have been serialized to a custom format. Time is saved by not serializing the result tree and having the application parse the reified file back into a memory representation; performance is enhanced by the application directly accessing the result of transformation (see Figure 1–11).

Consider the three scenarios in the diagram. At the top left a legacy application may already exist with the implementation of semantics triggered by a custom file format. Converting the application to accept

Figure 1–11   XSLT as an application front-end

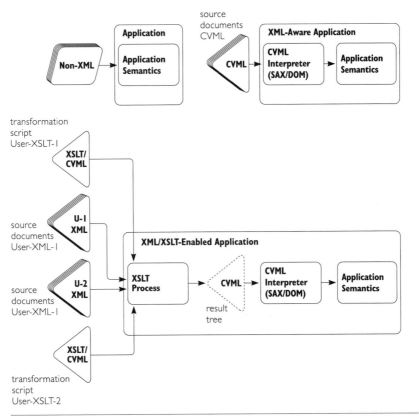

a single XML vocabulary would involved a programming interface, such as using the Document Object Model (DOM) representation of the input tree or using the Simple API for XML (SAX) events. The application shown in the second scenario acts on the presence of the markup in the CVML markup language.

When generalized using an XSLT processor, the third scenario shows an application can accommodate arbitrary customers' XML vocabularies merely by writing W3C conforming XSLT stylesheets as the "interpretation specification." Some XSLT processors can build a DOM of the result tree or deliver the result tree as SAX events thus giving an application developer standardized interfaces to the transformed information expressed using the application's custom semantics vocabulary. The developer's programming is then complete and the vendor accommodates each customer vocabulary with an appropriate stylesheet for translation to the application semantics.

1.2.5 Three-tiered architectures

A three-tiered architecture can meet technical and business objectives by delivering structured information to web browsers by using XSLT on the host, or on the user agent, or even on both.

Considering technical issues first, the server can perform the transformations centrally to accommodate those user agents supporting only HTML or HTML/CSS vocabularies. Alternatively, the server can distribute the processing load to XML/XSLT-aware user agents by delivering a combination of the stylesheet and the source information to be transformed on the recipient's platform, or even massaged before being sent to suppress or change the information as it is shown in Figure 1–12.

There may be good business reasons to selectively deliver richly-marked-up XML to the user agent or to arbitrarily transform XML to HTML on the server regardless of the user agent capabilities. Even if it is technically possible to send semantically-rich information in XML, protecting your intellectual property by hiding the richness behind the security of a "semantic firewall" must be considered. Perhaps there are revenue opportunities by only delivering a richly marked-up rendition of your information to your customers. Perhaps you could even scale the richness to differing levels of utility for customers who value your information with different granularity or specificity, while preserving the most detailed normative version of the data away of view.

Lastly, there are no restrictions to using two XSLT processes: one on the server to translate our organization's rich markup into an arbitrary delivery-oriented markup. This delivery markup, in turn, is translated using XSLT on the user agent for consumption by the operator. This approach can reduce bandwidth utilization and increase distributed processing without sacrificing privacy.

Note: There is no consensus in our XML community that semantic firewalls are a "good thing." Peers of mine preach that the World Wide Web must always be a semantic web with rich markup processed in a distributed fashion among user agents being de rigueur. Personally, I do not subscribe to this point of view. We have the flexibility to weigh the technical and business perspectives of our customers' needs for our information, our own infrastructure and processing capabilities, and our own commercial and

Figure 1–12   Server-side Transformation Architecture

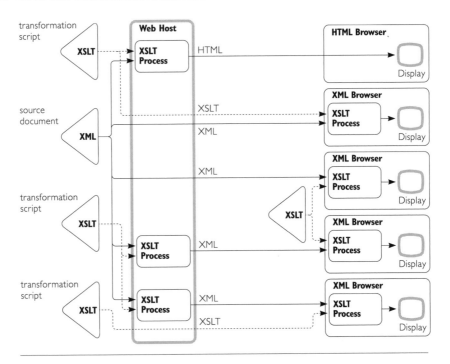

privacy concerns. We can choose to "dumb down" our information for consumption, and the installed base of user agents supporting presentation-oriented semantic-less HTML can be the perfect delivery vehicle to protect these concerns of ours.

2

Getting started
with XSLT
and XPath

2 Getting started with XSLT and XPath

Examining working stylesheets can help to understand how we use XSLT and XPath to effect our transformations. This chapter first dissects some example stylesheets before introducing basic terminology and design principles.

2.1 Stylesheet examples

Let's first look at some example stylesheets using two implementations of XSLT 1.0 and XPath 1.0: the XT processor from James Clark (`http://www.jclark.com/xml/xt.html`), and the third web release of Internet Explorer 5's (IE5) MSXML Technology Preview (`http://msdn.microsoft.com/xml`).

Note: The current (2001–06–01) IE5.5 *production* release supports only an archaic experimental dialect of XSLT based on an early working draft of the Recommendation. The examples in this book *will not* run on this production release of IE5. The production implementation of the old dialect is described in `http://msdn.microsoft.com/xml/XSLGuide/conformance.asp`.

These two processors were chosen merely as examples of, respectively, stand-alone and browser-based XSLT/XPath implementations, without prejudice to other conforming implementations. The code samples only use syntax conforming to XSLT 1.0 and XPath 1.0 Recommendations and will work with any conformant XSLT processor.

2.1.1   Some simple examples

Consider the following XML file `hello.xml` obtained from the XML 1.0 Recommendation and modified to declare an associated stylesheet:

Example 2–1   The first sample instance in XML 1.0 (modified)

```
Line 1  <?xml version="1.0"?>
     2  <?xml-stylesheet type="text/xsl" href="hello.xsl"?>
     3  <greeting>Hello world.</greeting>
```

We will use this simple file as the source of information for our transformation. Note that the stylesheet association processing instruction in line 2 refers to a stylesheet with the name "`hello.xsl`", of type XSL. Recall that an XSLT processor is *not* obliged to respect the stylesheet association preference, so let us first use a stand-alone XSLT processor with the following stylesheet `hellohtm.xsl`:

Example 2–2   A simple simplified stylesheet

```
Line 1  <?xml version="1.0"?>                              <!--hellohtm.xsl-->
     2  <!--XSLT 1.0 - http://www.CraneSoftwrights.com/training -->
     3  <html xmlns:xsl="http://www.w3.org/1999/XSL/Transform"
     4       xsl:version="1.0">
     5   <head><title>Greeting</title></head>
     6   <body><p>Words of greeting:<br/>
     7     <b><i><u><xsl:value-of select="greeting"/></u></i></b>
     8     </p></body>
     9  </html>
```

This file looks like a simple HTML file in XML markup conventions, but we are allowed to inject into the instance XSLT instructions using the prefix for the XSLT vocabulary declared on line 3. We can use any XML file as an XSLT stylesheet provided it declares the XSLT vocabulary within and indicates the version of XSLT being used. Any prefix can be used for XSLT instructions, though convention often sees xsl: as the prefix value.

Line 7 contains the only XSLT instruction in the instance. The xsl:value-of instruction uses an XPath expression in the select= attribute to calculate a string value from our source information. XPath views the source hierarchy using parent/child relationships. The XSLT processor's initial focus is the root of the document, which is considered the parent of the document element. Our XPath expression value "greeting" selects the element child node named "greeting" from the current focus, thus returning the value of the document element of type "greeting" from the instance.

Using an MSDOS command line invocation to execute the stand-alone processor we see the following result:

Example 2–3   Explicit invocation of Example 2–2

```
Line 1   X:\samp>xt hello.xml hellohtm.xsl hellohtm.htm
2   X:\samp>type hellohtm.htm
3   <html>
4   <head>
5   <title>Greeting</title>
6   </head>
7   <body>
8   <p>Words of greeting:<br>
9   <b><i><u>Hello world.</u></i></b>
10  </p>
11  </body>
12  </html>
13
14  X:\samp>
```

Note how the end result contains a mixture of the stylesheet markup and the source instance content, without any use of the XSLT vocabulary. The processor has recognized the use of HTML by the type of the document element and has engaged SGML markup conventions.

The SGML markup conventions are evidenced on line 8 where the <br> empty element has been serialized without the XML markup convention for the closing delimiter. This corresponds to line 6 of our stylesheet in Example 2–2 where this element is marked up as <br/> according to XML rules. Our inputs are always XML but the XSLT processor may recognize the output as being HTML and serialize the result following SGML rules.

Consider next the following XSLT file `hello.xsl` to produce XML output using the HTML vocabulary, where the output is serialized as XML:

Example 2–4   An explicitly-declared simple stylesheet

```
Line 1  <?xml version="1.0"?>                                  <!--hello.xsl-->
     2  <!--XSLT 1.0 - http://www.CraneSoftwrights.com/training -->
     3
     4  <xsl:transform xmlns:xsl="http://www.w3.org/1999/XSL/Transform"
     5                 version="1.0">
     6
     7  <xsl:output method="xml" omit-xml-declaration="yes"/>
     8
     9  <xsl:template match="/">
    10      <b><i><u><xsl:value-of select="greeting"/></u></i></b>
    11  </xsl:template>
    12
    13  </xsl:transform>
```

This file explicitly declares the document element of an XSLT stylesheet with the requisite XSLT namespace and version declarations. Line 7 declares the output to follow XML markup conventions and that the XML declaration is to be omitted from the serialized result. Lines 9 through 11 declare the content of the result that is added when the source information position matches the XPath expression in the `match=` on line 9. The value of "/" matches the root of the document, hence, this refers to the XSLT processor's initial focus.

The result we specify on line 10 wraps our source information in the HTML elements without the boilerplate used in the previous example. Line 13 ends the formal specification of the stylesheet content.

Using an MSDOS command line invocation to execute the XT processor we see the following result:

Example 2–5   Explicit invocation of Example 2–4

```
Line 1  X:\samp>xt hello.xml hello.xsl hello.htm
     2
     3  X:\samp>type hello.htm
     4  <b><i><u>Hello world.</u></i></b>
     5  X:\samp>
```

Figure 2–1 demonstrates what we see on the canvas (the child window is opened using the View/Source menu item) using a non-XML-aware browser to view the resulting HTML in Example 2–5.

Using the `msxml.bat` invocation batch file (described in) at an MSDOS command line to execute the MSXML processor:

Example 2–6   Example invocation of the MSXML processor for Example 2–4

```
Line 1  X:\samp>msxml hello.xml hello.xsl hello-ms.htm
     2
     3  X:\samp>type hello-ms.htm
     4  <b><i><u>Hello world.</u></i></b>
     5  X:\samp>
```

Figure 2–2 demonstrates the canvas painted with the HTML resulting from application of the stylesheet (the child window is opened using the View/Source menu item) using an XML-aware browser recognizing the W3C stylesheet association processing instruction in Example 2–1.

Figure 2–1   An non-XML-aware browser viewing the source of a document

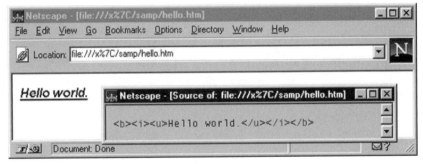

Figure 2–2   An XML-aware browser viewing the source of a document

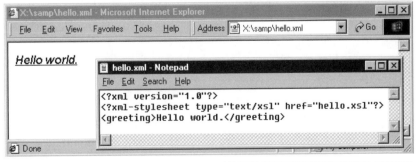

The canvas content matches what the non-XML browser rendered in Figure 2–1. Note that View/Source displays the raw XML source and not the transformed XHTML result of applying the stylesheet.

2.2 Syntax basics — stylesheets, templates, instructions

Next we'll look at some basic terminology both helpful in understanding the principles of writing an XSLT stylesheet and recognizing the constructs used therein. This section is not meant as tutelage for writing stylesheets, but only as background information, nomenclature and practice guidelines.

Note: I use two pairs of diametric terms not used as such in the XSLT Recommendation itself: simplified/composite stylesheets and push/pull design approaches. Actually, "simplified" is used in the Recommendation for this purpose, but "composite" is not and no other contrasting term is provided. Students of my instructor-led courses have found these distinctions helpful even though they are not official terms. Though these terms are documented here with apparent official status, such status is not meant to be conferred.

2.2.1 Stylesheet requirements

Every XSLT stylesheet must identify the namespace prefix used therein for XSLT instructions. The default namespace should not be used for this purpose as it prevents XSLT vocabulary attributes to be used at all places possible. The namespace URI associated with the prefix must be the value "`http://www.w3.org/1999/XSL/Transform`". It is a common practice to use the prefix "`xsl`" to identify the XSLT vocabulary, though this is only convention and any valid prefix can be used.

XSLT processor extensions are outside the scope of the XSLT vocabulary, so other URI values must be used to identify extensions.

The stylesheet must also declare the version of XSLT required by the instructions used therein. The attribute is named `version` and must accompany the namespace declaration in the an element as `version="version-number"` when the element is in the XSLT namespace. In a stylesheet where the XSLT namespace is declared in an element that is not an XSLT instruction, the namespace-qualified attribute declaration must be used as *prefix*:version="*version-number*".

The version number is a numeric floating-point value representing the latest version of XSLT defining the instructions used in the stylesheet. It need not declare the most capable version supported by the XSLT processor.

2.2.2 Instructions and literal result elements

XSLT instructions are only detected in the stylesheet tree and are not detected in the source tree. Instructions are specified using the namespace prefix associated with the XSLT namespace URI. The XSLT Recommendation describes the behavior of the XSLT processor for each of the instructions defined based on the instruction's element type (node name).

Top-level instructions are considered and/or executed by the XSLT processor before processing begins on the source information. For better performance reasons, a processor may choose to not consider a top-level instruction until there is need within the stylesheet to use it. All other instructions are found somewhere in a result tree template and are not executed until that point at which the processor is asked to add the instruction to the result tree. Instructions themselves are never added to the result tree.

Some XSLT instructions are control constructs used by the processor to manage our stylesheets. The wrapper and top-level elements declare our globally scoped constructs. Procedural and process-control constructs give us the ability to selectively add only portions of templates to the result, rather than always adding an entire template. Logically-oriented constructs give us facilities to share the use of values and declarations within our own stylesheet files. Physically-oriented constructs give us the power to share entire stylesheet fragments.

Other XSLT instructions are result tree value placeholders. We declare how a value is calculated by the processor, or obtained from a source tree, or both calculated by the processor from a value from a source tree. The value calculation is triggered when the XSLT processor is about to add the instruction to the result tree. The outcome of the calculation (which may be nothing) is added to the result tree.

All other instructions engage customized non-standard behaviors and are specified using extension elements in a standardized fashion. These elements use namespace prefixes declared by our stylesheets to be instruction prefixes. Extension instructions may be either control constructs or result tree value placeholders.

Consider the simple example in our stylesheets used earlier in this chapter where the following instruction is used:

Example 2–7   Simple value-calculation instruction in Example 2–4

```
<xsl:value-of select="greeting"/>
```

This instruction uses the `select=` attribute to specify the XPath expression of some value to be calculated and added to the result tree. When the expression is a location in the source tree, as is this example, the value returned is the value of the first location identified using the criteria. When that location is an element, the value returned is the concatenation of all of the #PCDATA text contained therein.

This example instruction is executed in the context of the root of the source document being the focus. The element child of the root of the document is the document element. The expression requests the value of the element child node named "`greeting`" of the root of the document, hence, the value of the document element of type "`greeting`". For any source document where "`greeting`" is not the document element, the value returned is the empty string. For any source document where it is the document element, as is our example, the value returned is the concatenation of all #PCDATA text in the entire instance.

A literal result element is any element in a stylesheet that is not a top-level element and is not either an XSLT instruction or an extension instruction. A literal result element can use the default namespace or any namespace not declared in the stylesheet to be an instruction namespace.

When the XSLT processor reads the stylesheet and creates the abstract nodes in the stylesheet tree, those nodes that are literal result elements represent the nodes that are added to the result tree. Though the definition of those nodes is dictated by the XML markup in the stylesheet entity, the markup used does not necessarily represent the markup that is serialized from the result tree nodes created from the stylesheet nodes.

Literal result elements marked up in the stylesheet entity may have attributes that are targeted for the XML processor used by the XSLT processor, targeted for the XSLT processor, or targeted for use in the result tree. Some attributes are consumed and acted upon as the stylesheet file is processed to build the stylesheet tree, while the others remain in the stylesheet tree for later use. Those literal result attributes remaining in the stylesheet tree that are qualified with an instruction namespace are acted on when they are asked to be added to the result tree.

2.2.3 Templates and template rules

Many XSLT instructions are container elements. The collection of literal result elements and other instructions being contained therein comprises the XSLT template for that instruction. A template can contain only literal result elements, only instruction elements, or a mixture of both. The behavior of the stylesheet can ask that a template be added to the result tree, at which point the nodes for literal result elements are added and the nodes for instructions are executed.

Consider again the simple example in our stylesheets used earlier in this chapter where the following template is used:

Example 2–8 Simple template in Example 2–4

```
<b><i><u><xsl:value-of select="greeting"/></u></i></b>
```

This template contains a mixture of literal result elements and an instruction element. When the XSLT processor adds this template to the result tree, the nodes for the `<b>`, `<i>`, and `<u>` elements are simply added to the tree, while the node for the `xsl:value-of` instruction triggers the processor to add the outcome of instruction execution to the tree.

A template rule is a result tree construction rule associated with source tree nodes. It is a declaration to the XSLT processor of a template to be added to the result tree when certain conditions are met by source locations visited by the processor. Template rules are either top-level elements explicitly written in the stylesheet or built-in templates assumed by the processor and implicitly available in all stylesheets.

The criteria for adding a written template rule's template to the result tree are specified in a number of attributes, one of which must be the match= attribute. This attribute is an XPath pattern expression, which is a subset of XPath expressions in general. The pattern expression describes preconditions of source tree nodes. The stylesheet writer is responsible for writing the preconditions and other attribute values in such a way as to unambiguously provide a single written or built-in template for each of the anticipated source tree conditions.

In a simplified stylesheet, the entire file is considered the template for the template rule for the root of the document. This template rule overrides the built-in rule implicitly available in the XSLT processor.

Back to the simple example in our composite stylesheet used earlier in this chapter, the following template rule is declared:

Example 2–9   Simple template rule in Example 2–4

```
Line 1  <xsl:template match="/">
     2      <b><i><u><xsl:value-of select="greeting"/></u></i></b>
     3  </xsl:template>
```

This template rule defines the template to be added to the result tree when the root of the document is visited. This written rule overrides the built-in rule implicitly available in the XSLT processor. The template is the same template we were discussing earlier: a set of result tree nodes and an instruction.

The XSLT processor beings processing by visiting the root of the document. This gives control to the stylesheet writer. Either the supplied template rule or built-in template rule for the root of the document is processed, based on what the writer has declared in the stylesheet. The writer is in complete control at this early stage and all XSLT processor behavior is dictated what the writer asks to be calculated and where the writer asks the XSLT processor to visit.

2.2.4 Simplified stylesheets

The simplest kind of XSLT stylesheet is an XML file implicitly representing the entire outcome of transformation. The result vocabulary is arbitrary, and the stylesheet tree forms the template used by the XSLT processor to build the result tree. The processor assumes the entire file is the template rule for the root node. If no XSLT or extension instructions are found therein, the stylesheet tree becomes the result tree. If instructions are present, the processor replaces the instructions with the outcomes of their execution (see Figure 2–3).

The XML declaration is consumed by the XML processor embedded within the XSLT processor, thus the XSLT processor never sees it. The remainder of the file is considered the result tree template for an implicit rule for the root of the document, describing the shape of the entire outcome of the transformation.

The document element is of type "html" and contains the namespace and version declarations of the XSLT language. Any element type within the result tree template that is qualified by the prefix assigned to the XSLT namespace URI is recognized as an XSLT instruction. No extension instruction namespaces are declared, thus all other element types in the instance are literal result elements. Indeed, the document element is a literal result element as it, too, is not an instruction.

Figure 2–3   Components of a Simplified Stylesheet

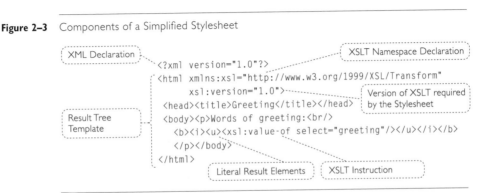

2.2.5 Composite stylesheets

A composite XSLT stylesheet is comprised of a distinct wrapper element containing the stylesheet specification. This wrapper element must be an XSLT instruction either of type `stylesheet` or `transform`, thus it must be qualified by the prefix associated with the XSLT namespace URI. This wrapper element is the document element in a stand-alone stylesheet, but may in other cases be embedded inside an XML document (see Figure 2–4).

The XML declaration is consumed by the XML processor embedded within the XSLT processor, thus the XSLT processor never sees it. The wrapper element must include the XSLT namespace and version declarations for the element to be recognized as an instruction.

The children of the wrapper element are the top-level elements, comprised of global constructs, serialization information, and certain maintenance instructions. Template rules supply the stylesheet behavior for matching source tree conditions. The content of a template rule is a result tree template containing both literal result elements and XSLT instructions.

The example above has only a single template rule, that being for the root of the document.

Figure 2–4   Components of a Composite Stylesheet

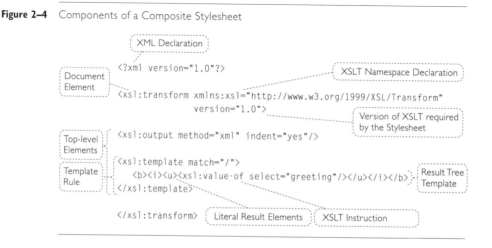

2.2.6 Approaches to stylesheet design

The last discussion in this two-chapter introduction regards how to approach using templates and instructions when writing a stylesheet. Two distinct approaches can be characterized. Choosing which approach to use when depends on your own preferences, the nature of the source information, and the nature of the desired result.

Note: In the text I refer to these two approaches as either stylesheet-driven or data-driven, though the former might be misconstrued. Of course all results are stylesheet-driven because the stylesheet dictates what to do, so the use of the term involves some nuance. By stylesheet-driven I mean that the order of the result is a result of the stylesheet tree having explicitly instructed the adding of information to the result tree. By data-driven I mean that the order of the result is a result of the source tree ordering having dictated the adding of information to the result tree.

2.2.6.1 *Pulling the input data*

When the stylesheet writer knows the location of and order of data found in the source tree, and the writer wants to add to the result a value from or collection of that data, then information can be pulled from the source tree on demand. Two instructions are provided for this purpose: one for obtaining or calculating a single string value to add to the result; and one for adding rich markup to the result based on obtaining as many values as may exist in the tree.

The writer uses the `<xsl:value-of select="`*XPath-expression*`"/>` instruction in a stylesheet element's content to calculate a single value to be added to the result tree. The instruction is always empty and therefore does not contain a template. This value calculated can be the result of function execution, the value of a variable, or the value of a node selected from the source tree. When used in the template of various XSLT instructions the outcome becomes part of the value of a result element, attribute, comment or processing instruction.

Note there is also a shorthand notation called an "attribute value template" that allows the equivalent to `<xsl:value-of>` to be used in a stylesheet's attribute content.

To iterate over locations in the source tree, the `<xsl:for-each select="`*XPath-node-set-expression*`">` instruction defines a template to be processed for each instance, possibly repeated, of the selected locations. This template can contain literal result elements or any instruction to be executed. When processing the given template, the focus of the processor's view of the source tree shifts to the location being visited, thus providing for relative addressing while moving through the information.

These instructions give the writer control over the order of information in the result. The data is being pulled from the source on demand and added to the result tree in the stylesheet-determined order. When collections of nodes are iterated the nodes are visited in document order. This implements a stylesheet-driven approach to creating the result.

A simplified stylesheet is obliged to use only these "pull" instructions and must dictate the order of the result with the above instructions in the lone template.

2.2.6.2   Pushing the input data

The stylesheet writer may not know the order of the data found in the source tree, or may want to have the source tree dictate the ordering of content of the result tree. In these situations, the writer instructs the XSLT processor to visit source tree nodes and to apply to the result the templates associated with the nodes that are visited.

The `<xsl:apply-templates select="`*XPath-node-expression*`">` instruction visits the source tree nodes described by the node expression in the `select=` attribute. The writer can choose any relative, absolute, or arbitrary location or locations to be visited.

Each node visited is pushed through the stylesheet to be caught by template rules. Template rules specify the template to be processed and added to the result tree. The template added is dictated by the template rule matched for the node being pushed, not by a template supplied by the instruction when a node is being pulled. This distinguishes the behavior as being a data-driven approach to creating the result, in that the source determines the ultimate order of the result.

A simplified stylesheet can only push information through built-in template rules, which is of limited value. As well, the built-in rules can be mimicked entirely by using pull constructs, thus they need never be used. There is no room in the stylesheet to declare template rules in a simplified stylesheet since there is no wrapper stylesheet instruction.

A composite stylesheet can either push or pull information because there is room in the stylesheet to define the top-level elements, including any number of template rules required for the transformation.

2.2.6.3 *Putting it all together*

We are *not* obliged to use only one approach when we write our stylesheets. It is very appropriate to push where the order is dictated by the source information and to pull when responding to a push where the order is known by the stylesheet. The most common use of this combination in a template is localized pull access to values that are relative to the focus being matched by nodes being pushed.

Note that push-oriented stylesheets more easily accommodate changes to the data and are more easily exploited by others who wish to reuse the stylesheets we write. The more granularity we have in our template rules, the more flexibly our stylesheets can respond to changes in the order of data. The more we pull data from our source tree, the more dependent we are on how we have coded the access to the information. The more we push data through our stylesheet, the less that changes in our data impact our stylesheet code.

Look again at the examples discussed earlier in this chapter and analyze the use of the above pull and push constructs to meet the objectives of the transformations.

These introductions and samples in the first two chapters have set the context and only scratch the surface of the power of XSLT to effect the transformations we need when working with our structured information. The rest of the chapters go into detail about the data model and access to information defined by XPath, and every instruction element and attribute value described by XSLT.

2.3 **More stylesheet examples**

The following more complex examples are meant merely as illustrations of some of the powerful facilities and techniques available in XSLT. These samples expose concepts such as variables, functions, and process control constructs a stylesheet writer uses to effect the desired result, but does not attempt any tutelage in their use.

Note: This subsection can be skipped entirely, or, for quick exposure to some of the facilities available in XSLT and XPath, only briefly reviewed. In the associated narratives I've avoided the precise terminology that hasn't yet been introduced and I overview the stylesheet contents and processor behaviors in only broad terms. Subsequent subsections of this chapter review some of the basic terminology and design approaches.

I hope not to frighten the reader with the complexity of these examples, but it is important to realize that there are more complex operations than can be illustrated using our earlier 3 line source file example. The complexity of your transformations will dictate the complexity of the stylesheet facilities being engaged. Simple transformations can be performed quite simply using XSLT, but not all of us have to meet only simple requirements.

2.3.1 Processing XML data with multiple XSLT stylesheets

The following XML source information in `prod.xml` is used to produce two very dissimilar renderings:

Example 2–10 Sample product sales source information

```
Line 1  <?xml version="1.0"?>                              <!--prod.xml-->
     2  <!DOCTYPE sales [
     3  <!ELEMENT sales ( products, record )>            <!--sales information-->
     4  <!ELEMENT products ( product+ )>                    <!--product record-->
     5  <!ELEMENT product ( #PCDATA )>                  <!--product information-->
     6  <!ATTLIST product id ID #REQUIRED>
     7  <!ELEMENT record ( cust+ )>                           <!--sales record-->
     8  <!ELEMENT cust ( prodsale+ )>                <!--customer sales record-->
     9  <!ATTLIST cust num CDATA #REQUIRED>             <!--customer number-->
    10  <!ELEMENT prodsale ( #PCDATA )>                 <!--product sale record-->
    11  <!ATTLIST prodsale idref IDREF #REQUIRED>
    12  ]>
    13  <sales>
    14    <products><product id="p1">Packing Boxes</product>
    15          <product id="p2">Packing Tape</product></products>
    16    <record><cust num="C1001">
    17          <prodsale idref="p1">100</prodsale>
    18          <prodsale idref="p2">200</prodsale></cust>
    19       <cust num="C1002">
```

```
20              <prodsale idref="p2">50</prodsale></cust>
21          <cust num="C1003">
22              <prodsale idref="p1">75</prodsale>
23              <prodsale idref="p2">15</prodsale></cust></record>
24  </sales>
```

Lines 2 through 11 describe the document model for the sales information. Lines 14 and 15 summarize product description information and have unique identifiers according to the ID/IDREF rules. Lines 16 through 23 summarize customer purchases (product sales), each entry referring to the product having been sold by use of the idref= attribute. Not all customers have been sold all products.

Consider the two renderings of the same data using two orientations, each produced with different stylesheets, shown in Figure 2–5.

Note how the same information is projected into a table orientation on the left canvas and a list orientation on the right canvas. The one authored order is delivered in two different presentation orders. Both results include titles from boilerplate text not found in the source. The table information on the left includes calculations of the sums of quantities in the columns, generated by the stylesheet and not present explicitly in the source.

Figure 2–5   Different HTML results from the same XML source

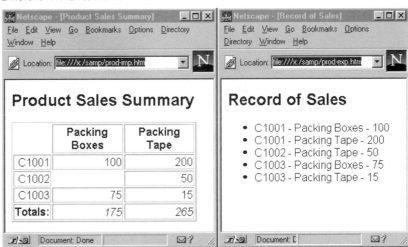

The simplified stylesheet `prod-imp.xsl` is an XHTML file utilizing the XSLT vocabulary for instructions to fill in the one result template by pulling data from the source:

Example 2–11   Tabular presentation of the sample product sales source information

```
Line 1  <?xml version="1.0"?>                              <!--prod-imp.xsl-->
     2  <!--XSLT 1.0 - http://www.CraneSoftwrights.com/training -->
     3  <html xmlns:xsl="http://www.w3.org/1999/XSL/Transform"
     4       xsl:version="1.0">
     5   <head><title>Product Sales Summary</title></head>
     6   <body><h2>Product Sales Summary</h2>
     7    <table summary="Product Sales Summary" border="1">
     8                                                        <!--list products-->
     9     <tr align="center"><th/>
    10        <xsl:for-each select="//product">
    11         <th><b><xsl:value-of select="."/></b></th>
    12        </xsl:for-each></tr>
    13                                                        <!--list customers-->
    14     <xsl:for-each select="/sales/record/cust">
    15       <xsl:variable name="customer" select="."/>
    16       <tr align="right"><td><xsl:value-of select="@num"/></td>
    17        <xsl:for-each select="//product">              <!--each product-->
    18         <td><xsl:value-of select="$customer/prodsale
    19                              [@idref=current()/@id]"/>
    20        </td></xsl:for-each>
    21       </tr></xsl:for-each>
    22                                                        <!--summarize-->
    23     <tr align="right"><td><b>Totals:</b></td>
    24        <xsl:for-each select="//product">
    25         <xsl:variable name="pid" select="@id"/>
    26         <td><i><xsl:value-of
    27                    select="sum(//prodsale[@idref=$pid])"/></i>
    28        </td></xsl:for-each></tr>
    29     </table>
    30   </body></html>
```

Recall that a stylesheet is oriented according to the desired result, producing the result in result parse order. The entire document is an HTML file whose document element begins on line 3 and ends on line 30. The XSLT namespace and version declarations are included in the document element. The naming of the document element as "html" triggers the default use of HTML result tree serialization conventions. Lines 5 and 6 are fixed boilerplate information for the mandatory `<title>` element.

Lines 7 through 29 build the result table from the content. A single header row `<th>` is generated in lines 9 through 12, with the columns of that row generated by traversing all of the `<product>` elements of the source. The focus moves on line 11 to each `<product>` source element in turn and the markup associated with the traversal builds each `<td>` result element. The content of each column is specified as ".", which for an element evaluates to the string value of that element.

Having completed the table header, the table body rows are then built, one at a time traversing each `<cust>` child of a `<record>` child of the `<sales>` child of the root of the document, according to the XPath expression "`/sales/record/cust`". The current focus moves to the `<cust>` element for the processing on lines 15 through 21. A local scope variable is bound on line 15 with the tree location of the current focus (note how this instruction uses the same XPath expression as on line 11 but with a different result). A table row is started on line 16 with the leftmost column calculated from the `num=` attribute of the `<cust>` element being processed.

The stylesheet then builds in lines 17 through 20 a column for each of the same columns created for the table header on line 10. The focus moves to each product in turn for the processing of lines 18 through 20. Each column's value is then calculated with the expression "`$customer/prodsale[@idref=current()/@id]`", which could be expressed as follows "from the customer location bound to the variable `$customer`, from all of the `<prodsale>` children of that customer, find that child whose `idref=` attribute is the value of the `id=` attribute of the focus element." When there is no such child, the column value is empty and processing continues. As many columns are produced for a body row as for the header row and our output becomes perfectly aligned.

Finally, lines 23 through 28 build the bottom row of the table with the totals calculated for each product. After the boilerplate leftmost column, line 24 uses the same "`//product`" expression as on lines 10 and 17 to generate the same number of table columns. The focus changes to each product for lines 25 through 28. A local scope variable is bound with the focus position in the tree. Each column is then calculated using a built-in function as the sum of all `<prodsale>` elements that reference the column being totaled. XPath provides the `sum()` function, preventing the stylesheet writer from having to implement complex counting and summing code; rather, the writer merely declares the need for the summed value to be added to the result on demand by using the appropriate XPath expression.

The file `prod-exp.xsl` is an explicit XSLT stylesheet with a number of result templates for handling source information:

Example 2–12   List-oriented presentation of the sample product sales source information

```
Line 1  <?xml version="1.0"?>                                    <!--prod-exp.xsl-->
     2  <!--XSLT 1.0 - http://www.CraneSoftwrights.com/training -->
     3  <xsl:stylesheet xmlns:xsl="http://www.w3.org/1999/XSL/Transform"
     4                  version="1.0">
     5
     6  <xsl:template match="/">                                  <!--root rule-->
     7    <html><head><title>Record of Sales</title></head>
     8      <body><h2>Record of Sales</h2>
     9        <xsl:apply-templates select="/sales/record"/>
    10      </body></html></xsl:template>
    11
    12  <xsl:template match="record">            <!--processing for each record-->
    13    <ul><xsl:apply-templates/></ul></xsl:template>
    14
    15  <xsl:template match="prodsale">              <!--processing for each sale-->
    16    <li><xsl:value-of select="../@num"/>          <!--use parent's attr-->
    17        <xsl:text> - </xsl:text>
    18        <xsl:value-of select="id(@idref)"/>                <!--go indirect-->
    19        <xsl:text> - </xsl:text>
    20        <xsl:value-of select="."/></li></xsl:template>
    21
    22  </xsl:stylesheet>
```

The document element on line 3 includes the requisite declarations of the language namespace and the version being used in the stylesheet. The children of the document element are the template rules describing the source tree event handlers for the transformation. Each event handler associates a template with an event trigger described by an XPath expression.

Lines 6 through 10 describe the template rule for processing the root of the document, as indicated by the "/" trigger in the `match=` attribute on line 6. The result document element and boilerplate is added to the result tree on lines 7 and 8. Line 9 instructs the XSLT processor in `<xsl:apply-templates>` to visit all `<record>` element children of the `<sales>` document element, as specified in the `select=` attribute. For each location visited, the processor pushes that location through the stylesheet, thus triggering the template of result markup it can match for each location.

Lines 12 and 13 describe the result markup when matching a `<record>` element. The focus moves to the `<record>` element being visited. The template rule on line 13 adds the markup for the HTML unordered list `<ul>` element to the result tree. The content of the list is created by instructing the processor to visit all children of the focus location (implicitly by not specifying any `select=` attribute) and apply the templates of result markup it triggers for each child. The only children of `<record>` are `<cust>` elements.

The stylesheet does not provide any template rule for the `<cust>` element, so built-in template rules automatically process the children of each location being visited in turn. Implicitly, then, our source information is being traversed in the depth-first order, visiting the locations in parse order and pushing each location through any template rules that are then found in the stylesheet. The children of the `<cust>` elements are `<prodsale>` elements.

The stylesheet does provide a template rule in lines 15 through 20 to handle a `<prodsale>` element when it is pushed, so the XSLT processor adds the markup triggered by that rule to the result. The focus changes when the template rule handles it, thus, lines 16, 18 and 20 each pull information relative to the `<prodsale>` element, respectively: the parent's `num=` attribute (the `<cust>` element's attribute); the string value of the target element being pointed to by the `<prodsale>` element's `idref=` attribute (indirectly obtaining the `<product>` element's value); and the value of the `<prodsale>` element itself.

3

XPath
data
model

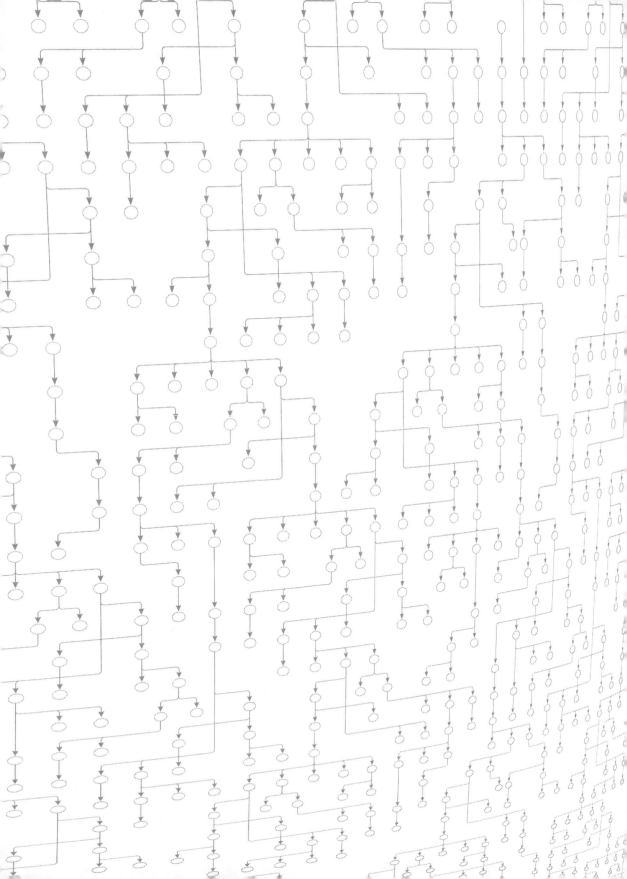

3 XPath data model

The basis of writing all stylesheets is an understanding of how our information is represented for us when we have to work with it. This chapter focuses on how XPath regards structured information through a model of XML data.

Dealing with information, not markup. All of the input and output information when using XSLT is manipulated in an abstract fashion using the XPath data model. There are three primary information structures to an XSLT processor: the source (the information being manipulated), the stylesheet (the manipulation instructions), and the result (the outcome of manipulating the information).

The stylesheet writer's frame of reference is always the information contained in an XML instance, not the markup used in the instance to represent that information. The information is dealt with as abstract nodes not the characters of markup.

The control a stylesheet writer has over the syntactic mechanisms used when serializing the result of transformation using XML or HTML is constrained by the premise that a subsequent process will be responsible for interpreting the serialized output. Since another processor is going to be interpreting the result, the syntactic constructs used in the serialization need only be correct, regardless of which of the correct methods are employed. Since any correct method can be employed, the processor decides which method is used and there is, therefore, no need to provide controls to the stylesheet writer to influence the syntactic constructs used in the result.

Traversing a source file or stylesheet file predictably. An XSLT processor regards a physical XML entity (a resource that often exists as a file) used as source or stylesheet input by using an abstraction model of a tree of nodes and set of associated information. The only content in these entities that we can see for our transformations is that which is represented in this model. This model does not have the same level of granularity as the markup syntax described by XML.

This abstraction is rigorously described in the XPath Recommendation. The Recommendation was, however, written before the formalisms being standardized in the XML Information Set Recommendation `http://www.w3.org/TR/xml-infoset` (a common abstract data set containing the information available from an XML document) were finalized. A future revision to the XPath Recommendation will recast the existing formalisms using the concepts and terminology of the finalized XML Information Set Recommendation when it is completed.

The nodes in this abstraction are typed, with each type describing a particular XML information construct. The XML processor being used by the XSLT processor derives each XML information construct from the markup being interpreted. All information about a node is well-defined, with no interpretation left open to an implementation. Every node type defines a string value of some kind for a node in the tree of that type. Some node types are named, while others are not. Some nodes have supplemental information made available through the XPath data model, but this information does not necessarily include aspects of the actual XML markup used to represent the construct.

This coarse-level abstraction helps the stylesheet writer, while at the same time hides some more granular information that would be useful in certain situations. This difference in granularity means there are particular classes of transformations unmet by the representation of XML data using the XPath model. Transformations requiring original markup syntax preservation cannot be implemented using XSLT because the syntactic XML markup used to represent the information constructs in an XML document is *not* saved in the data model.

The data model represents the information found in a well-formed XML instance. Validation is not required, though there are some aspects of the document model that influence the creation of the node tree and information set for an instance. A stylesheet may *require* information from the document model, that when missing will influence the behavior, but this is not an error condition. A well-written stylesheet can accommodate the absence of required information and inform the operator of missing input conditions.

A stylesheet traverses the data model of XML documents in the execution of its instructions. These instructions move the focus of processing from one node to another in the course of performing the stylesheet logic. From any one point of focus in the document, the stylesheet can locate information from or navigate about the data model of the document in one of thirteen possible directions, called axes. Eleven of these axes relate to ordered parent/child relationships of nodes in the tree, while two relate to attachment relationships. Each axis has a name and from any given point includes zero or some number of nodes in that axis direction. The stylesheet obtains nodes from an axis according to specified selection criteria and performs processing with the nodes found.

Consider the depiction of a node tree in Figure 3–1. In this example, the focus is considered the node in the middle of the diagram that is drawn with a thick outline. The collection of nodes on each of the parent/child-related axes is drawn by surrounding the nodes with a dotted line and enclosing the axis name within the dotted area. Some nodes can be found on different axes simultaneously.

Descriptions of each of the axes are detailed in this chapter. This diagram is a useful supplement to the descriptions when trying to remember which nodes are found along which axes. Note that the nodes addressed on each axis are proximity ordered relative to the focus, that is, the node addressed as the first node on the axis is the closest node on that axis to the focus (which in some cases is the focus node itself), while the node addressed as the last node on the axis is the furthest node on that axis from the focus.

Building a result predictably.   Our objective as stylesheet writers is to build our desired result as a tree using the same types of nodes used in the source and stylesheet trees. Nodes from the source and stylesheet trees are copied to the result tree, and nodes can be synthesized on demand for the result tree. The templates we write in our stylesheet describe the literal result elements and instructions that, respectively, represent nodes and perform instructions that may generate nodes. Stylesheets interpret templates and add nodes to the result tree in result tree parse order. The XSLT processor acts on the stylesheet in the same predictable fashion every time it accesses the source and stylesheet trees, thus ensuring our result is predictably created.

Figure 3–1   Nodes found along axes of different directions

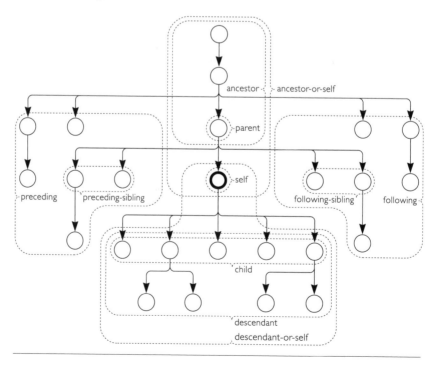

The resulting node tree that we build using our stylesheet may or may not be serialized into actual markup syntax as an output. When serializing our result tree, we can request certain serialization conventions be used, though the XSLT processor is not required to oblige our requests.

Included in this chapter. This chapter includes discussion of the following XSLT instructions regarding whitespace handling while building the data model representation of an instance.

- `<xsl:strip-space>`
  - indicates those source tree nodes in which whitespace-only text nodes are not to be preserved.
- `<xsl:preserve-space>`
  - indicates those source tree nodes in which whitespace-only text nodes are to be preserved.

3.1 XPath data model components

3.1.1 The file abstractions

XSLT describes 7 types of nodes present in node trees.

- Some node types are not visible in certain types of node trees.
- Some node types are only tree branches, or only tree leaves, or can be both.
- Some nodes are considered children.
- Some node types are named.
- All node types have a value of some kind —
  - either directly associated with the node or calculated from the values of descendent nodes.

3.1.2 Comment node and processing instruction node

There are two types of nodes visible in both the source tree and the result tree, but not visible in the stylesheet tree when copying stylesheet nodes to the result.

Comment:

- is a single unnamed node which is created from a single comment:

  ```
  <!--comment-value-string-->
  ```

- is a child of its parent node,
- is always a leaf of the tree and never has any child nodes of any type,
- has a value which is the content of the comment not including the opening and closing markup delimiters.
  - It is an error if a created comment node is supplied with the text string "--", though the XSLT processor may choose to not report the error and separate the two characters with a space.

Processing instruction node:

- is a single named node which is created from a single processing instruction:

```
<?piTarget?>

<?piTarget p-i-value-string?>
```

  - the name of the node is the XML Processing Instruction Target,
- is a child of its parent node,
- is always a leaf of the tree and never has any child nodes of any type,
- has a value which is the content of the processing instruction following the whitespace following the name, but not including the opening and closing markup delimiters.
  - It is an error if a created processing instruction node is supplied with the text string "?>", though the XSLT processor may choose to not report the error and separate the two characters with a space.

3.1.3   Element node:

- is a single named node created in "document order" for each element, which:
  - is the same order as the elements' start tags in the instance,
  - is a depth-first breadth-next tree order,
  - supports processing predictability;
    - many XPath facilities address document nodes in document order;
    - some facilities address document nodes in reverse document order,
- is a child of its parent node,
- may have *child* content nodes;
  - child nodes could be either text, or element, or comment, or processing instruction nodes;

- descendants of an element node are considered to be all the child nodes plus the descendants of child element nodes;
- an element node does not directly include any character data as any element's character data is found only in a child text node;
- an empty element does not have any child nodes,

- may have *attached* non-content nodes;
  - they are *not* considered to be child nodes of an element node;
  - the element node *is* considered to be the parent of an attached node;
  - two types of attached non-content nodes are:
    - specified or defaulted attributes as attribute nodes,
    - namespace declaration nodes;
  - an empty element may have attached nodes,

- may have a unique identifier useful for random access into a document;
  - this identifier is supplied by an attribute of type `ID` as detected by the XML processor;
  - this identifier is unique among all other elements with identifiers in the same source node tree;
  - neither the hierarchy from the root nor the relative position from the current node to an element with a unique identifier need to be known;
  - nodes distinguished by their unique identifier are returned from calling a function, not from using an axis,

- has a "Base URI" which:
  - is the URI of the physical entity in which the entity was parsed (either the document's URI or an external entity's URI),
  - is used when dealing with relative URI values in attached and descendent nodes,

- has the name which is the element type,
- has the value which is the concatenation, in document order, of all text nodes that are descendants of the element.

3.1.4 Namespace node:

- provides the definition of the URI to use in place of the namespace prefix:

  ```
  xmlns="default-namespace-URI"
  xmlns:namespace-prefix="namespace-URI"
  ```

- is such that every element has as many namespace nodes as it and its ancestors have namespace declarations,
- is not always addressable by a stylesheet writer, in particular it:
  - can never be used in a template matching pattern,

- can be used in a node set selection expression,
- is present in the source and stylesheet trees and the processor adds them to the result tree when copying element nodes;
  - a common problem when copying nodes to the result tree is the copying of unwanted namespace nodes that originate from ancestral declarations,
- can be arbitrarily ordered with regard to other namespace nodes,
- is always *attached* to element nodes;
  - it *is not* considered a child of the element node;
  - the element to which it is attached *is* considered its parent,
- is always a leaf of the tree and never has any child nodes of any type,
- has the name which is the namespace prefix,
- has the value which is the namespace URI,
- can be explicitly pruned from stylesheet literal result elements:

  ```
  xsl:exclude-result-prefixes="space-separated-names"
  ```

  - it suppresses the generation of the given namespace node for self and descendent stylesheet elements;
  - adding a stylesheet literal result element to the result tree does not copy any excluded namespace nodes,
- in a stylesheet, may use a different prefix to refer to a namespace URI than the prefix used in a source document for the URI being referred to;
  - each document has own set of prefixes;
  - stylesheet logic is based upon referenced URI values in each independent prefix space;
  - common mistake is to try to match a default namespace source element where the default namespace has a non-null namespace URI with a default namespace stylesheet element where the default namespace has a null namespace URI.

3.1.5 Attribute node:

- is a single attribute node attached to an element node for —
  - each attribute specified in the start tag of that element,
  - each attribute with a specified default value in the document model declaration for that element's attribute list;
    - for a document model expressed in a DTD (Document Type Definition), a node is *not* created for an attribute declared with an #IMPLIED default value,
- can be arbitrarily ordered with regard to other attribute nodes,

- *is* treated specially if it is the XML Namespace attribute `xmlns:prefix=`;
  - it creates a namespace node *only*;
  - an attribute node is *not* created,
- *is not* treated specially if it is the XML attribute `xml:space=` or `xml:lang=`;
  - it is the stylesheet's responsibility to copy or create such nodes in the result tree;
  - the presence of such attributes in XSLT instructions in the stylesheet does not implicitly reproduce the use of the attributes in the result,
- cannot be "global";
  - in XML 1.0 Recommendation there is no such construct as a "shared attribute" or "global attribute," which would be associated with more than one instantiated element or defined element type;
    - a defaulted or specified attribute of any given element type is instantiated for *every* such element in the instance;
    - a defaulted or specified attribute that may happen to have the identical declaration in each of two element types is not treated specially and is instantiated once for every element of each type in the instance,
- is always *attached* to element nodes;
  - it *is not* considered a child of the element node;
  - the element to which it is attached *is* considered its parent,
- is always a leaf of the tree and never has any child nodes of any type,
- has the name which is the name of the attribute,
- has the value which is the value of the attribute;
  - the value is normalized if required per the XML 1.0 Recommendation, Section 3.3.3,
- is significant when it is an attribute of *type* ID, as it confers a unique identifier to the element;
  - the element is assigned a unique identifier from the attribute value;
  - it requires the source file to have a document model whose declaration for the attribute is of type ID;
    - no special meaning is conferred for attributes named "id", only for attributes of type ID;
    - it is an error if there are two elements in the source tree with both an attribute of type ID and the same value for that attribute;
      - if the XSLT processor chooses to not report the error, the first element with the attribute of the given value is considered the element with the unique identifier;

- below are some well-formed document examples:

```
<!DOCTYPE prodsummary [
<!ATTLIST prod id ID #REQUIRED>
]>
```

and

```
<!DOCTYPE custsummary [
<!ATTLIST cust custNbr ID #REQUIRED>
]>
```

  - without a complete DTD it is sufficient to add only an attribute list declaration for the attribute in question;
  - not all XML processors used with XSLT processors communicate the required ID attribute type information without a complete DTD;
- it is a common error to process an input file that does not declare ID typed attributes with a stylesheet expecting to use unique identifiers;
  - function calls returning the sought nodes return the empty node set.

3.1.6   Text node:

- is a single unnamed node created for a string of adjacent character data;
  - it includes all text and character markup that is not any other kind of document markup;
    - characters are regarded in their abstract UCS (Universal Character Set) value, not by any entity that may have been used to specify the character in the instance;
      - e.g.: "<" in the instance is regarded as "<" in the text node;
      - this is an impediment to supporting markup preservation in stylesheets;
    - the XSLT processor can choose to serialize result tree text node characters using any escaping mechanisms appropriate to the active serialization method;
  - all entity references are expanded and their boundaries are not preserved;
    - all text is treated at the end result of parsing the instance;
  - all text not in markup before or after the document element is ignored whitespace;
    - by definition it must be whitespace and is, therefore, not considered part of the information;
  - see important detailed notes later in this section regarding whitespace preservation in text nodes,
- does *not* preserve any CDATA section boundaries;

- CDATA sections are considered only a syntactic sugar that reduces the amount of text escaping done in the creation of XML textual information;
- all text found in a CDATA section is added to the text node and is indistinguishable from text not found in a CDATA section,
- normalizes line endings from external entities to
 per XML 1.0,
- does not capture characters found inside comments and processing instructions as they are not considered character data, thus they are not captured in text nodes in the source tree;
  - note, however, that text nodes can be and are typically used in the stylesheet to specify the content of result tree comments and processing instructions,
- is a child of its parent node,
- is always a leaf of the tree and never has any child nodes of any type,
- has a value which is the string of character data in the node,
- is always combined in the result tree with adjacent text nodes.

3.1.7 Whitespace-only text nodes

Text nodes with any non-whitespace characters are always preserved and are not treated specially.

- All whitespace is preserved in every text node found to have at least one character other than #x20, #x9, #xD or #xA (as defined by XML; respectively these characters are space, horizontal tab, carriage return, and line feed).

Whitespace-only text nodes are treated specially.

- Such nodes are not necessarily created in both source and stylesheet documents.
  - The XML processor assumes most whitespace-only text in the stylesheet is not significant.
  - The stylesheet can specify which whitespace-only text in the source is or is not significant.
  - XML reserved attributes in either the source or stylesheet instances can indicate which whitespace-only text in the source is significant.

3.1.7.1 *Preservation in the stylesheet tree by the XSLT processor*

- `<xsl:text>` instruction's child text node is preserved.

- All whitespace is preserved in every text node that is a child of an `<xsl:text>` instruction found in stylesheet instance.
  - Note that `<xsl:text>` elements cannot have any elements in their content (e.g. XSLT instructions or literal result elements), they can only have text.

3.1.7.2 *Control in the source by the writer of the stylesheet*

- All element types are assumed to require whitespace-only child nodes to be preserved.
  - The list of element types for which whitespace-only child text nodes are stripped is initially empty.
- `<xsl:strip-space elements="`*names*`"/>` changes assumptions.
  - It grows the list of element types being stripped of whitespace-only child text nodes.
- `<xsl:preserve-space elements="`*names*`"/>` overrides changed assumptions.
  - It shrinks the list of element types being stripped of whitespace-only child text nodes.
  - The ability to grow the list after shrinking the list or shrink the list after growing the list is made available for stylesheets that are imported to other stylesheets.
  - The precedence rules for these instructions are the same as those for `<xsl:template>` described later for `<xsl:import>` in Chapter 6.
- This mechanism is applicable only to a given element's direct child text nodes.
  - It does not apply to other descendent text nodes.

3.1.7.3 *Overriding by the author of an XML instance*

- XML 1.0 reserved attributes can be used by the author of an instance.
  - `xml:space="preserve"` specifies that whitespace-only nodes be preserved.
  - `xml:space="default"` requests no special handling of whitespace-only nodes.
- This mechanism is applicable to all of a given element's descendant text nodes —
  - to the point at which a descendent element includes another whitespace XML declaration.
- According to the XML 1.0 Recommendation, any XML document can declare the intent that whitespace in document content be preserved by applications by using `xml:space="preserve"`, or can declare the application to do what it wishes with whitespace by using `xml:space="default"`.

- Text nodes under the influence of `xml:space="preserve"` are preserved regardless of stylesheet-specified controls, i.e. it overrides any other assumptions made by the XSLT processor.

3.1.8 Root node:

- is the only node in the tree without a parent;
    - the root node only occurs at the root of the tree as the parent of the document element,
- is a node whose child nodes in the source tree are restricted:
    - no text nodes,
    - exactly one element node (the document element),
    - any number of nodes needed for comments and processing instructions present in the XML instance outside of (either before or after), and in order with, the element node for the document element,
- is a node whose child nodes in the result tree are not restricted;
    - they can include any number of element, text, comment and processing instruction nodes;
    - the type and count of nodes dictates the serialization of the result —
        - either a well-formed document entity, with identical constraints as found in the source tree,
        - or a well-formed external general parsed entity, with the constraint of a single element node as a child of the root node being relaxed,
- is not named,
- has the value which is the value of the document element.

3.1.9 Summary of XPath data model nodes

The following summarizes how these node types compare in general:

Node type	Visible in node tree	Tree position	Child/ Attached	Named	Valued
Element	all node trees	leaf (empty) or branch (not empty)	child	element type	all descendent text node values
Attribute	all node trees	leaf	attached	attribute name	specified or defaulted string
Namespace	depends†	leaf	attached	prefix	URI string

Node type	Visible in node tree	Tree position	Child/ Attached	Named	Valued
Processing Instruction	not in stylesheet node tree	leaf	child	PI Target	character string after first whitespace
Comment	not in stylesheet node tree	leaf	child	no	character string
Text (whitespace-only)	depends††	leaf	child	no	character string
Text (non-whitespace-only)	all node trees	leaf	child	no	character string
Root	all node trees	branch	N/A	no	document element

† Namespace nodes:

- are duplicated in all element nodes descendent from the declaration of the namespace,
- are pruned from the stylesheet tree during tree creation by using:

  ```
  xsl:exclude-result-prefixes="names"
  ```

- cannot be pruned from the source tree during creation,
- are copied to the result tree when copying elements from the source tree or stylesheet tree.

†† Whitespace-only text nodes:

- are not made present in the stylesheet tree unless within the instruction:

  ```
  <xsl:text>
  ```

- can be pruned from the source tree during tree creation by using:

  ```
  <xsl:strip-space elements="names"/>
  ```

- can be protected from pruning from the source tree by using:

  ```
  <xsl:preserve-space elements="names"/>
  ```

- can be preserved in stylesheet or any source tree during tree creation when a descendant of an element using the attribute:

  ```
  xml:space="preserve"
  ```

- can always be in the result tree.

Specifically not included in the XPath data model but found in the Document Object Model (DOM):

- CDATA section nodes;
  - this is considered to be only syntactic sugar,
- document fragment and entity reference nodes;
  - this syntactic fragmentation is consumed by the XML processor within the XSLT processor,
- document type, entity and notation nodes;
  - there is no such information in XPath data model;
  - there is only a very limited access to unparsed entity URI strings through XSLT.

3.1.10 Depiction of a complete node tree

Consider the well-formed XML instance `partlist.xml`:

Example 3–1 An example XML instance without namespaces

```
Line 1  <?xml version="1.0"?>
     2  <!--start-->
     3  <part-list><part-name part-nbr="A123">bolt</part-name>
     4  <part-name part-nbr="B456">washer</part-name><warning type="ignore"/>
     5  <!--end of parts--><?cursor blink under?>
     6  </part-list>
```

A summary of each of the types of nodes in this instance and corresponding example values is as follows (other columns related to expressions are explained later in this chapter):

Node type	Node without specificity	Node in isolation	Isolation example	Example value
Element	*	*elementTypeName*	part-name	bolt
Attribute	@* or attribute::*	@*attributeName* or attribute:: *attributeName*	@part-nbr	A123
Namespace	namespace::*	namespace:: *prefix*	namespace::xml	http://www.w3.org/ XML/1998/namespace
Processing Instruction	processing-instruction ()	processing-instruction (*piTargetString*)	processing-instruction ('cursor')	blink under

Node type	Node without specificity	Node in isolation	Isolation example	Example value
Comment	`comment()`	N/A	N/A	`end of parts`
Text	`text()`	N/A	N/A	`bolt`
Root	`/`	N/A	N/A	`bolt` `washer`

These materials use the conventions shown in Figure 3–2 when depicting node trees.

It often helps when designing the stylesheet to sketch out the node tree of the source as shown in Figure 3–3.

Not depicted is the namespace node for the XML namespace. Such a node is attached to *every* element in the instance (see Figure 3–4).

Figure 3–2   Node tree depiction conventions

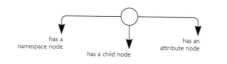

Figure 3–3   A depiction of the node tree of Example 3–1

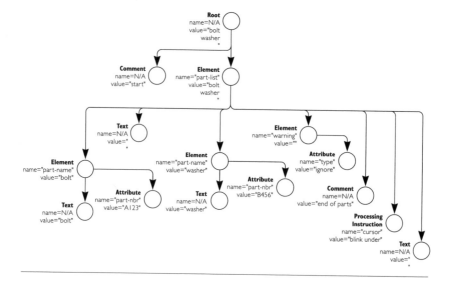

The following is a report of the content of the source node tree as generated by an XSLT processor:

Example 3–2   Report of node tree structure for Example 3–1

```
Line 1  SHOWTREE Stylesheet - http://www.CraneSoftwrights.com/resources/
     2  Processor: SAXON 5.3.2 from Michael Kay of ICL
     3  1  Comment: {start}
     4  2  Element 'part-list':
     5  2.I  Namespace 'xml': {http://www.w3.org/XML/1998/namespace}
     6  2.1  Element 'part-name' (part-list):
     7  2.1.I  Namespace 'xml': {http://www.w3.org/XML/1998/namespace}
     8  2.1.A  Attribute 'part-nbr': {A123}
     9  2.1.1  Text (part-list,part-name): {bolt}
    10  2.2  Text (part-list): {
    11  }
    12  2.3  Element 'part-name' (part-list):
    13  2.3.I  Namespace 'xml': {http://www.w3.org/XML/1998/namespace}
    14  2.3.A  Attribute 'part-nbr': {B456}
    15  2.3.1  Text (part-list,part-name): {washer}
    16  2.4  Element 'warning' (part-list):
    17  2.4.I  Namespace 'xml': {http://www.w3.org/XML/1998/namespace}
    18  2.4.A  Attribute 'type': {ignore}
    19  2.5  Text (part-list): {
    20  }
    21  2.6  Comment (part-list): {end of parts}
    22  2.7  Proc. Inst. 'cursor' (part-list): {blink under}
    23  2.8  Text (part-list): {
    24  }
```

Note that the above stylesheet is a free resource available from the given URL and is a useful diagnostic tool to report an XSLT processor's view of an arbitrary XML document.

- When a stylesheet does not behave as desired, it can help to see the nodes the processor can see in an XML document in case a visual inspection of that document is misinterpreted by the stylesheet writer.

Figure 3–4   Ever-present namespace node

3.1.10.1   *An example including namespace nodes*

Consider the well-formed instance `namespace.xml` that contains namespace declarations:

Example 3–3   An example XML instance with numerous namespaces

```
Line 1  <?xml version="1.0"?>
     2  <a>
     3    <b xmlns:x="http://x">
     4      <c xmlns:y="http://y">
     5        <d x:p="x-p" y:q="y-q" r="r" xmlns="http://z"/>
     6      </c>
     7    </b>
     8  </a>
```

Note in the instance that the `r=` attribute is not in any namespace; it is not in the default namespace that the `d` element is in.

The following is a report of the content of the source node tree as generated by an XSLT processor, revealing the replication of the namespace nodes:

Example 3–4   Report of node tree structure for Example 3–3

```
Line 1  SHOWTREE Stylesheet - http://www.CraneSoftwrights.com/resources/
     2  Processor: SAXON 5.3.2 from Michael Kay of ICL
     3  1 Element 'a':
     4  1.I  Namespace 'xml': {http://www.w3.org/XML/1998/namespace}
     5  1.1  Text (a): {
     6    }
     7  1.2  Element 'b' (a):
     8  1.2.I  Namespace 'xml': {http://www.w3.org/XML/1998/namespace}
     9  1.2.II  Namespace 'x': {http://x}
    10  1.2.1  Text (a,b): {
    11    }
    12  1.2.2  Element 'c' (a,b):
    13  1.2.2.I  Namespace 'xml': {http://www.w3.org/XML/1998/namespace}
    14  1.2.2.II  Namespace 'x': {http://x}
    15  1.2.2.III  Namespace 'y': {http://y}
    16  1.2.2.1  Text (a,b,c): {
    17        }
    18  1.2.2.2  Element '{http://z}d' (a,b,c):
    19  1.2.2.2.I  Namespace 'xml': {http://www.w3.org/XML/1998/namespace}
    20  1.2.2.2.II  Namespace 'x': {http://x}
    21  1.2.2.2.III  Namespace 'y': {http://y}
    22  1.2.2.2.IV  Namespace: {http://z}
    23  1.2.2.2.A  Attribute '{http://x}x:p': {x-p}
    24  1.2.2.2.B  Attribute '{http://y}y:q': {y-q}
    25  1.2.2.2.C  Attribute 'r': {r}
```

```
26  1.2.2.3  Text (a,b,c): {
27       }
28  1.2.3  Text (a,b): {
29     }
30  1.3  Text (a): {
31  }
```

Note how there are two namespaces for b on lines 8 and 9 and three namespaces for c on lines 13 through 15. Every element has the xml namespace node and each of b, c, and d have the namespace nodes of all ancestral elements.

3.2 XPath expressions and patterns

3.2.1 Expressions

XPath defines core data types used in expressions.

- Boolean values:
  - are the traditional true and false values used in logical arithmetic.
- Number values:
  - are floating point numbers as defined by IEEE.
- String values:
  - are sequences of UCS characters represented by their character codes.
- Nodes from the source tree (location paths made up of location steps);
  - location paths specify sets of nodes (primarily treated in document order);
  - location steps specify nodes from an axis (primarily treated in proximity order).

XSLT extends XPath data types and expressions to include —

- fragments of the result tree,
  - which are packages of result tree nodes representing information that can be added to the result tree on demand.

XSLT expressions are used for:

- selecting nodes from the source tree —
  - using a location path expression,
    - e.g.: `<xsl:apply-templates select="part-name/@*"/>`,
      - i.e. add to the result tree the template for each of the attributes of all part-name children,
  - executing a function returning nodes,

- specifying matching source node conditions —
  - choosing between alternative template rules,
  - using a subset of location path expressions,
    - e.g.: `<xsl:template match="@part-nbr">`,
      - i.e. specify the result tree template for the `part-nbr` attribute of any element,
    - e.g.: `<xsl:template match="part-name/@part-nbr">`,
      - i.e. specify the result tree template for the `part-nbr` attribute of a `part-name` element,
  - node counting,
  - key collection membership,
- evaluating the value of some formulation —
  - adding the result of an expression evaluation as a string of generated text to the result tree,
  - using an arbitrary XSLT or XPath expression,
    - e.g.: `<xsl:value-of select="sum(`*`node-set-expression`*`)"/>`
      - i.e. find all the nodes specified in the node-set expression,
      - convert the string value of each node to a number,
      - sum the numbers into a total,
      - return the number total as the result of the `sum()` expression evaluation,
      - the instruction converts the number to a string for use in the result tree,
  - key collection member valuation.

3.2.1.1   *Formal expression grammar in Recommendations:*

- is only summarized in this book.
  - See Appendix C for cross-referenced list of productions.
    - They are not cross-referenced in the actual Recommendations.
  - Formal language is not copied from Recommendations into this material.
  - This book does not attempt to be as rigorous as the Recommendations.

3.2.1.2   *Two basic kinds of expressions*

- Pattern expression:
  - specifies a node-set;
    - it is a subset of location path expressions;
    - no variable references are allowed anywhere in the expression;
    - if the first step is a function it can only be `id()` or `key()` but not any other function;
    - steps can only use `child::` or `attribute::` axes,
  - supports either matching or evaluation:
    - supports only *matching* when used in a context that requires a pattern —
      - as such returns a boolean value,
    - supports only *evaluation* in all other contexts —

- as such returns a node-set.
- Non-pattern expression:
  - specifies and returns any XPath or XSLT data type —
    - all location paths,
    - other XSLT and XPath expressions,
  - supports only evaluation,
  - can use parentheses for grouping —
    - by isolating the result of an expression's value within another expression —
      - e.g. when using operators,
    - to coerce processing of location path expressions to document order.

3.2.2 Location path expression evaluation context

XPath defines a context for evaluating location path expressions.

- Context node:
  - is a node in the tree.
- Context position:
  - is a non-zero positive integer.
- Context size:
  - is a non-zero positive integer greater than or equal to the context position.
- Variable bindings:
  - are used when variables are referenced.
- Function library:
  - is used when functions are called.
- Namespace declarations:
  - are used when namespace prefixes are specified.

XSLT sub-expression is evaluated in an XSLT context.

- Aspects that may change at each step are as follows:
  - the current node:
    - defines the XPath context node,
  - the current node list:
    - is the set of nodes being acted upon;
      - it always contains the current node;
      - the 1-origin location of the current node in the list defines the XPath value for context position;
      - the size of the list defines the XPath value for context size.
- Aspects that do not change at each step are as follows:
  - variable bindings:
    - include XSLT-specific data types,

- XPath core functions,
- namespace declarations,
- those specific to XSLT and not XPath:
  - XSLT-specific and processor-defined extension functions,
  - a node key set of source tree nodes.

XSLT current node list is a critically important concept, which:

- is redefined for every `select=` expression:
  - `<xsl:apply-templates>` — pushing nodes,
  - `<xsl:for-each>` — pulling nodes,
- is temporarily changed throughout evaluation of a location path expression —
  - refined as each intermediate result in between two location steps of a location path,
  - the result of specifying a node test and filtering by the predicates on each of the nodes from the previous step in the path,
- supersedes previous current node list until finished being processed;
  - when done, current node restores to previous position in previous node list,
- does not allow to halt processing of the current node list part way;
  - all members of the current node list are processed in sequence.

Functions returning information regarding the current node list are as follows:

- `position()`
  - returns the position of the current node in the current node list,
  - uses the number 1 for the first position, not zero as in many programming languages;
- `last()`
  - returns the number of nodes in the current node list.

3.2.3 Location path expression structure

3.2.3.1 *Location path expressions:*

- specify nodes from the source node tree by the relationships of nodes to each other;
  - arbitrary location from well-defined position:
    - is usable in pattern expressions —
      - if it begins with a function returning a node-set from the initial source node tree:
        - `key()`

- - id()
  - is not usable in pattern expressions —
    - if it begins with a function returning a node-set from other than the initial source node tree:
      - document()
    - if it begins with a node-set variable:
      - $variable-name
  - may be followed by a relative location expression,
  - cannot be used as a location step or preceded by a location path in an expression,
  - absolute location from root of tree containing the current node:
    - begins with "/",
    - may be followed with a relative location expression,
    - must be used with care as to which tree is being accessed when dealing with multiple source node trees;
      - the stylesheet can store the root of the initial source node tree in a top-level variable in order to always have access to the starting tree,
  - relative location from current position:
    - does not begin with "/",
    - evaluates relative node relationships to current node,
- evaluate multiple location steps from left to right;
  - steps are separated using "/";
  - each step refines the node-set based on specified criteria,
- may be a single expression formed as a union of multiple expressions;
  - complete location expressions are separated with "|";
  - logical or can be used for union of node-sets (not logical and for intersection)
  - behavior "feels" different based on where used;
    - it acts like the natural language "or" (choice) when performing pattern matching;
      - match="a | b" matches element nodes named "a" or element nodes named "b";
    - but it acts like the natural language "and" (aggregate) when performing node selection for evaluation;
      - select="a | b" selects child element nodes named "a" and child element nodes named "b".

3.2.3.2 Location steps

Each non-function location step in a location path is comprised of (see Figure 3–5):

- an axis identifier —
  - indicating the direction from current node,

- a node test —
  - filtering nodes by type and name,
- zero or more predicates —
  - filtering nodes by qualifying expressions tested against each node.

The current node list changes at and during every step evaluation (see Figure 3–6).

- It changes at every node test.
- It changes after every predicate.
- In the end, the resulting node list contains the nodes of the type of the rightmost node test.

For example, the following single location path has 4 steps:

```
id(parent::*/@idref)/ancestor-or-self::frame
                    /descendant::fig[caption]
                    /@image
```

- Arbitrary whitespace can be added to try to make location paths more legible.
- The first step jumps to an arbitrary location based on the unique identifier of an element being equal to the `idref=` attribute of the parent of the current node.
- The second step moves up the hierarchy, if necessary, to the `frame` element.
- The third step uses a predicate to filter from all descendent `fig` elements only those with child `caption` elements.
- The fourth step moves to the `image` attribute of each of the `fig` elements selected.

Figure 3–5   Components of a location step

axis :: *nodetest* [*predicate*][*predicate*]

Figure 3–6   Node-set changes and bases of relative evaluation

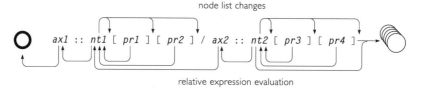

- Note that the expression uses some abbreviations described later in this section.

3.2.3.3 *Axes*

- There are thirteen axis directions from current node, each in proximity order.
- The use of a double colon "::" immediately follows the use of an axis name.
  - `ancestor::`
    - the parent and its ancestors (the chain of parents up to *and including* the root), in reverse document order,
  - `ancestor-or-self::`
    - the current node and its ancestors, in reverse document order,
  - `attribute::`
    - attached attribute nodes, in an implementation-defined order,
  - `child::`
    - immediate child nodes, in document order,
  - `descendant::`
    - all descendent nodes (children and their children), in document order,
  - `descendant-or-self::`
    - the current node and its descendent nodes, in document order,
  - `following::`
    - all nodes after the end of the current node, in document order,
  - `following-sibling::`
    - all following nodes that are siblings of the current node, in document order,
  - `namespace::`
    - attached namespace nodes, in an implementation-defined order,
  - `parent::`
    - the parent node (or the attaching node for attached attribute and namespace nodes),
  - `preceding::`
    - all nodes wholly contained (constructs start and end) before the start of the current node, in reverse document order,
  - `preceding-sibling::`
    - all preceding nodes that are siblings of the current node, in reverse document order,
  - `self::`

- the current node.

A depiction of each of the axes is at Figure 3–1.

3.2.3.4 *Node tests*

Node tests determine what type and optionally which name of node to look for along the direction of the axis specified or implied.

- A node by its type along any axis:
  - `processing-instruction()`
    - a processing instruction node (regardless of name),
  - `comment()`
    - a comment node,
  - `text()`
    - a text node,
  - `node()`
    - a node of any type (the wildcard);
  - note that even though the above can be used on any axis, the attached axes will never have processing instruction, comment, or text nodes,
- a name: "`processing-instruction(name-string-expression)`":
  - a processing instruction node by its name,
- a name: "*name*":
  - when using the namespace axis: a namespace node,
  - when using the attribute axis: an attribute node not in any namespace,
  - otherwise: an element node not in any namespace;
  - note that "not in any namespace" also means not in the default namespace,
- a namespace-qualified name: "*prefix:name*":
  - when using the namespace axis: empty node-set,
  - when using the attribute axis: an attribute node in the given prefix's namespace,
  - otherwise: an element node in the given prefix's namespace,
- the character "`*`":
  - when using the namespace axis: all namespace nodes,
  - when using the attribute axis: all attribute nodes,
  - otherwise: all element nodes in any namespace (including the default namespace),
- the sequence "*prefix:*`*`":
  - when using the namespace axis: empty node-set,
  - when using the attribute axis: all attribute nodes in the given prefix's namespace,
  - otherwise: all element nodes in the given prefix's namespace.

Important namespace nuances:

- Recall that elements in the default namespace do not have a namespace prefix but a namespace URI is defined for them.
- Node tests without a namespace prefix do not use the default namespace of the stylesheet.
  - Thus, such nodes tested are considered as not being in any namespace.
  - If the stylesheet declares the default namespace, this is not used in expression evaluation for non-prefixed node tests.
- Source tree nodes not in any namespace are only matched by node tests that do not have a namespace prefix.
  - Source tree nodes in the default namespace *are* considered to be in a namespace.
- Source tree nodes in any namespace are only matched by node tests that have a namespace prefix.
  - Any namespace prefix can be used in a node test provided the namespace URI is identical to the namespace URI of the node being matched in the source tree.
  - All namespace-qualified source tree nodes can only be matched with namespace-qualified node tests.
    - Those elements are included in the default namespace.
    - Attributes without a prefix are never considered to be in any namespace and thus are not considered to be in the default namespace even if one is defined.

3.2.3.5 *Abbreviations*

- Several abbreviations can make writing expressions more succinct.
- Some abbreviations are only an axis specification, which:
  - requires a node test,
  - allows predicates to be used within the step,
  - includes the following cases:
    - omitted axis specification:
      - denotes nodes along `child::` axis according to the node test and optional predicates,
    - the character "@":
      - denotes nodes along the `attribute::` axis according to the node test and possible predicate.
- Other abbreviations are complete location steps and:
  - prohibit the direct use of predicates within the step,
  - include the following cases:
    - the character ".":
      - `self::node()`
        - the current node regardless of the node type;
      - can be used stand-alone in the expression,

- the sequence "..":
  - `parent::node()`
    - the parent node if the current node is not an attached node (element, text, processing instruction, or comment),
    - the attaching node if the current node is an attached node (attribute or namespace),
    - the empty node-set if the current node is the root node,
  - can be used standalone in the expression,
- the sequence "//":
  - `/descendant-or-self::node()/`
  - abbreviates absolute location path when used at the start of an expression,
  - abbreviates relative location path when used elsewhere in an expression,
  - must be followed by another location step in the expression.

3.2.3.6 *Predicates*

- ## Predicates are qualifying expressions to filter nodes.
  - A node is considered qualified to be in the node-set if the filter expression evaluates as a boolean value to `true`.
- ## Predicates are specifiable on any node set:
  - a node test in a location step,
  - the resulting set of an entire location path;
    - a location path result can be specified by placing the location path in parentheses,
  - the return node-set from a function (e.g. `id()`, `key()`),
  - a node-set variable.
- ## Predicates are specified within square brackets "[" and "]" and can be:
  - a numeric value: `question[3]` or `question[last()]`;
    - it specifies the ordinal position (1-origin) in the current node list;
    - the predicate is `true` for only the node with the given ordinal position,
  - node-set expression value: `question[@answer]` or `question[guess]`;
    - it specifies node presence test;
    - the predicate is `true` only if the selection of nodes specified returns a non-empty set of nodes,
  - other expression value: `question[count(guess)=5]`;
    - it is converted to boolean according to `boolean()`;
    - the predicate is `true` only if the expression evaluates to `true`.
- ## For numeric predicates, the node ordering depends on the source of the node-set.
  - Nodes specified in a location step expression are treated in proximity order.

- Nodes selected along the reverse axes (towards the start of the document) are counted in reverse document order and nodes selected along forward axes (towards the end of the document) are counted in document order.
- When the axis includes the context node, the context node is at position one and the node in the set closest to the context node is at position two, and so on through the list.
- When the axis does not include the context node, the node in the set closest to the context node is at position one, the next closest is at position two, and so on through the list.
- Nodes returned by a location path expression are treated in document order.
  - Confusingly described in the recommendation as "filters the node-set with respect to the child axis".
- `preceding-sibling::*[1]` does not necessarily select the same node as `(preceding-sibling::*)[1]`.
  - The first is a complete location step expression while the second is a predicate applied to a location path expression.

- Multiple predicates are cumulative and are —
  - evaluated left to right in the syntax,
  - specified in adjacent predicate expressions,
  - applied in turn to each node in the resulting set from applying the previous predicate.

- All predicates are applied to each node in current node list or set.
  - The predicate is evaluated in the context of each node in turn.
    - The predicate expression temporarily changes the context of evaluation to produce the result.
    - The resulting context at the end of a given predicate's evaluation is not material.
  - The node stays in set if the predicate's result boolean value is `true`.
  - Otherwise, the node is removed from the list.

3.2.4 Example node-set and pattern expressions

Some example node-set and pattern expressions expressed as a selection attribute:

- `select="child::partNbr"`
  - child element nodes from the current node with the name "`partNbr`",
- `select="partNbr"`
  - child element nodes from the current node with the name "`partNbr`",
- `select="./partNbr"`
  - child element nodes from the current node with the name "`partNbr`",
- `select=".//partNbr"`

- descendent element nodes from the current node with the name "partNbr",
- select="//partNbr"
  - descendent element nodes from the root with the name "partNbr" (i.e. all such element nodes in the entire document),
- select="../partNbr"
  - sibling (and possibly self) element nodes with the name "partNbr" by first going to the parent with ".." and then to the parent's children,
- select="self::partNbr"
  - the current node if the current node name is "partNbr", otherwise the empty node-set,
- select="@type"
  - attached attribute nodes with the name "type",
- select="../@type"
  - the parent's attached attribute nodes with the name "type",
- select="../partNbr/@type"
  - the attribute nodes with the name "type" of the sibling element nodes with the name "partNbr",
- select="partNbr/@type"
  - the attribute nodes named "type" of the child element nodes with the name "partNbr",
- select="/.."
  - a guaranteed empty node-set (the root never has a parent node).

Example node-set and pattern expressions incorporating predicates:

- select="partNbr[@type]"
  - the child element nodes with the name "partNbr" that have the attribute named "type",
- select="partNbr[@type='cots']/@price"
  - the attribute node named "price" of the child element nodes with the name "partNbr" that have the attribute named "type" equal to the string "cots",
- select="partNbr[position()=3]"
  - the third child element node named "partNbr",
- select="partNbr[3] | partNbr[5]"
  - the third and fifth child element nodes named "partNbr",
- select="partNbr[position()>=3 and position()<=5]"
  - the third through fifth child element nodes named "partNbr",
- select="partNbr[@type][3]"

- the third child element node named "partNbr" that has an attached attribute node named "type",
- select="partNbr[3][@type]"
  - the third child element node named "partNbr" *if* that node has an attached attribute named "type", otherwise, it indicates the empty set,
- select="partNbr[position()=last()]"
  - the last child element node named "partNbr",
- select="(//partNbr)[1]"
  - the first element node with the name "partNbr" in the entire document,
- select="//partNbr[1]"
  - descendent element nodes from the root with the name "partNbr" that are the first amongst sibling partNbr elements,
- select="*[not(self::partNbr | self::partList)]"
  - all children elements except elements named "partNbr" or "partList".

Example node-set expressions that are not patterns:

- select="preceding::partNbr"
  - the set of all preceding element nodes with the name "partNbr",
- select="preceding::partNbr[1]"
  - the closest preceding element node with the name "partNbr",
- select="preceding::partNbr[@type]"
  - the set of all preceding element nodes with the name "partNbr" that have an attribute named "type",
- select="preceding-sibling::partNbr/@type"
  - the attributes named "type" of all the preceding element sibling nodes with the name "partNbr",
- select="preceding-sibling::partNbr[@type][1]"
  - the closest preceding sibling element node with the name "partNbr" that has an attribute named "type",
- select="preceding-sibling::partNbr[1][@type]"
  - the closest preceding element sibling node with the name "partNbr" if and only if that element has an attribute named "type" (if the closest does not have the attribute, the result is the empty set of nodes),
- select="preceding-sibling::partNbr[@type][1]/@type"
  - the attribute named "type" of the closest preceding sibling element node with the name "partNbr" that has an attribute named "type",
- select="preceding-sibling::partNbr/@type[1]"
  - the attributes named "type" of all the preceding element sibling nodes with the name "partNbr" (the predicate has no effect),

- `select="(preceding-sibling::partNbr/@type)[1]"`
  - the attribute named "type" of the furthest preceding element node with the name "partNbr" (the set is in document order),
- `select="(preceding-sibling::partNbr/@type)[last()]"`
  - the attribute named "type" of the closest preceding element node with the name "partNbr" (the set is in document order),
- `select="id(@reference)/@type"`
  - the attribute named "type" of the element node (returned by the id() function) with the unique identifier equal to the value of the "reference" attribute attached to the current node.

3.2.5 Location path expression evaluation summary

XSLT begins XPath location path expression evaluation at the first step which can be:

- an arbitrary location —
  - oriented to the node or nodes resulting from executing a function or the reference to a node-set variable,
- an absolute location —
  - oriented to the root node,
- a relative location —
  - oriented to the current node.

Each step is evaluated.

- Resulting node list of previous step is the current node list for given step.
- Step conditions are evaluated for each member of node list.
  - Each evaluation uses each member as current node.
  - Each evaluation returns a set of nodes.
- Resulting step node list is union of all evaluations in the step.

Evaluation continues as follows.

- Steps are evaluated left-to-right.
- Evaluation terminates when current node list is empty.
  - Resulting node list for the entire expression is the empty node list.
- The final step's result becomes the expression's result.
  - The current node list after the last step is evaluated.

The stepwise evaluation of the expression utilizing predicates is shown in Figure 3–7.

3.2.6 Processing of node-sets from reverse axes

Important nuances regarding the processing of nodes selected by axes are as follows.

- Recall that predicates are oriented by proximity to the current node, thus predicates applied to nodes found on reverse axes act on the node-sets in reverse document order, while predicates applied to nodes found on forward axes act on the node-sets in document order.

- When the resulting set selected by the given location step is processed *as a collection of nodes*, it is processed in document order, not in axis order —

  - when a predicate is applied to a node-set expression containing nodes selected by axes,
  - in an intermediate step for a following location step expression.

Figure 3–7   An example multi-step location path

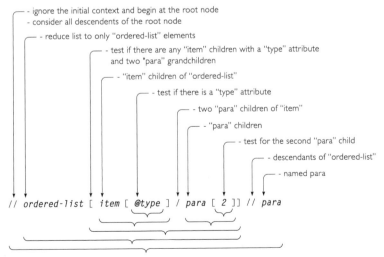

all "para" element nodes that are descendents of all "ordered-list" element nodes
of the entire document node tree that have at least two "para" element node
children of an "item" child that has a "type" attribute specified or defaulted

Consider the XML file `nodeset.xml`:

Example 3–5   An example instance for processing using the `preceding-sibling::` axis

```
Line 1  <?xml version="1.0"?>
     2  <set>
     3  <item>A</item>
     4  <item>B</item>
     5  <item>C</item>
     6  </set>
```

It is processed with the XSLT file `nodeset.xsl`:

Example 3–6   Processing the example instance using the `preceding-sibling::` axis

```
Line 1  <?xml version="1.0"?>                                      <!--nodeset.xsl-->
     2  <!--XSLT 1.0 - http://www.CraneSoftwrights.com/training -->
     3  <!DOCTYPE xsl:stylesheet [<!ENTITY nl "&#xd;&#xa;">]>
     4  <xsl:stylesheet xmlns:xsl="http://www.w3.org/1999/XSL/Transform"
     5                  version="1.0">
     6
     7  <xsl:output method="text"/>
     8
     9  <xsl:template match="/">                                   <!--root rule-->
    10    <xsl:for-each select="//item[last()]">           <!--work from the end-->
    11      <xsl:text>"preceding-sibling::item[1]": </xsl:text>
    12      <xsl:value-of select="preceding-sibling::item[1]"/>
    13      <xsl:text>&nl;"(preceding-sibling::item)[1]": </xsl:text>
    14      <xsl:value-of select="(preceding-sibling::item)[1]"/>
    15      <xsl:text>&nl;for each "preceding-sibling::item":</xsl:text>
    16      <xsl:for-each select="preceding-sibling::item/text()">
    17        <xsl:text>&nl;   Item: </xsl:text><xsl:value-of select="."/>
    18      </xsl:for-each>
    19    </xsl:for-each>
    20  </xsl:template>
    21
    22  </xsl:stylesheet>
```

It produces the following result:

Example 3–7   Results of processing the example with the `preceding-sibling::` axis

```
Line 1  "preceding-sibling::item[1]": B
     2  "(preceding-sibling::item)[1]": A
     3  for each "preceding-sibling::item":
     4    Item: A
     5    Item: B
```

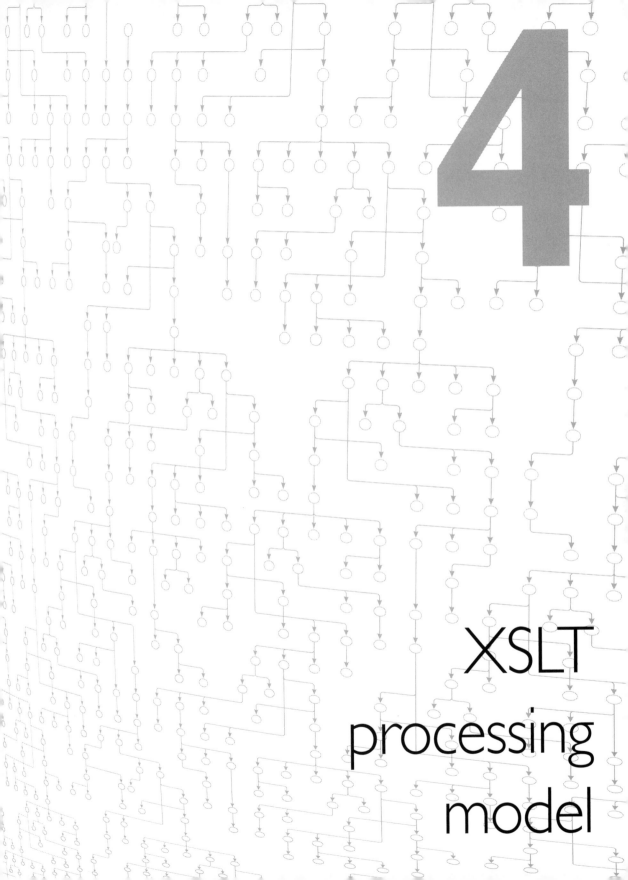

4

XSLT
processing
model

4 XSLT processing model

Understanding the XSLT process model helps us build our stylesheets according to the nature of the information we are working with, and the nature of our desired result.

XSLT is designed to ensure predictability. XSLT specifies well-defined predictable behaviors for all of the instructions. This ensures that random factors do not impact the processing of our information with our stylesheets. Note, however, that there are some behaviors that are specified to be implementation dependent, therefore the actual process using a given XSLT processor may be different than the same process using another XSLT processor, though both processors implement the well-defined behavior according to the Recommendation.

Note: The above paragraph may seem contradictory. Many behaviors in XSLT are described indicating what an XSLT processor must do based on whether or not the processor chooses to respond to certain conditions or to offer to the operator. For each such behavior the stylesheet writer can rely on a well-defined process, though the writer may not know which process is actually being used by a given processor.

In my early stages of learning to write XSLT stylesheets, I found this difficult to understand.

The XSLT processor reads the stylesheet resource, interpreting the contents as an abstract node tree according to the data model rules for a stylesheet. The resulting tree includes instructions (either from the XSLT vocabulary or an extension vocabulary) to be executed and literal result elements to be added to the result tree as required. Some top-level instructions are interpreted in order to know how to build the node tree for the source resource.

The XSLT processor then reads the source resource, interpreting the contents as an abstract node tree according to both the data model rules for a source resource and certain top-level instructions in the stylesheet. A source resource can include any vocabulary, including an instruction vocabulary, without the processor regarding the node tree in any way special.

The processing of the source resource then begins by the XSLT processor identifying the template rule for the root node and starting the result tree with the associated template. No other assumptions are made by the processor. All other behavior is dictated by the stylesheet.

The stylesheet templates shape the content of the result tree. Any instructions found in a template being included in the result tree are executed, with the result of each instruction being used in the result tree rather than the instruction itself. It is the stylesheet writer's responsibility to ensure the templates are added in the desired result tree parse order. This requires the stylesheet writer to visit the trigger nodes for matching templates in the required order to produce the desired result. Once a portion of the result tree is completed, there is no method of returning to modify that portion of the result. The boundaries of these portions are well defined.

If the XSLT processor offers the operator to act on the resulting tree created by the stylesheet, a number of possible actions can result. The result may be interpreted as XSL formatting and flow objects to effect a rendering to some target device. The result could be directly interpreted by an application utilizing the XSLT processor in a custom fashion as an XML processing front end.

The result may also be serialized into an external resource, thereby reifying the abstract node tree into actual physical syntax according to certain lexical rules. If a processor offers serialization, it is only obliged to support XML conventions, though it may also choose to offer HTML, text or an extension output method implemented by the processor.

A simple illustration of the basic process. Consider the flow of information depicted in the diagram in Figure 4–1.

The node trees created by the stylesheet file, the source file and by the result of stylesheet execution present the actual resources according to the XPath data model.

The diagram attempts to illustrate how literal result elements from the stylesheet node tree are copied to the result tree and how instruction elements from the stylesheet node tree are interpreted by instruction execution. This execution in this example results in a particular node from the source tree being added to the result tree. Descendent nodes making up that source node's sub-tree are copied to the result along with the apex.

Figure 4–1   Process model illustration

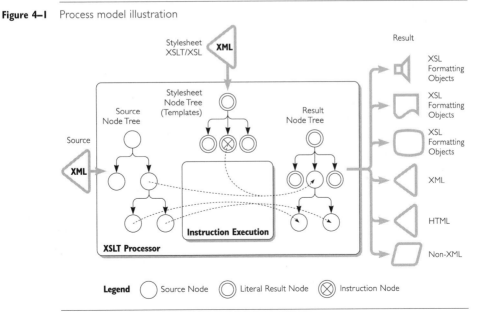

The normative result of transformation is the abstract result node tree. The processor may then offer to interpret the result node tree by effecting a rendering of the XSL formatting semantics, or by reifying the result tree as markup or custom syntax, or by interpreting the result for some custom application means, or a combination of the above.

Included in this chapter. This chapter includes discussion of the following XSLT instructions regarding processing of source instances by stylesheet logic.

Instructions to pull information from the source tree or to calculate values are as follows.

- `<xsl:for-each>`
  - iterates over a selection of source tree nodes using a supplied template.
- `<xsl:value-of>`
  - adds to the result tree the evaluation of an expression or the value of a source tree node.

Instructions to push information from the source tree through the stylesheet are as follows.

- `<xsl:apply-templates>`
  - supplies a selection of source tree nodes to push through template rules.
- `<xsl:template>`
  - defines a template rule.

4.1 XSLT processing model

4.1.1 Example transformation requirement

To illustrate various aspects of the XSLT processing model, examine the different requirements presented by the following transformation of information from a source instance into a desired result in HTML.

Consider the following XML source instance `card.xml`:

Example 4–1   An example business card XML instance

```
Line 1   <?xml version="1.0"?>
     2   <?xml-stylesheet type="text/xsl" href="cardpush.xsl"?>
     3   <card><name>G. Ken Holman</name>
     4   <address>Box 266, Kars, Ontario CANADA K0A-2E0</address>
```

```
5  <email type="Main">gkholman@CraneSoftwrights.com</email>
6  <email type="Backup">gkholman@CanadaMail.com</email>
7  </card>
```

The source tree of nodes is as follows:

Example 4–2   The XPath data model of the example instance

```
Line 1   SHOWTREE Stylesheet - http://www.CraneSoftwrights.com/resources/
     2   Processor: SAXON 5.3.2 from Michael Kay of ICL
     3   1  Proc. Inst. 'xml-stylesheet': {type="text/xsl" href="cardpush.xsl"}
     4   2  Element 'card':
     5   2.I  Namespace 'xml': {http://www.w3.org/XML/1998/namespace}
     6   2.1  Element 'name' (card):
     7   2.1.I  Namespace 'xml': {http://www.w3.org/XML/1998/namespace}
     8   2.1.1  Text (card,name): {G. Ken Holman}
     9   2.2  Text (card): {
    10   }
    11   2.3  Element 'address' (card):
    12   2.3.I  Namespace 'xml': {http://www.w3.org/XML/1998/namespace}
    13   2.3.1  Text (card,address): {Box 266, Kars, Ontario CANADA K0A-2E0}
    14   2.4  Text (card): {
    15   }
    16   2.5  Element 'email' (card):
    17   2.5.I  Namespace 'xml': {http://www.w3.org/XML/1998/namespace}
    18   2.5.A  Attribute 'type': {Main}
    19   2.5.1  Text (card,email): {gkholman@CraneSoftwrights.com}
    20   2.6  Text (card): {
    21   }
    22   2.7  Element 'email' (card):
    23   2.7.I  Namespace 'xml': {http://www.w3.org/XML/1998/namespace}
    24   2.7.A  Attribute 'type': {Backup}
    25   2.7.1  Text (card,email): {gkholman@CanadaMail.com}
    26   2.8  Text (card): {
    27   }
```

The objective is to render the result shown in Figure 4–2.

Of note:

- There is boilerplate text on the canvas that doesn't come from the source tree.
- Attribute values and element values are being displayed on the canvas.
- The name is only in the instance once and is rendered twice.
- Each pass of the information duplicates some data and suppresses or selects other data.

- The email addresses are hyperlinked (see status bar at bottom) thus requiring an element's content from the source to appear simultaneously in both an attribute (with a prefix) and content of the result.

One HTML encoding is the following result instance:

Example 4–3   Desired HTML markup for display of the example

```
Line 1  <center>
     2  <b><u>Electronic Contact Information</u></b>
     3  </center>
     4  <p>Name: G. Ken Holman</p>
     5
     6  <p>Main Email: <a href="mailto:gkholman@CraneSoftwrights.com"
     7  >gkholman@CraneSoftwrights.com</a>
     8  </p>
     9  <p>Backup Email: <a href="mailto:gkholman@CanadaMail.com"
    10  >gkholman@CanadaMail.com</a>
    11  </p>
    12  <center>
    13  <b><u>Postal Contact Information</u></b>
    14  </center>
    15  <p>Name: G. Ken Holman</p>
    16  <p>Address: Box 266, Kars, Ontario CANADA K0A-2E0</p>
```

Figure 4–2   The desired rendering of the example

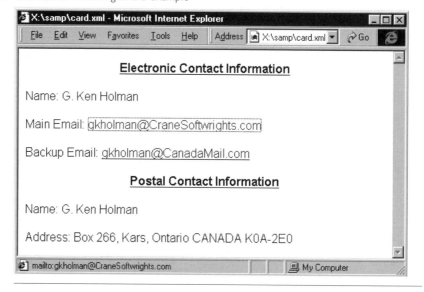

4.1.2 Approaches to transformation

There are two approaches:

- "pulling" information from the source tree —
  - adding the values into the result tree where desired,
  - by obtaining the values of or iterating over the presence of source tree nodes under stylesheet control,
- "pushing" the source tree through the stylesheet —
  - triggering events by the source tree to be caught by template rules waiting in the stylesheet.

Choosing which approach to use depends on the nature of the source data.

- Use pull when the source data order is known.
  - The kind and order of the nodes in the source tree are as expected by the stylesheet writer.
  - The stylesheet writer dictates the creation of the result tree.
    - The source nodes can be accessed on command.
    - The data is pulled by obtaining values from each of the nodes at the required locations of the result.
    - The count of source nodes at each location doesn't necessarily need to be known, only the location.
      - It is possible to iterate over an unknown number of source nodes characterized only by their location.
- Use push when the source data order is unknown or arbitrary.
  - The source tree dictates the creation of the result tree.
    - The kind and order of the nodes in the source tree are not expected by the stylesheet writer.
    - The writer chooses which portions of the source node tree are pushed through the stylesheet —
      - simply by name or by some other selection pattern for source tree nodes.
    - The stylesheet provides handlers for the events triggered by the source tree nodes.
      - The handlers are called template rules.
      - The triggers are called match patterns.
        - They characterize the relationships of source tree nodes to other source tree nodes.
      - Groups of template rules can be named —
        - to engage a stylesheet-defined "mode" of transformation,
        - to make it possible to selectively engage a particular mode when pushing a given set of source tree nodes.
    - The stylesheet may rely on built-in templates;

- not all source tree conditions have to be explicitly accommodated.
- Push supports source information from different document models —
  - if it is necessary to accommodate different input hierarchies with a given transformation.
- Push promotes customization and adaptation of other stylesheets;
  - Fine-grained push-oriented templates can be exploited more easily than monolithic pull-oriented templates.

Very often a mixture can best produce the result required.

- Pushing nodes through node event handlers:
  - accommodates the data in the order that it arrives,
  - flexibly allows instances from different document models to be accommodated.
- Pulling nodes from within the node event handlers:
  - enables accessing information from relative locations to those nodes that are being pushed.

4.1.3   Calculating result text

To build result information from source —

- when using *element* content in the stylesheet —
  - use this XSLT instruction:

    ```
    <xsl:value-of select="XPath-expression"/>
    ```

    - this instruction is always empty and never has a template;
- when using *attribute* content in the stylesheet —
  - use an attribute value template (AVT):

    ```
    attr="{XPath-expression}"
    ```

    - typically it is used in the attributes of literal result elements;
    - it is supported in the attributes of a small number of XSLT instructions;
    - an example is:

      ```
      attr="http://{expression-1}/{expression-2}"
      ```

      - multiple expressions in separate sets of brackets are allowed in a single attribute;
      - brace brackets surround each expression;
    - it allows to use any XPath expression, as in:

      ```
      total="{($base + @fixed) *
              (1 + ancestor::order/@tax)}"
      ```

      - an evaluated expression can be specified;
      - the total attribute is calculated as the sum of the base variable and the current node's fixed attribute multiplied by the order ancestor's tax attribute;

- literal brace brackets "{" and "}" must be specified as "{{" and "}}".

A stand-alone node-set expression is used to access a value from the source node tree.

- Only first node in set is used —
  - based on document order.
- Value calculated is the empty string if the set of nodes is empty.
  - This is not an error.

Consider the source fragment `<email type="Main">...</email>`.

- To use it in the following content of an element:

```
<b>The type is: Main</b>
```

  - we can use either a literal result element:

Example 4–4   Accessing an attribute when in a literal result element's content

```
<b>The type is: <xsl:value-of select="@type"/></b>
```

  - or an element instruction:

Example 4–5   Accessing an attribute when in an instruction element's content

```
Line 1   <xsl:element name="b">
     2     <xsl:text>The type is: </xsl:text>
     3     <xsl:value-of select="@type"/>
     4   </xsl:element>
```

- To use it in the following attribute content:

```
<order email-info="The type is: Main">ELECTRONIC</order>
```

  - we can use either a literal result element and attribute value template:

Example 4–6   Accessing an attribute when in literal result element attribute content of the stylesheet

```
Line 1   <order email-info="The type is: {@type}">
     2     <xsl:text>ELECTRONIC</xsl:text>
     3   </order>
```

  - or element and attribute instructions:

Example 4–7   Accessing an attribute when in an instruction element's content

```
Line 1   <xsl:element name="order">
     2     <xsl:attribute name="email-info">
     3       <xsl:text>The type is: </xsl:text>
     4       <xsl:value-of select="@type"/>
     5     </xsl:attribute>
```

```
6        <xsl:text>ELECTRONIC</xsl:text>
7    </xsl:element>
```

Other examples of obtaining source node tree values are as follows:

- `<xsl:value-of select="."/>`
  - injects the value of the current source tree node,
- `<xsl:value-of select="name(.)"/>`
  - injects the expanded name "*prefix:local*" of the current node,
- `<xsl:value-of select=".//partNbr"/>`
  - injects the value of the first of all descendent elements named partNbr,
- `<repair ref="{//partNbr}"/>`
  - injects the value of the first of all elements named partNbr from the entire instance,
- `<xsl:value-of select="//module[3]`
  `                     /lesson[@type='exercise'][last()]`
  `                     /frame/title"/>`
  - injects the title of the frame of the last lesson with an attribute node named "type" with the value "exercise", where that lesson is found in the third chapter,
    - note the arbitrary use of whitespace between tokens of the XPath expression.

Serialization of the result text obeys the following rules.

- If appropriate to the output method, all sensitive characters added to the result tree are escaped when serialized.
- "<" in the tree is escaped as "<" or "<" or "<" or "<".
- "&" in the tree is escaped as "&" or "&" or "&".
- ">" in the tree is escaped as ">" or ">" or ">" or ">".
- CDATA sections are serialized as in "<![CDATA[<&>]]>".

Sometimes escaping needs to be avoided.

- The stylesheet can request escaping be suppressed on any sequence of text added to result tree:
  ```
  <xsl:value-of select="expression"
                disable-output-escaping="yes"/>
  ```
- The processor can choose to ignore the request;

- stylesheet writer takes the risk;
  - disabling the escaping of characters can result in the output not being well-formed;
  - it is not a typical requirement when transforming information for the purposes of rendering;
  - not using this feature will result in all output being well-formed.

It is often necessary to access information more than once.

- source XML:

  ```
  <email type="Backup">gkholman@CanadaMail.com</email>
  ```

- desired result:

  ```
  <a href="mailto:gkholman@CanadaMail.com">
  gkholman@CanadaMail.com</a>
  ```

  - Note how the element's content from the source has been used twice in the result —
    - prefixed by "mailto:" in the attribute,
    - in the element's content.

This can be achieved using an attribute value template:

Example 4–8   Using an attribute value template in a literal result element

```
Line 1   <a href="mailto:{.}">
     2     <xsl:value-of select="."/>
     3   </a>
```

This can also be achieved using only instructions:

Example 4–9   Using an instruction to define an attribute value

```
Line 1   <xsl:element name="a">
     2     <xsl:attribute name="href">
     3       <xsl:text>mailto:</xsl:text>
     4       <xsl:value-of select="."/>
     5     </xsl:attribute>
     6     <xsl:value-of select="."/>
     7   </xsl:element>
```

Note again the attribute to `<xsl:value-of>` is assumed to be an expression and therefore that attribute *cannot* be specified with an attribute value template.

4.1.4 Iterative template instantiation

One can iterate over a set of selected source tree nodes:

Example 4–10 Attribute of the `<xsl:for-each>` instruction

```
Line 1    <xsl:for-each select="node-set-expression">
    2        template
    3    </xsl:for-each>
```

- Instruction element encapsulates a template to add for each iteration.
- Instruction attribute specifies which source tree nodes make up the selected node set.
- The stylesheet dictates the order and content of the result tree.

An example:

Example 4–11 An example of iterating over child element nodes

```
Line 1    <xsl:for-each select="email">
    2        <p><xsl:value-of select="@type"/> Email:
    3          <a>
    4            <xsl:attribute name="href">
    5              <xsl:text>mailto:</xsl:text>
    6              <xsl:value-of select="."/>
    7            </xsl:attribute>
    8            <xsl:value-of select="."/>
    9          </a>
    10       </p>
    11   </xsl:for-each>
```

The focus for XPath evaluation changes within the template.

- The `<xsl:for-each>` instruction's attribute is evaluated with the current node in the current node list of the template in which it is found.
  - In the example above "@type" is evaluated relative to the "email" element node, not to the parent node that was the current node when the iteration was executed.
- Instructions *within* the template are evaluated using each of the nodes selected.
  - The set of nodes selected becomes the current node list.
  - Each member of the set takes a turn as the current node.

- The nodes are in document order unless the first instructions of the template are sort instructions.
- The evaluation context is restored at the end of `<xsl:for-each>` to that context in place when the instruction was executed.

4.1.5   Template rules

The classical event-processing scheme goes as follows.

- Generate events:

Example 4–12   The generation of template rule events

```
<xsl:apply-templates select="node-set-expression">
```

- the instruction determines which nodes to visit;
- the set of nodes selected becomes the current node list for the processing of each node;
  - each member of the set takes a turn as the current node;
- the nodes are in document order unless the first instructions of the template are sort instructions;
- the `select=` attribute is optional;
  - it assumes `select="node()"` when absent;
    - the current node list becomes all child nodes of the current node;
  - attribute and namespace nodes of the source node tree *are not implicitly visited*;
    - they must be visited explicitly under stylesheet control by selecting the nodes desired;
- the data dictates the order and content of the result tree;
- the evaluation context is restored at the end of `<xsl:apply-templates>` to that context in place when the instruction was executed.
- Handle events:

Example 4–13   The components of a template rule

```
Line 1    <xsl:template match="node-set-pattern">
     2        template
     3    </xsl:template>
```

- this provides the template to be injected in the result tree when given nodes are visited;
  - the `match=` pattern does not need to be equivalent to the `select=` pattern that was used in `<xsl:apply-templates>`;
  - nodes and their contexts as described in the pattern are evaluated in the context of the source tree;

- the template rules can be grouped;
  - collections of template rules are called "modes" (described later in this chapter);
- template conflict resolution rules apply;
  - you cannot have more than one event handler that is a candidate for being triggered for visiting a given node (described later in this chapter);
  - the nature of the pattern and additional attributes in the stylesheet control matching nuances;
- the template rule can be named;
  - invoked on demand by the stylesheet as well as required by the nodes selected from the source node tree (described later in Chapter 6);
- the template rule's template can be parameterized;
  - variables whose bound values can be passed by the process invoking the template (described later in Chapter 6).

For example, in the objective of this sample the processing of the root node can ask the XSLT processor to look for template rules for all child element nodes named "card", thus the document element must be named "card":

Example 4–14   Pushing the document element of the example instance

```
Line 1   <xsl:template match="/">                          <!--process root node-->
     2     <xsl:apply-templates select="card"/>        <!--assume doc. element name-->
     3   </xsl:template>
```

The XSLT processor finds the template rule for a document element named card, adds to the result tree and then processes child nodes:

Example 4–15   Matching the document element of the example instance

```
Line 1   <xsl:template match="/card">
     2     <center><b><u>Electronic Contact Information</u></b></center>
     3     <xsl:apply-templates/>
     4   </xsl:template>
```

In turn, having found an email child element node, the processor will find the template rule for that element:

Example 4–16   Matching the email element nodes of the example instance

```
Line 1   <xsl:template match="email">                       <!--generate a mailto:-->
     2     <p><xsl:value-of select="@type"/>
     3     <xsl:text> Email: </xsl:text>
     4     <a href="mailto:{.}">
     5       <xsl:apply-templates/>
     6     </a>
```

```
7    </p>
8  </xsl:template>
```

In this recursive-like process —

- the `<xsl:template>` constructs set up the event handlers to handle the set of nodes selected in `<xsl:apply-templates>` —
    - either explicitly (a node set using a `select=` expression) or implicitly (just the child nodes);
- the context is continually changed and restored as the node tree is traversed;
- the data dictates the order in which templates are processed;
- each template is added to the result tree thus creating the result tree parse order.

Note that the example above of explicitly processing the named document element in the root rule limits the processing of this stylesheet to instances beginning with that element, which:

- prevents unexpected behavior from processing other instances with the stylesheet,
- results in the empty result when not processing expected instances.

4.1.6 Modes

Modes allow collections of template rules to be made.

- The `mode="mode-name"` attribute can be used:
    - in `<xsl:apply-templates/>` to indicate which collection to use,
    - in `<xsl:template>` to indicate the collection to which this template belongs.
- When `mode=` is not specified, the unnamed collection is used.

For example, consider in the objective to process one set of templates for the electronic information and a second set of templates for the postal information where the same match patterns are needed in both processes:

Example 4–17 Processing the entire example instance twice in a single stylesheet

```
Line 1  <xsl:template match="/">                    <!--process entire instance twice-->
     2    <xsl:apply-templates select="card"/>
     3    <xsl:apply-templates select="card" mode="addr"/>
     4  </xsl:template>
     5                                                 <!--electronic info-->
```

```
 6  <xsl:template match="card">
 7                                                          <!--template here-->
 8  </xsl:template>
 9                                                          <!--postal info-->
10  <xsl:template match="card" mode="addr">
11                                                          <!--template here-->
12  </xsl:template>
```

The root rule above processes the document element twice, once in each of two different modes.

- Every execution of `<xsl:apply-templates>` will only use those `<xsl:template>` rules with the matching mode attribute.

Without modes each template would have complex context calculations.

- By using separate collections, each collection can be treated as a mini-stylesheet.
- Modes can be changed at any time.
- There can be any number of modes each reflecting different requirements of the stylesheet without having to accommodate other requirements.

4.1.7   Empty templates

Sometimes necessary to add nothing to the result tree.

- All events must be handled even if not wanted.
    - Built-in template rules may add information to the result tree when not desired.
    - A stylesheet template rule overrides a built-in template rule.
- This case is no different in principle than a non-empty template.
    - The instruction itself is empty (i.e. has no children), so the empty template is added to the result.

Example 4–18   Suppressing a node using an empty template rule

```
Line 1                                                      <!--suppress the address-->
     2  <xsl:template match="address"></xsl:template>
```

According to XML rules for empty elements, the above markup is no different than the following (though the preceding may be more easily comprehended by a reader of the stylesheet):

Example 4–19   Alternative XML markup for an empty template rule

```
<xsl:template match="address"/>          <!--suppress the address-->
```

According to XSLT rules for ignored comments and whitespace-only text nodes, the above markup is no different than the following (though they are distinctly different in XML terms):

Example 4–20   Alternative XSLT markup for an empty template rule

```
Line 1  <xsl:template match="address">          <!--suppress the address-->
     2  </xsl:template>
```

4.1.8 Built-in template rules

XSLT specifies built-in template rules that are assumed to be a part of all stylesheets.

- When the processor can't match a stylesheet template rule to a given node, a built-in template rule is used.

When there is no explicit template rule for the root node or an element node, the following built-in rule will be assumed by the XSLT processor with an implicit mode= attribute of the current mode.

- Note how attributes are not pushed by built-in templates, they must be explicitly pushed or processed by the stylesheet.

Example 4–21   The built-in rules for element and root nodes in the unnamed and named modes

```
Line 1  <xsl:template match="*|/">
     2    <xsl:apply-templates/>
     3  </xsl:template>
     4
     5  <xsl:template match="*|/" mode="mode-name">
     6    <xsl:apply-templates mode="mode-name"/>
     7  </xsl:template>
```

When there is no explicit template rule for a text or attribute node, the following built-in rule will be assumed by the XSLT processor to add the leaf node's value to the result tree:

Example 4–22   The built-in rules for text and attribute nodes in the unnamed and named modes

```
Line 1  <xsl:template match="text()|@*">
     2    <xsl:value-of select="."/>
     3  </xsl:template>
```

```
4
5    <xsl:template match="text()|@*" mode="mode-name">
6      <xsl:value-of select="."/>
7    </xsl:template>
```

When there is no explicit rule for a comment or processing instruction node, the following empty built-in rule will be assumed by the XSLT processor and, when triggered, it specifies that nothing is to be added to the result tree:

Example 4–23   The built-in rules for the comment and processing instruction nodes in the unnamed and named modes

```
Line 1    <xsl:template match="comment()|processing-instruction()"/>
2
3         <xsl:template match="comment()|processing-instruction()"
4                        mode="mode-name"/>
```

All namespace nodes are also ignored (as there is no pattern with which to recognize them in a match attribute). Namespace nodes are added to the result tree piggybacked on element nodes being copied to the result tree and as a result of instructions synthesizing result tree nodes.

4.1.9   Template rule conflict resolution

Template rule selection must be unambiguous.

- Separate collections of rules are distinguished by the mode used at select time.
- More than one matching rule in a given collection of rules is an error.
  - The XSLT process must only match a single template rule for each event.
  - It is the stylesheet writer's responsibility to not confuse the processor.
    - You must only supply a single template rule for every event or rely on the built-in templates for an event not explicitly handled.
- Multiple hierarchical relationships can often be ambiguous.
  - Template rule matching patterns are often written with hierarchies specifying the context of nodes.
  - When one hierarchy is a strict subset of the other hierarchy then both hierarchies are candidates for a node that is found in the subset.

An important portability issue is as follows:

- the XSLT processor is *not* required to report a template conflict error condition.
  - If not reported, it is required to use the *last* template rule found in the stylesheet that matches the source tree node;
  - A stylesheet apparently successfully running using one XSLT processor not reporting template conflict errors *will not run* in another XSLT processor that chooses to report such errors.

Every template rule has a priority.

- Priorities are used by the XSLT processor to avoid conflict within a given collection of template rules.
  - They are helpful when specifying multiple template rules with subsets of matching conditions.
- The highest priority wins.
  - The processor chooses the matching template rule within the given collection that has the highest explicit or implicit numeric priority value.
- An explicit priority can be specified by user.
  - Its value is a floating point number:
    ```
    <xsl:template match="match-pattern"
                  priority="numeric-value">
    ```
- An implicit priority is assumed based on pattern specificity when `priority=` is not specified:
  - −.5 for patterns comprised of *only* a wildcard or node type:
    - wildcards: "`*`" or "`@*`",
    - node types: `node()`, `comment()`, `processing-instruction()` or `text()`,
  - −.25 for patterns comprised of a namespace prefix and a wildcard:
    - "`prefix:*`",
  - 0 for patterns comprised of *only* a node's name:
    - un-prefixed or `child::` axis for an element,
    - prefixed with "`@`" or `attribute::` axis for an attribute,
    - with or without a namespace prefix,
    - a literal in `processing-instruction(PI-target)`,
  - .5 for all other patterns.

A union match pattern for a template rule is handled severally.

- The processor will regard each of the patterns separately as if they were present individually in copies of the template rule.

Consider an example of a typographical vocabulary.

- The element `figure` specifies a figure reference.

- The element `para` specifies a paragraph of content.
- The element `margin` specifies a marginalia construct.
- The elements are in the vocabulary identified by URI associated with the stylesheet's `b:` prefix.

The rendering of figures differs based on context.

- When found *outside* a paragraph, perhaps it is rendered centered on the line, with a hotlink to a description.
- When found *inside* a paragraph, perhaps it is rendered inline to the paragraph, with a hotlink to a description.
- When found inside a paragraph that is *marginalia*, perhaps it is rendered inline to the paragraph, without a hotlink to a description.
- Each of the above contexts requires a different template rule, but all must be active to accommodate all of the different situations.
  - These contexts can only be distinguished unambiguously by using priority.

Without priority, the following rules would conflict for the processing of a figure when that figure is in a paragraph in marginalia:

Example 4–24 Five distinct patterns matching the element `b:margin/b:para/b:figure`

```
Line 1   <xsl:template match="b:margin/b:para/b:figure" priority="2">
   2
   3   <xsl:template match="b:para/b:figure">                    <!--priority=".5"-->
   4
   5   <xsl:template match="b:figure">                           <!--priority="0"-->
   6
   7   <xsl:template match="b:*">                                <!--priority="-.25"-->
   8
   9   <xsl:template match="*">                                  <!--priority="-.5"-->
```

Note that without explicit priority —

- the first two rules above would both have the implicit value of .5 for priority;
- a processor not reporting the conflict would always process the second of the two rules for figures found in paragraphs.

As a general rule of thumb —

- the more specific the matching pattern, the higher the specified priority must be.

4.1.10 Processing model summary

The XSLT processor must produce the same effect as the following.

- Read the stylesheet file into a node tree.
  - Tree contains instruction elements and literal result elements.
- Read the source file into a node tree.
  - Only instructions found in the stylesheet tree are acted upon.
- Implicitly execute `<xsl:apply-templates select="/"/>`.
  - Instantiate the template for the root node as the start of the result tree.
  - Note that in an implicitly declared stylesheet, the one result template found in the stylesheet is assumed to be the template for a template rule for the root node, thus satisfying the above instruction.
- For each `<xsl:apply-templates>` and `<xsl:for-each>` instruction do the following.
  - `select=` defines the current node list.
  - The current node list may be sorted (described later in Chapter 9).
  - For each of the nodes in the current node list:
    - visit that node as the current node,
    - determine the template to be added to the result tree;
      - if using `<xsl:apply-templates>`:
        - match the template rule of highest priority in the `mode=` collection,
        - pass all parameterized variable binding values (described later in Chapter 6);
      - if using `<xsl:for-each>`:
        - use the template of the instruction itself,
    - execute XSLT and extension instructions found in the template,
      - replace instruction in situ with the template result of instruction execution,
    - add literal result elements and results of instruction execution to the result tree.

Note that the processor is not required to be implemented explicitly in any particular way.

- A given implementation can produce the identical result following any algorithm.
- The Recommendations describe the desired end effect, not the method of implementation.

4.1.11   Parallelism

An XSLT processor implementation has the latitude to process the input in any fashion, including in a parallel fashion, as long as the result is the same as when processed serially as described in the Recommendation.

- The side-effect free nature of the XSLT expression language allows an implementation to simultaneously process multiple nodes of the tree without impacting on expression evaluation.
  - By design, the processing of any one template rule on a given node of the source tree cannot have any impact on the processing of any other template rule or the same template rule on any other node of the source tree.
- The end result of the parallel processes must be assembled *as if* the source tree nodes were processed sequentially.

For example, consider a book with a number of chapters.

- Each chapter node can be processed in parallel on different computers or processors.
- The completed result sub-trees for each chapter are assembled in the order of the corresponding source tree chapter nodes.
- The end result is achieved in a time related to the longest processing of one chapter, not on the sum of the processing of all chapters.

4.1.12   Suggested stylesheet development approach

Always remember it is the stylesheet's responsibility (thus the stylesheet writer's responsibility) to create the result tree in result tree document order.

- What is the document element of the result?
- What is the first content that belongs in the result?
- What comes next, and next, and next, to the end of the result?
- For each piece of content that belongs in the result —
  - is it found in the source tree?
    - If so, then that part of the source tree must be the next part that is accessed and processed.
    - If not, then the content must be put directly in the stylesheet for adding to the result.
  - Ensure all attribute nodes for a result element are added before its content.

An iterative approach to stylesheet development:

- begins by developing templates with instructions that handle high level constructs in the source node,
- progresses by developing templates for successively lower level constructs within each high level construct,
- shows small results quickly with simple stylesheets before growing into complex stylesheets,
- will allow you to build on previous successes and recognize pitfalls early.

Note that even if some high level constructs will be invisible in the final stylesheet, revealing their presence in the output at early stages of development helps with diagnosing problems in the templates.

The following is a helpful technique when working with an XSLT processor that does not report template conflict errors.

- In the physical order of templates in the stylesheet file, order templates with more specificity before templates with less specificity.
- As new templates are added, neglecting to attach priority will produce no change to the results as the processor will fall back to the latter templates (thus indicating the newly added template isn't being processed and requires priority).

4.2 Sample XSLT stylesheets

4.2.1 Card sample stylesheets

Recall the transformation objective in Section 4.1.1.

The file `cardpull.xsl` illustrates the pull approach using an implicit stylesheet with only a result tree template:

Example 4–25 Using a pull approach to solve the business card example

```
Line 1  <?xml version="1.0"?>                                    <!--cardpull.xsl-->
     2  <!--XSLT 1.0 - http://www.CraneSoftwrights.com/training -->
     3  <html xmlns:xsl="http://www.w3.org/1999/XSL/Transform"
     4        xsl:version="1.0">
     5  <center><b><u>Electronic Contact Information</u></b></center>
     6  <p>Name: <xsl:value-of select="/card/name"/></p>
     7  <xsl:for-each select="/card/email">
     8    <p><xsl:value-of select="@type"/>
```

```
 9          <xsl:text> Email: </xsl:text>
10          <a href="mailto:{.}"><xsl:value-of select="."/></a></p>
11      </xsl:for-each>
12      <center><b><u>Postal Contact Information</u></b></center>
13      <p>Name: <xsl:value-of select="/card/name"/></p>
14      <p>Address: <xsl:value-of select="/card/address"/></p>
15  </html>
```

The file `cardpush.xsl` illustrates the push approach using an explicit
stylesheet with a number of template rules and named modes (collections of template rules):

Example 4–26   Using a push approach to solve the business card example

```
Line 1  <?xml version="1.0"?>                                  <!--cardpush.xsl-->
     2  <!--XSLT 1.0 - http://www.CraneSoftwrights.com/training -->
     3  <xsl:stylesheet xmlns:xsl="http://www.w3.org/1999/XSL/Transform"
     4                  version="1.0">
     5
     6  <xsl:template match="/">                    <!--process entire instance twice-->
     7    <html><xsl:apply-templates select="card"/>
     8          <xsl:apply-templates select="card" mode="addr"/></html>
     9  </xsl:template>
    10                                                          <!--electronic info-->
    11  <xsl:template match="card">
    12    <center><b><u>Electronic Contact Information</u></b></center>
    13    <xsl:apply-templates/>
    14  </xsl:template>
    15
    16  <xsl:template match="name"><p>Name: <xsl:apply-templates/></p>
    17  </xsl:template>
    18
    19  <xsl:template match="address"/>                     <!--suppress the address-->
    20
    21  <xsl:template match="email">                        <!--generate a mailto:-->
    22    <p><xsl:value-of select="@type"/>
    23        <xsl:text> Email: </xsl:text>
    24        <a href="mailto:{.}"><xsl:apply-templates/></a></p>
    25  </xsl:template>
    26                                                          <!--postal info-->
    27  <xsl:template match="card" mode="addr">
    28    <center><b><u>Postal Contact Information</u></b></center>
    29    <xsl:apply-templates select="name"/>
    30    <xsl:apply-templates select="address" mode="addr"/>
    31  </xsl:template>
    32                                                              *
    33  <xsl:template match="address" mode="addr">
    34    <p>Address: <xsl:apply-templates/></p>
    35  </xsl:template>
    36  </xsl:stylesheet>
```

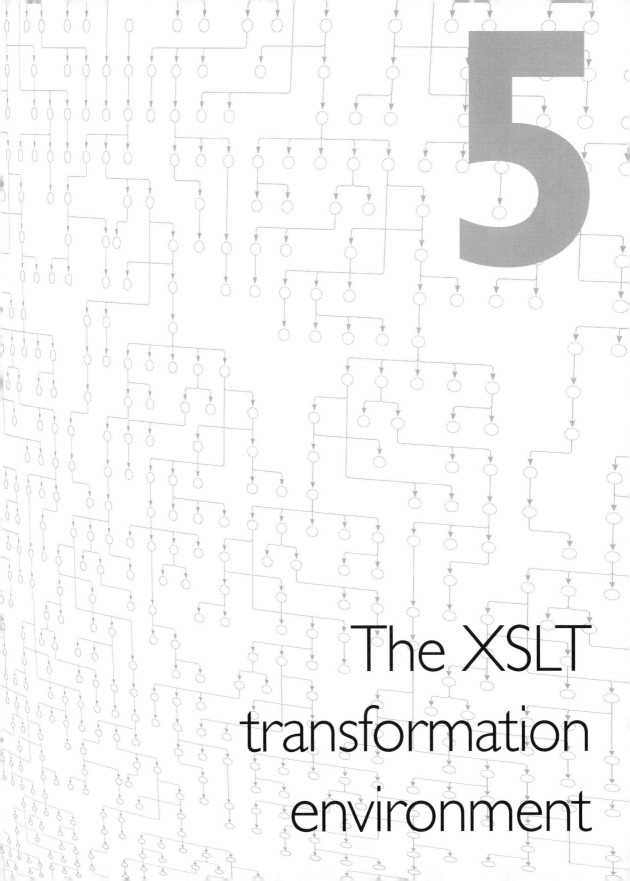

5

The XSLT transformation environment

5 The XSLT transformation environment

Some aspects of our stylesheets are of a global nature that we must consider before we delve into the details of template instruction execution and behaviors. This chapter overviews the aspects of our environment in which we use our XSLT processor from the perspectives of the stylesheet contents, the serialized output (if any), and the operator invoking the processor.

All explicitly declared stylesheets follow a required shape of container and top-level (container children) elements. Methods are also specified for including arbitrary information in a stylesheet file, useful for supplemental information for processing, or as documentation of the stylesheet content.

The stylesheet can declare its desire for values of certain parameters of the output serialization that influence the contents of the reified result node tree.

In addition, there are a number of ways available to communicate with an XSLT processor that is interpreting a stylesheet resource against a source resource. Communication to the processor can be engaged at invocation as well as from the processor during execution.

Finally, this chapter reviews aspects of the transformation environment that cannot be controlled by the operator or the stylesheet. It is important to understand the limitations of what can be asked for or even supported by the XSLT processor.

This chapter includes discussion of the following XSLT instructions regarding the transformation environment in which a stylesheet is used.

Instructions for wrapping the content of a stylesheet are as follows.

- `<xsl:stylesheet>`
  - encapsulates a stylesheet specification.
- `<xsl:transform>`
  - encapsulates a stylesheet specification.

Instructions for serializing the result tree are as follows.

- `<xsl:namespace-alias>`
  - specifies a result tree namespace translation.
- `<xsl:output>`
  - specifies the desired serialization of the result tree.

Instructions for communicating with the operator are as follows.

- `<xsl:message>`
  - reports a stylesheet condition to the operator.
- `<xsl:param>`
  - supplies a parameterized value from the operator.

5.1 Stylesheet basics

5.1.1 The stylesheet document/container element

Two identical and interchangeable choices for the document element are:

- `<xsl:stylesheet>`
- `<xsl:transform>`

They can also be used as a container element for a stylesheet embedded in another context.

- They may use id="*unique identifier*".
  - It identifies the stylesheet when there are multiple ones from which to choose.
  - The use of this XML ID attribute is outside the scope of the Recommendation.
  - It could be used as a fragment identifier by the stylesheet association processing instruction or by other techniques to identify a given stylesheet among many.

Controls available on container element or any literal result element are:

- exclude-result-prefixes="*whitespace-separated-prefixes*"
  - scope of influence is all descendent elements in stylesheet;
  - this declaration indicates which stylesheet namespace prefixes are not expected in the result, thus are not to be included in the stylesheet tree;
    - a list of whitespace-separated namespace prefixes specifies prefixes that are to be explicitly excluded from the stylesheet tree (using #default as the name to reference the default namespace, which is sometimes unofficially called the null namespace);
  - user-specified prefixes and associated namespace declarations are often used in XSLT stylesheets (but not desired in the result) for various purposes such as:
    - top-level documentation,
    - embedded structured data,
    - named XSLT constructs;
  - recall that copying an element node from the stylesheet to the result will copy all attached namespace nodes, thus stylesheet namespace declarations can easily end up in the result tree;
    - a stylesheet wrapper-element namespace declaration is typically used for top-level namespace usage, thus the document element of the result will typically end up with the same declarations;
  - this exclusion declaration tells the XSLT processor to not include the specified namespace nodes on descendent nodes of the stylesheet tree;
  - this exclusion declaration has no effect on namespace nodes of the source tree,
- extension-element-prefixes="*whitespace-separated-prefixes*"
  - scope of influence is all descendent elements in stylesheet;
  - this declaration indicates which stylesheet namespace prefixes are instruction prefixes;
    - a list of whitespace-separated namespace prefixes specifying prefixes that are extension namespaces to be recognized by the XSLT processor (using #default as the name to reference the default namespace);
  - recall that everything that is not an instruction is considered to be a literal result element;

- elements prefixed with the namespace prefix associated with the XSLT URI are interpreted as instructions;
- this declaration tells the XSLT processor what other prefixes are to be interpreted as instructions because they are extension elements required by the stylesheet;
- the processor need not implement the extension elements (detailed in Chapter 6).

Child elements of the document or container element are referred to as "top-level" elements.

- If present, the following must occur before all other top-level elements:
  - `xsl:import`
    - see Chapter 6.
- If present, the following (listed alphabetically) may occur in any order as top-level elements:
  - `xsl:attribute-set`
    - see Chapter 7,
  - `xsl:include`
    - see Chapter 6,
  - `xsl:key`
    - see Chapter 8,
  - `xsl:decimal-format`
    - see Chapter 8,
  - `xsl:namespace-alias`
    - see this chapter,
  - `xsl:output`
    - see this chapter,
  - `xsl:preserve-space`
    - see Chapter 3,
  - `xsl:strip-space`
    - see Chapter 3,
  - `xsl:template`
    - see Chapter 4.
- The following are used not only as top-level elements, while all others listed above are only used as top-level elements:
  - `xsl:param`
    - see Chapter 6,
  - `xsl:variable`
    - see Chapter 6.

5.1.2 Documenting stylesheets

Because an XSL stylesheet is an XML document —

- XML comments can be used to provide documentation about the stylesheet,
- all XML comments and processing instructions found in an XSL stylesheet are ignored.
  - Note that some XML editing tools may leave processing instructions in files for remembering locations such as the last cursor position.

Adding richly marked up documentation to a stylesheet:

- allows the stylesheet to be run through a documenting stylesheet to extract the documentation in any fashion desired,
- is accomplished by including non-XSLT constructs as top-level elements (children of the stylesheet document element) provided that the default namespace is not used as the namespace for such constructs, as in the following example:

Example 5–1   Using non-XSLT constructs as top-level elements

```
Line 1  <?xml version="1.0"?>                                   <!--hellodoc.xsl-->
     2  <!--XSLT 1.0 - http://www.CraneSoftwrights.com/training -->
     3
     4  <xsl:transform xmlns:xsl="http://www.w3.org/1999/XSL/Transform"
     5                 version="1.0" exclude-result-prefixes="mydoc"
     6                 xmlns:mydoc="http://www.mycompany.com/mydoc">
     7
     8  <xsl:output method="html"/>
     9
    10  <mydoc:para>
    11  The following construct is the root template.
    12  </mydoc:para>
    13
    14  <xsl:template match="/">                                  <!--root rule-->
    15      <b><i><u><xsl:value-of select="greeting"/></u></i></b>
    16      <?test a processing instruction here?>
    17  </xsl:template>
    18
    19  </xsl:transform>
```

Note the use of exclude-result-prefixes= in the document element above to tell the XSLT processor to not emit a namespace declaration for the prefix of the documentation namespace —

- if the stylesheet writer knows that namespace will never be needed in the result;
- because the XSLT processor doesn't know when creating the document element node of the result tree whether the namespace will ever be needed in the instance, so by default the declaration is emitted.

5.1.3   Namespace protection

Some special concern regarding the use of namespaces are as follows.

- The "transformation by example" paradigm utilizes literal result elements.
  - It represents result tree element nodes with associated attribute nodes.
    - An element is written with associated attributes in a template in the stylesheet and can use —
      - the default namespace,
      - a namespace prefix and associated namespace URI.
    - An alternative described later is the use of XSLT instructions to synthesize result tree nodes.
- Some namespaces can be sensitive in the document processing environment;
  - this includes automatically-triggered platform services;
  - for example: digital signature processing.
- If the result tree requires a sensitive namespace, the stylesheet can't use the namespace in a literal result element —
  - to produce an XSLT script as the output of translation;
    - the XSLT processor would incorrectly interpret the result vocabulary as input,
  - to use a platform service for the output of translation;
    - the stylesheet use of the URI would incorrectly trigger the service.
- The `<xsl:namespace-alias` *attributes*`/>` top-level element can be used, which:
  - is an instruction to translate a namespace prefix in the stylesheet into another namespace prefix when used in the result;
  - with attribute `stylesheet-prefix="`*prefix*`"`:
    - specifies the prefix used in the stylesheet tree that is being added to the result tree by the stylesheet,
      - has no influence or recognition in the source tree,
  - with attribute `result-prefix="`*prefix*`"`:

- specifies the prefix of the stylesheet tree whose URI is to be used for the result tree prefix,
- must have this attribute declared in the stylesheet even if no element in the stylesheet uses the prefix.

Note in the example below how the XSLT namespace URI cannot be used for the declaration for the xslo prefix, otherwise the xslo prefixed elements would be interpreted as XSLT instructions.

Example 5–2   A stylesheet that produces a stylesheet

```
Line 1  <?xml version="1.0"?>                                         <!--xsl.xsl-->
     2  <!--XSLT 1.0 - http://www.CraneSoftwrights.com/training -->
     3
     4  <xsl:stylesheet xmlns:xsl="http://www.w3.org/1999/XSL/Transform"
     5              xmlns:xslo="any-URI" version="1.0">
     6
     7  <xsl:output indent="yes"/>
     8
     9  <xsl:namespace-alias stylesheet-prefix="xslo"
    10                  result-prefix="xsl"/>
    11
    12  <xsl:template match="/">                                      <!--root rule-->
    13    <xslo:stylesheet version="1.0">
    14      <xslo:template match="/">
    15        <html>
    16          <p>Hello world</p>
    17        </html>
    18      </xslo:template>
    19    </xslo:stylesheet>
    20  </xsl:template>
    21
    22  </xsl:stylesheet>
```

- When this particular stylesheet is run with itself (or any XML file) as the source, the XSLT processor will assign the "xslo:" prefix's URI used in the result tree with the URI for the "xsl" prefix as indicated in the <xsl:namespace-alias> instruction, thus using the XSLT URI when the result tree is serialized as XML markup:

Example 5–3   A stylesheet produced by a stylesheet

```
Line 1  <xslo:stylesheet version="1.0"
     2  xmlns:xslo="http://www.w3.org/1999/XSL/Transform">
     3  <xslo:template match="/">
     4  <html>
     5  <p>Hello world</p>
     6  </html>
```

```
7  </xslo:template>
8  </xslo:stylesheet>
```

- When run with itself (or any XML file) as the source, the output will be:

Example 5–4   The result produced by the produced stylesheet

```
Line 1  <!DOCTYPE html PUBLIC "-//W3C//DTD HTML 4.0 Transitional//EN">
2  <html>
3  <p>Hello world</p>
4  </html>
```

5.2 **Communicating with the XSLT processor**

5.2.1 Serializing the result tree

The `<xsl:output>` top-level element:

- is a request to serialize the result tree as a sequence of bytes.
    - The XSLT processor *may* choose to respect the request, but is not obliged.

All attributes of `<xsl:output>` are optional.

- The `method="method-indication"` attribute may take these values:
    - `method="html"`
        - uses the HTML vocabulary and SGML markup conventions, namely:
            - empty elements,
            - attribute minimization,
            - built-in character entity referencing (ISO Latin 1),
            - the entire set of HTML conventions (you cannot selectively turn on only a subset of them);
                - all conventions are used according to common practice,
        - is considered the default in certain result tree conditions;
            - the name of the document element node is HTML (case insensitive);
            - the null namespace URI is used for the name (i.e.: there is no namespace prefix);
            - any preceding text nodes contain only whitespace,
    - `method="xml"`
        - uses arbitrary vocabulary and XML markup conventions, namely:
            - empty elements,
            - built-in character entity referencing,
        - is the default when the default isn't HTML,
    - `method="text"`
        - uses no vocabulary and no lexical or syntactic conventions,

- serializes only the text nodes of every element in the result tree,
  - outputs all characters in clear text (no entities of any kind),
- is never the default,
- `method="prefix:processor-recognized-method-name"`
  - uses the prefix defined by `xmlns:prefix="processor-recognized-URI-reference"`;
  - uses lexical and syntactic conventions recognized by the XSLT processor;
    - in particular, serialization can be arbitrary (it is out of the scope of XSLT);
  - is never the default.

- Attributes related to the method are as follows:
  - `version="numeric-version"`
    - specifies the version of the output method,
  - `omit-xml-declaration="yes"` or `omit-xml-declaration="no"`
    - specifies the absence or presence of the XML declaration (if the result tree represents a document entity) or the text declaration (if the result tree represents an external general parsed entity),
  - `standalone="yes"` or `standalone="no"`
    - specifies the presence or absence of a standalone document declaration,
  - `doctype-system="system-identifier"`
    - specifies the system identifier to use in the DOCTYPE declaration,
  - `doctype-public="public-identifier"`
    - specifies the public identifier to use in the DOCTYPE declaration,
    - requires `doctype-system=` to also be specified if the output method is XML.

- Attributes related to the serialized markup syntax are as follows:
  - `indent="yes"`
    - asks the XSLT processor (at its discretion) to indent the result "nicely" with additional whitespace when using the `xml` method;
      - this may have implications for the downstream parsing processes if the whitespace is considered significant,
  - `cdata-section-elements="list-of-element-type-names"`
    - gives a whitespace separated list of element types possibly used in the result,
    - specifies those result tree elements whose text content is serialized within a CDATA section.

- Attributes related to the encoding are as follows:
  - `encoding="encoding"`
    - requests (if supported by the processor) the character set encoding output of the emitted result tree,
    - has the value which should match the `encoding=` pseudo-attribute described by the XML Recommendation for the XML declaration,
  - `media-type="media-type"`
    - specifies the MIME content type (without specifying the `charset` parameter).

5.2.2 Illustration of output methods

Consider a simple XML file `nodein.xml` created using the 8-bit ISO character set for Western European languages Latin–1, a.k.a. ISO–8859–1 (note the copyright symbol seen here is encoded in the file using the hexadecimal character `0xA9`):

Example 5–5 An XML source file with characters sensitive to processing

```
Line 1  <?xml version="1.0" encoding="iso-8859-1"?>
     2  <p>Test with © and &lt; and &amp; in it</p>
```

Figure 5–1 illustrates the node tree that is created by the XSL processor.

Note how the markup used to represent the sensitive XML characters is lost. The node tree shown would also be created identically by the following markup:

Example 5–6 The same information using a CDATA section

```
Line 1  <?xml version="1.0" encoding="iso-8859-1"?>
     2  <p><![CDATA[Test with © and < and & in it]]></p>
```

All character values in text nodes are maintained as UCS–2 (Universal Character Set — Two Octet) characters. The UCS character set is a 32-bit (4 octet) repertoire with a 16-bit (2 octet) repertoire subset (equivalent to Unicode) that can be serialized as either 16-bit (2 octet) characters or, using an encoding called UTF–8, as a sequence of 8-bit (1 octet) characters.

Utilizing an extension element defined in XT providing for multiple result trees, one can copy the source node tree to each of three result

Figure 5–1 Illustration of Node Tree Characters

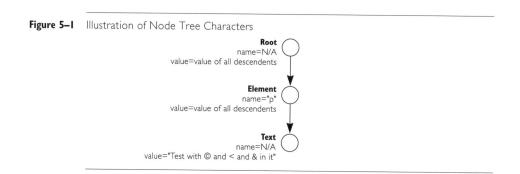

trees, such that each result tree is identical to the source tree, and interpret each result tree differently:

Example 5–7   Emission of the source tree using three different output methods

```
Line 1  <?xml version="1.0"?>                                    <!--nodeout.xsl-->
    2   <!--XSLT 1.0 - http://www.CraneSoftwrights.com/training -->
    3   <!--XT (see http://www.jclark.com/xml/xt.html)-->
    4   <xsl:stylesheet xmlns:xsl="http://www.w3.org/1999/XSL/Transform"
    5                   version="1.0"
    6                   xmlns:xt="http://www.jclark.com/xt"
    7                   extension-element-prefixes="xt">
    8
    9   <xsl:template match="/">
   10     <xt:document method="xml"  href="nodeout.xml"
   11                  omit-xml-declaration="yes">
   12       <xsl:copy-of select="."/>
   13     </xt:document>
   14     <xt:document method="html" href="nodeout.htm">
   15       <xsl:copy-of select="."/>
   16     </xt:document>
   17     <xt:document method="text" href="nodeout.txt">
   18       <xsl:copy-of select="."/>
   19     </xt:document>
   20   </xsl:template>
   21
   22   </xsl:stylesheet>
```

There is a nuance here regarding the use of the extension element: the `<xt:document>` element creates a separate result tree, and is not a result tree element itself that resides in a single "master" result tree as might be evident.

The use of `method="xml"` emits the same nodes using the UCS characters of the text nodes while using the built-in XML entities where necessary:

Example 5–8   XML output method emission of sample instance

```
<p>Test with © and &lt; and &amp; in it</p>
```

- Note the two-character UTF–8 hexadecimal representation of the copyright symbol is `0xC2 0xA9` which would both be revealed in a non-UTF–8 presentation environment such as an ISO–8859–1 Latin–1 environment as follows:

```
<p>Test with Â© and &lt; and &amp; in it</p>
```

The use of `method="html"` recognizes known built-in HTML entities and uses the entity references where necessary:

Example 5–9   HTML output method emission of sample instance

```
<p>Test with &copy; and &lt; and &amp; in it</p>
```

The use of `method="text"` ignores all element start and end tags and puts out the UCS characters of all the text nodes while not using any built-in entities:

Example 5–10   Text output method emission of sample instance

```
Test with © and < and & in it
```

- Note again in a non-UTF–8 environment this text file would appear as two characters as in the ISO–8859–1 Latin–1 environment:

```
Test with Â© and < and & in it
```

5.2.3   Communicating with the outside environment

These instructions are used for communication between the stylesheet and the XSLT processor and the operator:

- stylesheet to operator: `<xsl:message>`
  - it contains an arbitrary message such as —
    - status of progress,
    - content violation;
  - the specific mechanism of communication is not standardized;
  - the processor may choose to not support relating the message,
  - the content is any template (static or calculated),
  - this instruction can contain the `terminate="yes"` attribute —
    - which gives an instruction to stop any further processing of the stylesheet and source files,
  - this instruction allows the stylesheet to report on semantic validation;
    - when content has been detected as being incorrect, messages can report problems to the operator;
    - structural well-formedness correctness has already been determined by the XML processor inside the XSLT processor;
    - stylesheet could also use XPath to determine structural validity if the XSLT processor does not use a validating XML processor;
  - this instruction allows the stylesheet to report progress when manipulating large data sets,
- operator to stylesheet: `<xsl:param>`

- it provides an invocation-time parameterized value for a globally scoped bound variable;
- the specific mechanism of communication is not standardized;
- the processor may choose to not support value specification;
- a default value can be specified should no value be supplied at invocation,

- processor to stylesheet:
  - to obtain the value of a system property, use:

        system-property('*prefix:property-name*')

  - use XSLT namespace to indicate reserved system properties:
    - xsl:version
      - returns a decimal number (not a string) of the XSLT processor's implementation level in order to test the level of functionality for a given stylesheet;
    - xsl:vendor and xsl:vendor-url
      - each returns a string indicating, respectively, the name and URL (Uniform Resource Locator — RFC–1738/RFC–1808/RFC–2396) of the vendor of the executing XSL processor;
  - use other namespaces to indicate extension system properties:

        xmlns:*prefix*="*processor-recognized-URI-reference*"

        system-property('*prefix:property-name*')

    - the processor returns the empty string for an unrecognized property.

The following example illustrates how to tell the operator the stylesheet uses features not supported by the processor.

| Example 5–11 | An example of utilizing available system properties |

```
Line 1   <xsl:choose>
  2        <xsl:when test="system-property('xsl:version') >= 2.0">
  3          <xsl:feature-of-2.0/>
  4        </xsl:when>
  5        <xsl:otherwise>
  6          <xsl:message terminate="yes">
  7   Sorry, this stylesheet requires XSLT 2.0
  8   Complain to: '<xsl:value-of
  9                     select="system-property('xsl:vendor')"/>'
 10   at '<xsl:value-of select="system-property('xsl:vendor-url')"/>'.
 11          </xsl:message>
 12        </xsl:otherwise>
 13   </xsl:choose>
```

5.2.4 Uncontrolled processes

There is no recommendation-based user or stylesheet control over or communication available regarding the following processes implemented by the XSLT processor.

- Result tree attribute order:
  - the XSLT processor may choose to serialize attribute nodes found in the result tree in any order.
- Result tree serialization instance markup:
  - the XSLT processor may choose any way it desires to serialize the content of text nodes when the stylesheet does not instruct a given element to be emitted as a CDATA section —
    - using XML built-in character entities for markup-sensitive characters,
    - using numeric character entities for markup-sensitive characters or characters not present in the encoding character set,
    - using piecemeal CDATA sections;
  - any original markup syntax from the source file is lost when the source file is abstracted into the source node tree;
  - other than an entire element emitted as a CDATA section, there is no control available in the stylesheet over which serialization methods are used for text content.
- Result tree construction:
  - the stylesheet writer is responsible for dictating the final content of the result tree;
  - the XSLT processor can use any means to effect the final result as described in the Recommendation without necessarily implementing the prose description found therein;
  - the side-effect free nature of the XSLT design (including the inability to change the value of bound variables) allows an XSLT processor to process portions of the input in parallel and combine the intermediate results into the single final result tree;
  - the of XSLT allows the processor to choose to not preserve the result node tree when serializing the transformed information to an output instance, thus the result may never actually exist as a complete tree within the processor.

6

XSLT
stylesheet
management

6 XSLT stylesheet management

A very important aspect of writing stylesheets is the maintenance of the stylesheet resources themselves. There are a number of modularization techniques when designing stylesheet code that help the writer work within their own stylesheets as well as sharing stylesheets and stylesheet fragments with others. This chapter reviews facilities that promote modularization of stylesheet resources.

Note: Too often we jump into new technologies without thinking of the best ways we can exploit what we do beyond the straightforward tasks addressed by the objectives of the technologies. An investment in XSLT can be tapped by others and leveraged across an organization's deployment of this technology. I feel that stylesheet maintenance techniques are as important, if not more important, than the transformation facilities themselves: if we can write fancy stylesheets but are not able to maintain them (or have others maintain what we write), or we are not able to leverage what we have done with our colleagues, then we will have less success with the technology than otherwise.

Others judging how successful we are with XSLT could also better accept this new technology if proper software engineering practices are demonstrated. Establishing organization-wide strategies for deploying how XSLT can be successfully used by others will help entrench this technology and gain more benefit than working in isolation.

All physical XSLT entities are XML entities. Remember that while physical entities are files for most users, many users may be obtaining their entities from virtual resources and may not be dealing with actual physical files. In either case, though, the entities can be regarded as we regard XML files. Thus, when considering both logical and physical modularization, there are opportunities and facilities in both the XML markup constructs and in the XSLT language specification.

The XML-related facilities are markup-oriented in nature regarding how portions of stylesheet markup can be used in many areas of the stylesheet itself. The XML processor within the XSLT processor loses the boundaries of syntactic modularization such that the XSLT processor sees all of the markup as a single entity regardless of how it was expressed.

XSLT-related facilities are semantic in nature regarding shared functionality and reuse of stylesheet concepts. The XSLT processor can mix and match semantic constructs in a well-defined manner, thus supporting both logical and physical modularization of the operations of our stylesheets.

Modularizing the logical structure supports development.   The logical structure (see Figure 6–1) includes constructs found within a single resource. Schemes for localizing reused information into a single location support maintenance within a given stylesheet file by leveraging any changes made in the one shared construct.

Figure 6–1   Exploiting logical modularization

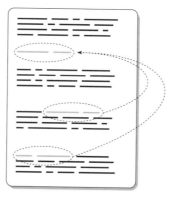

This chapter overviews logical modularization techniques utilizing —

- XML internal general entities,
- XML internal general entities in marked sections in external parameter entities,
- XSLT variable bindings,
- XSLT named templates.

Modularizing the physical entity structure supports reuse. The physical structure (see Figure 6–2) includes external resources referenced and used by a given resource. Schemes for localizing reused information into a shared location support maintenance within an organization's deployment of stylesheets. Organizational investment in common fragments is leveraged when any development or change in a given shared resource is made.

This chapter overviews physical modularization techniques utilizing —

- XML external parsed general entities,
- XSLT included files,
- XSLT imported files,
- XSLT extension functions,
- XSLT extension elements (instructions).

Figure 6–2   Exploiting physical modularization

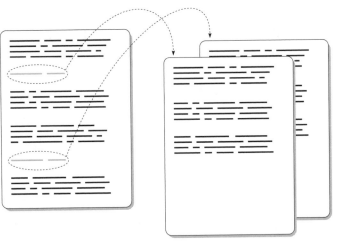

Included in this chapter. This chapter includes discussion of the following XSLT instructions regarding logical and physical modularization of stylesheets.

Instructions related to logical modularization are as follows.

- `<xsl:call-template>`
  - processes a stand-alone template on demand.
- `<xsl:template>`
  - declares a template to be called by name.
- `<xsl:variable>`
  - declares a non-parameterized variable and its bound value.
- `<xsl:param>`
  - declares a parameterized variable and its default bound value.
- `<xsl:with-param>`
  - specifies a binding value for a parameterized variable.

Instructions related to physical modularization are as follows.

- `<xsl:include>`
  - includes a stylesheet without overriding stylesheet constructs.
- `<xsl:import>`
  - imports a stylesheet while overriding stylesheet constructs.
- `<xsl:apply-imports>`
  - bypasses the importation of template rules.
- `<xsl:fallback>`
  - accommodates the lack of implementation of an instruction element.

6.1   Modularizing the logical structure of stylesheets

6.1.1   Internal general entities

An XSLT stylesheet is an XML document, hence:

- general entities can be declared in the document model defined —
  - in the associated schema or Document Type Definition (DTD),
  - in the internal declaration subset,
  - in an external file of declarations;
- entities can be used in the body of the stylesheet logic;
  - textual replacement allows common sequences of markup to be packaged;
  - instructions, content or any text can be defined and re-used;

- the use of entities is not preserved;
  - the XML processor provides the parsed information to the XSLT processor without distinguishing text encoded with or without entities.

Example 6–1   Using internal parsed general entities

```
Line 1  <?xml version="1.0"?>                                    <!--entisamp.xsl-->
2  <!--XSLT 1.0 - http://www.CraneSoftwrights.com/training -->
3  <!DOCTYPE xsl:stylesheet [
4  <!ENTITY Module-word "Module">                   <!--boilerplate text in English-->
5  <!ENTITY Lesson-word "Lesson">
6  <!ENTITY nl "&#xd;&#xa;">                              <!--DOS newline-->
7  ]>
8  <xsl:stylesheet xmlns:xsl="http://www.w3.org/1999/XSL/Transform"
9                  version="1.0">
10  <xsl:output method="text"/>
11  <xsl:template match="/">                              <!-- root rule -->
12    <xsl:for-each select="//module">
13      <xsl:text>&Module-word;: </xsl:text>
14      <xsl:value-of select="title"/>
15      <xsl:apply-templates select="."/><xsl:text>&nl;</xsl:text>
16    </xsl:for-each>
17  </xsl:template>
18  <!-- ... -->
19  <xsl:template match="lesson">
20   <xsl:text>&Lesson-word;: </xsl:text>
21   <xsl:value-of select="title"/>
22   <xsl:text> - &Module-word;: </xsl:text>
23   <xsl:value-of select="../title"/>
24   <xsl:apply-templates/>
25   <xsl:text>&nl;</xsl:text>
26  </xsl:template>
27  </xsl:stylesheet>
```

The declarations of internal general entities can be influenced by parameter entity declarations in an external declaration to control the XSLT processor matching of source nodes.

- The XSLT processor acts on the presence of nodes in the source node tree, not on the types of elements found in the document model, hence one can have match patterns for elements never expected to be found.
- Conditional marked sections are only allowed in external declaration subsets, not in internal declaration subsets, nor in the document element itself.

- Consider the need to have an XSLT processor behave in two different ways for a given element type;
  - it can manipulate the element node names being matched by templates in match=;
  - it can manipulate the names of modes in which the templates are collected in mode=.

Using a conditional marked section with a parameter entity in an external declaration subset, one could have:

Example 6–2   Conditionally modifying internal parsed general entities used in match patterns

```
Line 1    <!--
     2       marksamp.ent - External declaration subset example.
     3    -->
     4
     5    <!ENTITY % style2 "IGNORE">          <!--assume without decl means default 1-->
     6    <![%style2;[                          <!--requesting override of 1 with 2-->
     7      <!ENTITY pane-style-1 "zzz-ignore-pane">
     8      <!ENTITY pane-style-2 "pane">
     9    ]]>
    10    <!ENTITY pane-style-1 "pane">         <!--used if not already defined-->
    11    <!ENTITY pane-style-2 "zzz-ignore-pane">
    12
    13    <!--end of file-->
```

In this example, the value of the %style2; parameter entity dictates the value of the two general entities when used in the body of the stylesheet.

Referring to the external declaration subset, one could then have:

Example 6–3   Using internal parsed general entities in match patterns

```
Line 1    <?xml version="1.0"?>                              <!--marksamp.xsl-->
     2    <!--XSLT 1.0 - http://www.CraneSoftwrights.com/training -->
     3
     4    <!DOCTYPE xsl:stylesheet [
     5    <!ENTITY % style2 "INCLUDE">
     6    <!ENTITY % marksamp-ent SYSTEM "marksamp.ent">
     7    %marksamp-ent;
     8    ]>
     9    <xsl:stylesheet xmlns:xsl="http://www.w3.org/1999/XSL/Transform"
    10                    version="1.0">
    11
    12    <xsl:output method="text"/>
    13
    14    <xsl:template match="&pane-style-1;">
    15      <xsl:text>Pane Style 1: </xsl:text>
```

```
16    <xsl:apply-templates/>
17  </xsl:template>
18
19  <xsl:template match="&pane-style-2;">
20    <xsl:text>Pane Style 2: </xsl:text>
21    <xsl:apply-templates/>
22  </xsl:template>
23
24  </xsl:stylesheet>
```

The end result reveals the use of the general entities:

Example 6–4   Example end result

```
Line 1    Pane Style 2: Pane 1
     2    Pane Style 2: Pane 2
     3    Pane Style 2: Pane 3
```

This technique is also useful when wanting to conditionally not process an element by selectively defining the following &notes-element; general entity to engage the higher priority template rule, or defaulting with a bogus name to engage the lower priority template rule:

Example 6–5   Using internal parsed general entities in a match pattern with priority

```
Line 1  <xsl:template match="&notes-element;" priority="1">
     2    <hr noshade="noshade"/>
     3    <i>Notes:</i><br/>
     4    <xsl:apply-templates/>
     5  </xsl:template>
     6
     7  <xsl:template match="notes"/>                     <!--assume empty-->
```

6.1.2 Variables and parameters:

- are values which are reused multiple times without recalculation;
  - once a value is bound to a variable in a given scope, that value cannot change;
  - note the use of the word "variable" is in the mathematical sense of a placeholder or a symbol, not in the traditional programming sense of a storage location that can be modified,
- when defined in a template are locally scoped;
  - the scope is only the following siblings of the declaration and their descendants,
- when defined with a top-level declaration are globally scoped;
  - the scope is all templates and other globally scoped variables;
  - locally scoped declarations can override global declarations,

- can be of any type returned by an expression:
  - XPath data types:
    - source tree node set,
    - string,
    - number,
    - boolean,
  - result tree fragment (specific to XSLT and not defined in XPath):
    - is created by a direct assignment of rich markup described by the template;
      - the exception of an empty result tree fragment is treated as an empty string,
    - during assignment, may use conditional processing of the assigned value in the template,
- are named using namespace-qualified names;
  - the default namespace is not used when not using a namespace prefix;
  - this can prevent inadvertent variable name collision when mixing stylesheet fragments,
- are referenced in expressions prefixed with "$",
  - cannot be referenced when the expression is a match pattern, for example in —
    - template rules,
    - a key collection declaration,
- can have their value used in the stylesheet with either

  ```
  <xsl:value-of select="$variable-name"/>
  ```

  or

  ```
  <element attribute="{$variable-name}"/>
  ```

  - note that the value of a variable that is a result tree fragment is the value of all the descendent text nodes in the markup stream of the fragment;
  - note that the value of a variable that is a source tree node set is the value of the first member of the node set,
- can have their node structure copied to the result tree with:

  ```
  <xsl:copy-of select="$variable-name"/>
  ```

Classical programming approaches do not apply.

- The theory behind this approach is referred to as side-effect free programming which:
  - is an important implementation constraint that supports parallelism,
  - has a robust heritage in LISP-like languages and their derivatives.
- One must use "identification of quantity" rather than "counting".
  - There is no variable assignment construct in XSLT.
  - Variables cannot vary in the global scope or any given local scope.

- You must use an approach similar to "what is the current chapter number amongst the chapter siblings?";
    - a global chapter number variable incremented at the start of each chapter cannot be implemented in XSLT.
- The XSLT processor has built-in numbering facilities.
    - They identify for the stylesheet writer the quantity of nodes or values required.
    - They supplant the need to do a lot of programming in the stylesheet.
    - The act of counting in a stylesheet is awkward when using bound variables as opposed to classical schemes of using global variables that are not available in XSLT;
        - typically, recursively called templates are used, sometimes with axes;
            - a recursively called template introduces a new local scope of variable bindings.
        - Stylesheets with explicit counting logic are typically very verbose and difficult to follow;
            - they are typically more complex than classical programming approaches.
    - Numbering facilities are declarative and easy to follow;
        - you don't need to debug algorithm implementations in stylesheet.

Examples below demonstrate declaring and binding fixed values to variables and parameters (parameterized variables).

Binding a value to a variable:

Example 6–6   Instructions to bind a value to a variable

```
Line 1  <xsl:variable name="variable-name"
     2              select="expression-value"/>
     3
     4                          <!--binding an empty string to a variable-->
     5  <xsl:variable name="variable-name"/>
     6
     7  <xsl:variable name="variable-name">
     8    result-tree-fragment-value-template
     9  </xsl:variable>
```

- Binding specifies the value associated with a given variable's name.
- The expression value may be an explicit value or the end result of an expression evaluation.
- An empty result-tree fragment value is interpreted as an empty string value.
- The result-tree fragment value may be the end result of a conditional statement or any template execution.

A parameter (short for parameterized variable) is identical to a variable except that the expression supplied is considered a default value if a value has not been supplied to override the use of the default.

Parameterized variables:

- are identical to a variable in syntax and use,
- have a default value which is bound to the variable when a parameter value is not supplied at invocation;
  - top-level parameterized variables are bound at stylesheet invocation;
    - an XSLT processor can choose to not support this;
  - template parameterized variables are bound at template invocation.

Defaulting a parameterized variable to a value:

Example 6–7   Instructions to bind a default value to a parameterized variable

```
Line 1  <xsl:param name="variable-name"
     2              select="expression-value"/>
     3
     4                                 <!--defaulting an empty string to a parameter-->
     5  <xsl:param name="variable-name"/>
     6
     7  <xsl:param name="variable-name">
     8    result-tree-fragment-value-template
     9  </xsl:param>
```

XSLT notes the semantics of variable assignment are similar to the semantics of Java final local variable declaration with an initialization value, as in:

Example 6–8   Java final variable assignment

```
final Object x = "value";
```

as opposed to Java variable assignment that is *not* available in XSLT:

Example 6–9   Java variable assignment

```
x = "value";
```

An XSLT processor may offer an invocation-time facility to supply values to bind to top-level global parameters.

An example of the direct assignment of a result tree fragment to a variable, then two ways to access the variable is as follows:

Example 6–10   Comparing `<xsl:copy-of>` with `<xsl:value-of>`

```
Line 1   <xsl:variable name="test">                          <!--variable assignment-->
     2     <para>test para 1</para>                          <!--of rich structure-->
     3     <para>test para 2</para>
     4   </xsl:variable>
     5   <xsl:copy-of select="$test"/>                       <!--add fragment to result-->
     6   <xsl:copy-of select="$test"/>                       <!--again-->
     7   <value><xsl:value-of select="$test"/></value>       <!--add value-->
```

The resulting markup (two copies and concatenated text node value) is:

Example 6–11   Results of comparing `<xsl:copy-of>` with `<xsl:value-of>`

```
Line 1   <para>test para 1</para>
     2   <para>test para 2</para>
     3   <para>test para 1</para>
     4   <para>test para 2</para>
     5   <value>test para 1test para 2</value>
```

Consider the following stylesheet `varsamp.xsl` that reports sample assigned values to variables of each type (note that while in this example the top-level variable assignments follow the reporting in the flow of the stylesheet source, the top-level variables are assigned before the processing of the source node tree begins):

Example 6–12   Illustration of values of variables of all types

```
Line 1   <?xml version="1.0"?>                               <!--varsamp.xsl-->
     2   <!--XSLT 1.0 - http://www.CraneSoftwrights.com/training -->
     3
     4   <xsl:stylesheet xmlns:xsl="http://www.w3.org/1999/XSL/Transform"
     5                   version="1.0">
     6
     7   <xsl:template match="/">                            <!--report variables-->
     8     <root example="{{{$var3a}}} - attribute">
     9   Var1a (result-tree copy-of): {<xsl:copy-of select="$var1a"/>}
    10   Var1a (result-tree value-of): {<xsl:value-of select="$var1a"/>}
    11   Var1b (result-tree copy-of): {<xsl:copy-of select="$var1b"/>}
    12   Var1b (result-tree value-of): {<xsl:value-of select="$var1b"/>}
    13   Var1c (result-tree value-of): {<xsl:value-of select="$var1c"/>}
    14   Var2a (node set copy-of): {<xsl:copy-of select="$var2a"/>}
    15   Var2a (node set value-of): {<xsl:value-of select="$var2a"/>}
    16   Var2b (node set value-of): {<xsl:value-of select="$var2b"/>}
    17   Var3a (string value-of): {<xsl:value-of select="$var3a"/>}
    18   Var3b (string value-of): {<xsl:value-of select="$var3b"/>}
    19   Var3c (string value-of): {<xsl:value-of select="$var3c"/>}
    20   Var4a (number value-of): <xsl:value-of select="$var4a"/>
```

```
21  Var4b (number value-of): <xsl:value-of select="$var4b"/>
22  Var5a (boolean var1a value-of): <xsl:value-of select="$var5a"/>
23  Var5b (boolean var1b value-of): <xsl:value-of select="$var5b"/>
24  Var5c (boolean var1c value-of): <xsl:value-of select="$var5c"/>
25  Var5d (boolean var2a value-of): <xsl:value-of select="$var5d"/>
26  Var5e (boolean var2b value-of): <xsl:value-of select="$var5e"/>
27  Var5f (boolean var3a value-of): <xsl:value-of select="$var5f"/>
28  Var5g (boolean var3b value-of): <xsl:value-of select="$var5g"/>
29  Var5h (boolean var4a value-of): <xsl:value-of select="$var5h"/>
30  Var5i (boolean var4b value-of): <xsl:value-of select="$var5i"/>
31  Var5j (boolean value-of): <xsl:value-of select="$var5j"/>
32  Var5k (boolean value-of): <xsl:value-of select="$var5k"/>
33    <xsl:text>&#xa;</xsl:text></root>
34  </xsl:template>
35
36  <xsl:variable name="var1a">                          <!--result tree-->
37    <xyz attr1="test">This is test 1</xyz>
38    <xyz>This is test 2</xyz>
39  </xsl:variable>
40  <xsl:variable name="var1b">
41    <xsl:apply-templates select="//abc"/>             <!--processing result-->
42  </xsl:variable>
43  <xsl:variable name="var1c">
44    <xsl:apply-templates select="//def"/>             <!--processing result-->
45  </xsl:variable>
46  <xsl:variable name="var2a" select="//abc"/>              <!--node list-->
47  <xsl:variable name="var2b" select="//def"/>
48  <xsl:variable name="var3a" select="'string1-val'"/>        <!--string-->
49  <xsl:variable name="var3b" select="''"/>
50  <xsl:variable name="var3c"/>
51  <xsl:variable name="var4a" select="42"/>                 <!--number-->
52  <xsl:variable name="var4b" select="0"/>
53  <xsl:variable name="var5a" select="boolean($var1a)"/>       <!--bool.-->
54  <xsl:variable name="var5b" select="boolean($var1b)"/>
55  <xsl:variable name="var5c" select="boolean($var1c)"/>
56  <xsl:variable name="var5d" select="boolean($var2a)"/>
57  <xsl:variable name="var5e" select="boolean($var2b)"/>
58  <xsl:variable name="var5f" select="boolean($var3a)"/>
59  <xsl:variable name="var5g" select="boolean($var3b)"/>
60  <xsl:variable name="var5h" select="boolean($var4a)"/>
61  <xsl:variable name="var5i" select="boolean($var4b)"/>
62  <xsl:variable name="var5j" select="true()"/>
63  <xsl:variable name="var5k" select="false()"/>
64
65  <xsl:template match="abc">
66    <out attr2="val"><xsl:apply-templates/></out>
67  </xsl:template>
68
69  </xsl:stylesheet>
```

When acting on the following simple instance `varsamp.xml`:

Example 6–13   Sample data for variable value illustration

```
Line 1   <?xml version="1.0"?>
     2   <test>Test
     3   <abc test="attr">(abc 1 value)</abc> input.
     4   <abc>(abc 2 value)</abc></test>
```

The stylesheet produces the following result:

Example 6–14   Sample results for variable value illustration

```
Line 1   <?xml version="1.0" encoding="utf-8"?>
     2   <root example="{string1-val} - attribute">
     3   Var1a (result-tree copy-of):
            {<xyz attr1="test">This is test 1</xyz>
                                    <xyz>This is test 2</xyz>}
     4   Var1a (result-tree value-of): {This is test 1This is test 2}
     5   Var1b (result-tree copy-of):
            {<out attr2="val">(abc 1 value)</out>
                              <out attr2="val">(abc 2 value)</out>}
     6   Var1b (result-tree value-of): {(abc 1 value)(abc 2 value)}
     7   Var1c (result-tree value-of): {}
     8   Var2a (node set copy-of):
            {<abc test="attr">(abc 1 value)</abc><abc>(abc 2 value)</abc>}
     9   Var2a (node set value-of): {(abc 1 value)}
    10   Var2b (node set value-of): {}
    11   Var3a (string value-of): {string1-val}
    12   Var3b (string value-of): {}
    13   Var3c (string value-of): {}
    14   Var4a (number value-of): 42
    15   Var4b (number value-of): 0
    16   Var5a (boolean var1a value-of): true
    17   Var5b (boolean var1b value-of): true
    18   Var5c (boolean var1c value-of): true
    19   Var5d (boolean var2a value-of): true
    20   Var5e (boolean var2b value-of): false
    21   Var5f (boolean var3a value-of): true
    22   Var5g (boolean var3b value-of): false
    23   Var5h (boolean var4a value-of): true
    24   Var5i (boolean var4b value-of): false
    25   Var5j (boolean value-of): true
    26   Var5k (boolean value-of): false
    27   </root>
```

6.1.3   Named templates

A named template:

- has presence in the node structure of the stylesheet,
- is unlike internal entities because of parameterized variables,

- has the ability to be invoked (called) from many places —
  - each time, with the same or different invocation parameter binding values;
  - each time, introducing a new local scope within which variables can have different bound values than used in previously engaged local scopes,
- is added to the result tree when invoked,
- can have any content:
  - nothing at all,
  - simple text,
  - a full result tree template with instructions (including invocations of other named templates).

The instruction `<xsl:template name="`*`template-name`*`">`:

- gives the template a label to use when being called,
- can also specify a `match=` attribute;
  - using both allows a template to be used in either or both push and pull approaches simultaneously.

The instruction `<xsl:call-template name="`*`template-name`*`"/>`:

- adds the named template to the result node tree.

Here are three examples of passing a value to bind to a parameterized variable in the template.

Example 6–15   Instructions to supply a value for a parameterized variable

```
Line 1  <xsl:with-param name="variable-name"
     2                  select="expression-value"/>
     3
     4                                              <!--empty string binding value-->
     5  <xsl:with-param name="variable-name"/>
     6
     7  <xsl:with-param name="variable-name">
     8    result-tree-fragment-value-template
     9  </xsl:with-param>
```

Invoking a named template with parameter binding values:

Example 6–16   Supplying values when calling a named template

```
Line 1  <xsl:call-template name="template-name">
     2    optional <xsl:with-param> parameter binding values
     3  </xsl:call-template>
```

- supplies values to bind to variables in the called template for its use,

- adds the resulting template to the result node tree.

During push, the identical scheme of passing parameter values to override templates can be used.

- The values get bound to parameterized variables declared in the template rules invoked by the XSLT processor for each given node selected.
- Passing parameter binding values can reduce the amount of calculation performed by an XSLT script if values can be calculated at an early step in the process and passed on.
- Built-in template rules *do not* support the passing of parameter values.

Example 6–17   Supplying values when pushing nodes

```
Line 1   <xsl:apply-templates select="node-set-expression">
     2     optional <xsl:with-param> parameter binding values
     3   </xsl:apply-templates>
```

Here is a named template declaration defining the nodes to be added to the result tree when the template is called:

Example 6–18   Declaring a named template

```
Line 1   <xsl:template name="template-name">
     2     optional <xsl:param> parameterized variable declarations
     3     optional <xsl:variable> variable declarations
     4     optional template content
     5   </xsl:template>
```

The processor ignores `<xsl:with-param>` when certain conditions are not met, namely when —

- attempting to pass a binding value for a variable that isn't parameterized, i.e. —
  - one declared in the template using `<xsl:variable>`,
- attempting to pass a binding value for a variable that doesn't exist, i.e. —
  - any variables in built-in templates,
  - variables omitted as an oversight by the stylesheet writer.

Using an argument value in a template is no different than with a variable.

- To use the value in an element's content, write:

```
<xsl:value-of select="$variable-name"/>
```

- To use the value in a literal result element's attribute by using an attribute value template, write:

```
<some-element some-attribute="{$variable-name}"/>
```

Consider the following input file ntempsamp.xml:

Example 6–19　Sample data for illustration of supplying parameterized values

```
Line 1  <?xml version="1.0"?>
     2  <course>
     3  <module>
     4  <title>The First Module</title>
     5  <lesson><title>Lesson 1 of First Module</title></lesson>
     6  <lesson><title>Lesson 1 of First Module</title></lesson>
     7  </module>
     8  <module>
     9  <title>The Second Module</title>
    10  <lesson><title>Lesson 1 of Second Module</title></lesson>
    11  <lesson><title>Lesson 2 of Second Module</title></lesson>
    12  </module>
    13  </course>
```

We need to go over the data twice and the following output to be produced:

Example 6–20　Sample result illustrating supplying parameterized values

```
Line 1  <result>
     2  {The First Module - Lesson 1 of First Module - }
     3  {The First Module - Lesson 1 of First Module - }
     4  {The Second Module - Lesson 1 of Second Module - }
     5  {The Second Module - Lesson 2 of Second Module - }
     6  (The First Module - Lesson 1 of First Module - again! - The Course)
     7  (The First Module - Lesson 1 of First Module - again! - The Course)
     8  (The Second Module - Lesson 1 of Second Module - again! - The Course)
     9  (The Second Module - Lesson 2 of Second Module - again! - The Course)
    10  </result>
```

The result is accomplished with the following stylesheet ntempsamp.xsl:

Example 6–21　Sample stylesheet illustrating supplying parameterized values

```
Line 1  <?xml version="1.0"?>                              <!--ntempsamp.xsl-->
     2  <!--XSLT 1.0 - http://www.CraneSoftwrights.com/training -->
     3  <xsl:stylesheet xmlns:xsl="http://www.w3.org/1999/XSL/Transform"
     4                  version="1.0">
```

```
5
6    <xsl:output omit-xml-declaration="yes"/>
7
8    <xsl:template match="/">                              <!-- root rule -->
9     <result><xsl:text>&#xd;&#xa;</xsl:text>
10      <xsl:apply-templates select="//lesson"/>
11      <xsl:apply-templates select="//lesson" mode="second"/>
12     </result></xsl:template>
13
14   <xsl:template match="lesson">                     <!--for each lesson first-->
15     <xsl:call-template name="lesson-title"/></xsl:template>
16
17   <xsl:template match="lesson" mode="second">            <!--second time-->
18     <xsl:call-template name="lesson-title">
19       <xsl:with-param name="start-delimiter" select="'('"/>
20       <xsl:with-param name="end-delimiter" select="')'"/>
21       <xsl:with-param name="suffix">
22         <xsl:text>again! - </xsl:text>
23         <xsl:value-of select="/course/title"/>
24       </xsl:with-param>
25     </xsl:call-template></xsl:template>
26
27   <xsl:template name="lesson-title">                  <!--content for suffix-->
28     <xsl:param name="start-delimiter" select="'{'"/>
29     <xsl:param name="end-delimiter" select="'}'"/>
30     <xsl:param name="suffix"/>
31     <xsl:value-of select="$start-delimiter"/>
32     <xsl:value-of select="../title"/><xsl:text> - </xsl:text>
33     <xsl:value-of select="title"/><xsl:text> - </xsl:text>
34     <xsl:value-of select="$suffix"/>
35     <xsl:value-of select="$end-delimiter"/><xsl:text>
36   </xsl:text></xsl:template>
37
38   </xsl:stylesheet>
```

6.1.4 Explicit loop repetition

It is often a requirement to loop a specified number of times to build the result tree.

- You cannot use an `<xsl:for-each>` because the number of loops is based on the count of nodes triggered by the select=.
- A template can call itself recursively for the number of additions required to the result tree.
  - This may require the processor to implement "tail recursion" to avoid the recursive calls exceeding the available stack space;
    - tail recursion can only be exploited if there are no components targeted for the result tree after the recursive call in the template.

- Each call indicates one fewer repeats are required.

| **Example 6–22** | Using recursive template calls for iteration |

```
Line I   <?xml version="1.0"?>                                    <!--loop.xsl-->
     2   <!--XSLT 1.0 - http://www.CraneSoftwrights.com/training -->
     3   <!DOCTYPE xsl:stylesheet [ <!ENTITY nl "&#xd;&#xa;"> ]>
     4
     5   <xsl:stylesheet xmlns:xsl="http://www.w3.org/1999/XSL/Transform"
     6                   version="1.0">
     7   <xsl:output method="text"/>
     8
     9   <xsl:param name="count" select="3"/>                      <!--allow override-->
    10
    11   <xsl:template match="/">
    12     <xsl:text>Dan:   "Say goodnight, Dick."&nl;</xsl:text>
    13     <xsl:call-template name="countdown">                   <!--begin countdown-->
    14                       <!--convert to number in case supplied as string-->
    15       <xsl:with-param name="countdown" select="number($count)"/>
    16     </xsl:call-template>
    17   </xsl:template>
    18
    19   <xsl:template name="countdown">                          <!--recursive loop until done-->
    20     <xsl:param name="countdown"/>
    21     <xsl:if test="$countdown">                             <!--count not zero; more work-->
    22       <xsl:text>Dick:  "Goodnight Dick!"&nl;</xsl:text>
    23       <xsl:call-template name="countdown">                 <!--next; one less-->
    24         <xsl:with-param name="countdown" select="$countdown - 1"/>
    25       </xsl:call-template>
    26     </xsl:if>
    27   </xsl:template>
    28
    29   </xsl:stylesheet>
```

6.2   Modularizing the physical structure of stylesheets

6.2.1   External parsed general entities

An XML external parsed general entity:

- is a stand-alone XML stream of data suitable for referencing from within another XML entity;
  - by XML 1.0 rules (Section 4.3.2) the content of the entity must be well formed;
  - the reference is resolved by the XML processor within the XSLT processor,
- can contain any stylesheet fragment residing outside of the stylesheet that invokes it;
  - the entity could represent a portion of or an entire template;

- the entity might be synthesized by some pre-process that is used to parameterize the behavior of the stylesheet or the nature of the result markup,
- supports management of very large stylesheets —
  - breaking the entire work into manageable fragments,
- is a syntactic fragmenting method;
  - it is *not* designed for stylesheet fragment re-use between different stylesheets;
  - see `<xsl:include>` and `<xsl:import>` for semantic stylesheet fragment re-use.

All boundaries of external parsed general entities are lost.

- The XSLT processor cannot distinguish between markup having been found in the main stylesheet entity from markup having been found in an entity outside the main stylesheet entity.
- Any stylesheet nodes created from the external parsed general entity are added to the stylesheet node tree as if found within the main stylesheet entity itself.

6.2.2 Included files

Semantic inclusion of stylesheets:

- is performed by `<xsl:include href="`*uniform-resource-identifier*`"/>`,
- results in wholly incorporating another stylesheet;>
  - the external file itself is a complete XSLT stylesheet with requisite declarations;
  - the external XSLT stylesheet may have its own internal declaration subset;
    - an internal subset cannot be used in an external file when that file is included as an external general entity;
    - the internal subset used in the included file may have own general entities,
- adds included stylesheet nodes to the stylesheet tree in situ;
  - any stylesheet nodes created from the included file are added to the stylesheet node tree as if found within the stylesheet itself at the point of inclusion,
- provides no special accommodation of template conflicts;
  - there is no distinction of included constructs from those in the main stylesheet entity;
  - location of inclusion is important for error recovery during template conflict resolution;
  - this method is ideal for sharing small working stylesheet fragments,
    - is dedicated to commonly used document model fragments,
    - is targeted for different transformation purposes.

6.2.3   Imported files

Semantic importation of stylesheets:

- is performed by `<xsl:import href="uniform-resource-identifi-er"/>`,
- results in partially incorporating another stylesheet;
  - the external file itself is a complete XSLT stylesheet with requisite declarations;
    - the internal subset used in the included file may have own general entities,
- makes constructs in the importing stylesheet override constructs in the imported stylesheet,
- uses importation order to define "importance" for template conflict resolution;
  - stylesheet constructs in the imported file are considered less important;
    - they are less important than any corresponding constructs in the importing stylesheet;
      - thus they are not available to be used when there are identically-identified constructs found in the importing stylesheet;
    - corollary: importing stylesheet constructs are more important than imported constructs;
      - they are chosen before (without being considered a conflict) any identically-identified constructs found in an imported stylesheet;
  - order increases in importance for multiple importation;
    - when more than one file is being imported, former importation confers less importance than latter importation;
      - corollary: latter imported stylesheet constructs from a given importing file are considered more important;
        - they are chosen before (without being considered a conflict) any identically-identified constructs found in former imported stylesheets;
      - importance is transitive;
        - all stylesheet constructs from latter imported stylesheets (including those that may be imported into the imported stylesheet) are more important than constructs from prior imported stylesheets,
- is ideal for tweaking large working stylesheets;
  - suppose a new stylesheet needs 95% of an existing stylesheet;
  - only 5% written as overriding constructs are more important than those found in the imported stylesheet;
  - this is an acceptable method for encapsulating semantic validation algorithms for re-use by multiple stylesheets.

An illustration of the transitive nature of importation is shown in Figure 6–3.

The order of importance of these files in which a given construct is found is:

- `file.xsl`,
- `file2.xsl`,
- `file2a.xsl`,
- `file1.xsl`,
- `file1a.xsl`.

Note that the above order is exactly the reverse order of parsing the imported files when parsed at the point they are declared, and since all imported files are declared in a stylesheet before any other stylesheet content, this makes it straightforward for implementers to simply override a given construct's definition with a subsequent definition in parse order.

Other importation requirements are as follows.

- All imported stylesheets must be declared at the start of the importing stylesheet —
  - before *any* other construct is declared.
- Imported stylesheets from included stylesheets are imported after imported stylesheets of the including stylesheet.
  - All included stylesheets are examined in order, looking for imported stylesheets.

Figure 6–3 Importation precedence

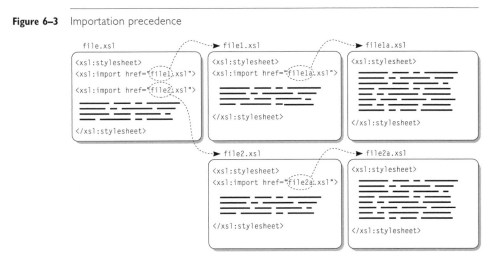

Bypassing importance is possible using `<xsl:apply-imports/>` which:

- is useful to supplement existing processing available from an imported stylesheet,
- has no attributes to be specified and can define no content,
- acts a lot like `<xsl:apply-templates select="." mode="`*mode-name*`">` but not quite:
  - does not respect any template rules in the importing stylesheet, only in the imported stylesheet,
  - does not change the XPath context as would the instruction above,
- is used to bypass the template rules of the importing stylesheet,
  - only uses the template rules of the imported stylesheet normally ignored due to importance,
  - reprocesses the current node;
    - the current node is not changed;
    - the current node list is not changed;
    - the mode is not changed,
- cannot be used within an `<xsl:for-each>` template.

6.2.4   Extension mechanisms

XSLT is extensible in design.

- A stylesheet can reference functions and instructions not defined by XSLT.
- Techniques are specified for —
  - declaring an extension,
  - invoking an extension,
  - accommodating a processor that hasn't implemented an extension.
- No techniques are specified for implementation.

Important portability issue:

- An XSLT processor is *not* required to support any extension at all.
- A stylesheet that must be portable across different XSLT implementations cannot rely on the implementation of extensions mechanisms.

6.2.4.1   *Extension Functions*

Extension functions are evaluated by a custom implementation within the XSLT processor.

- They are called by referencing their namespace-qualified names, optionally providing parameters to be used by the function:

  ```
  xmlns:function-namespace-prefix = "processor-recognized-URI"
  ```

- There is a built-in function `function-available( 'function-namespace-prefix:function-name' )`.

  - It is used to determine if the given function is available to be called.
  - Note that this function can also be used to test the availability of an XSLT function defined in the Recommendation:

    ```
    function-available( 'XSLT-function-name' )
    ```

  - It returns `false` if function is not implemented or available.
    - It must be available in the XPath function library context.

- Extension function is invoked by:

  ```
  function-namespace-prefix:function-name( )
  ```

  or

  ```
  function-namespace-prefix:function-name( function-arguments )
  ```

- Invocation returns `false` if function is not implemented or available.

6.2.4.2 Extension Instruction Elements

Extension instructions are evaluated by a custom implementation within the XSLT processor.

- They are executed by an element with a namespace-qualified element type name,
  - may have attributes that may or may not allow attribute value templates,
  - are considered as instructions and are not considered the same as literal result elements,
  - are not allowed as top-level elements,
    - can only be used as instructions within templates.
- They must have their namespace prefix declared by `xmlns:instruction-namespace-prefix="processor-recognized-URI"`.
- They must have their namespace prefix listed in `xsl:extension-element-prefixes="whitespace-separated-prefixes"`.
  - An ancestral element in the stylesheet must declare the namespace prefix;
    - if not declared, stylesheet node is assumed to represent a literal result element;
    - `#default` is used to specify the default namespace as an extension element namespace.

- There is a built-in function `element-available('prefix:element-type')`;
  - it is used to determine if a given element type is an instruction.
  - note that this function can also be used to test the availability of an XSLT element defined in the Recommendation, not just an extension element:

    ```
    element-available(XSLT-prefix:element-type)
    ```

  - invocation returns `false` if instruction is not implemented or available.
- Generally an extension instruction has the following structure:

  ```
  <instruction-namespace-prefix:instruction-name optional-attrs>
      optional-instruction-content-and-fallback
  </instruction-namespace-prefix:instruction-name>
  ```

Accommodating unimplemented extension instruction elements is performed as follows.

- Invocation instantiates `<xsl:fallback>` stylesheet templates in the result tree if the instruction is not implemented or available.
  - Fallback element or elements must be an immediate child or multiple immediate children of either an XSLT element or an extension element in the stylesheet.
    - Other descendent fallback templates are not added to the result tree.
  - Fallback templates are used only when the processor doesn't implement the instruction element;
  - they are ignored when the processor does implement the instruction element.
  - All fallback element templates are instantiated in order when the instruction element is executed.
  - It is an error if there are no fallback child elements when trying to execute an unimplemented instruction element.

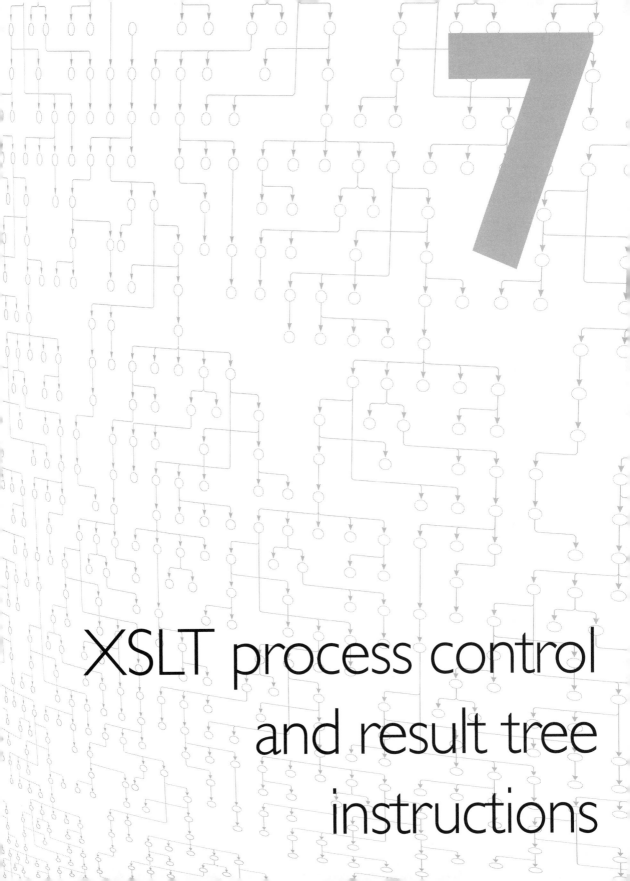

7

XSLT process control and result tree instructions

7 XSLT process control and result tree instructions

Sometimes our result correlates one-to-one with our source and we can merrily transform each of our input constructs into output constructs. More often, our result does not correlate one-for-one with our source and we have to make decisions on-the-fly about what content goes in our result and what content does not. XSLT includes process control constructs allowing us to selectively process portions of our templates based on criteria we choose to test.

Recognizing that people unfamiliar with programming style and algorithms still need to fulfill transformation requirements, XSLT provides a powerful instruction for identifying the quantity of constructs we find in our source resources. This declarative facility supplants many of the needs to implement counting algorithms in our stylesheet code by asking the XSLT processor to add a string representing the count of our source information to our result tree.

Finally, though we can rely on literal result elements to express many of our needs for instantiating result tree nodes, we are sometimes obliged to specifically instruct the XSLT processor to instantiate nodes when we cannot be satisfied by this simple syntactic shortcut.

Included in this chapter.   This chapter includes discussion of the following XSLT action instructions.

Instructions related to process control are as follows.

- `<xsl:if>`
  - performs single-state conditional inclusion of a template.
- `<xsl:choose>`
  - performs multiple-state conditional inclusion of one of a number of templates.
- `<xsl:when>`
  - performs single-state conditional inclusion of a template within a multiple-state condition.
- `<xsl:otherwise>`
  - performs default-state conditional inclusion of a template within a multiple-state condition.

Instructions related to building the result tree are as follows.

- `<xsl:number>`
  - adds a string to the result tree representing the position of the current node.
- `<xsl:attribute>`
  - instantiates an attribute node in the result tree.
- `<xsl:attribute-set>`
  - declares a set of attribute nodes for use in the result tree.
- `<xsl:comment>`
  - instantiates a comment node in the result tree.
- `<xsl:element>`
  - instantiates an element node in the result tree.
- `<xsl:processing-instruction>`
  - instantiates a processing instruction node in the result tree.
- `<xsl:text>`
  - instantiates a text node in the result tree.
- `<xsl:copy>`
  - instantiates a copy of the current node in the result tree.
- `<xsl:copy-of>`
  - instantiates a complete copy of a specified node in the result tree.

7.1 **Conditional control instructions**

7.1.1 "If — Then" conditionality

You can conditionally add a template chosen from a single alternative:

Example 7–1   The structure of the if-then construct

```
Line 1   <xsl:if test="expression-converted-to-boolean">
   2        template
   3     </xsl:if>
```

- Expression can be simple or complex.
  - A presence test is performed by a node-set expression.
    - The instruction attempts to select from the source node tree according to the expression.
      - The test determines success if at least one node from the tree would be selected or failure if no nodes from the tree would be selected.
  - Arbitrary tests can be performed with other expressions.
  - Boolean operators can combine multiple criteria into a single testing alternative.
- `true` test result adds template to the result tree.
  - The XPath context for the template does not change.
    - Current node and current node list do not change.
  - Any instructions found therein are processed in the usual way.
- `false` test result continues processing after instruction.

An example of use with a node selection test expression:

Example 7–2   Testing the presence of a child element node

```
Line 1   <xsl:if test="module">              <!--show title if module child exists-->
   2        <xsl:text>&Module-word;: </xsl:text>
   3        <xsl:value-of select="module/title"/>
   4     </xsl:if>
```

An example of use with a function test expression to create a comma-separated list:

Example 7–3   Testing the current location during an iteration

```
Line 1   <xsl:for-each select="//item">
   2        <xsl:value-of select="."/>            <!--all in comma-separated list-->
   3        <xsl:if test="position()!=last()">, </xsl:if>
   4     </xsl:for-each>
```

7.1.2 "If — Else If — Else" conditionality

You can conditionally add a template chosen from multiple alternatives:

Example 7–4 The structure of the if-else-if-else construct

```
Line 1  <xsl:choose>
    2     <xsl:when test="expression-converted-to-boolean">
    3       template
    4     </xsl:when>
    5     ...
    6     <xsl:when test="expression-converted-to-boolean">
    7       template
    8     </xsl:when>
    9     <xsl:otherwise>
   10       template
   11     </xsl:otherwise>
   12  </xsl:choose>
```

- You can have one or more `<xsl:when>` constructs.
  - Each construct contains a boolean expression specified in a `test=` attribute.
  - Each construct is tested in turn until first expression evaluates to `true`.
    - The XPath context for the template does not change.
      - Current node and current node list do not change.
    - Any instructions found therein are processed in the usual way.
  - The template may be empty.
    - It is useful when you need not to add anything in certain conditions and add something when all other conditions are tested.
- At most one `<xsl:otherwise>` construct may be present.
  - It is used when all `<xsl:when>` constructs evaluate to `false`.
  - It follows all `<xsl:when>` constructs.
  - If absent when conditions require it to be used, nothing is added to the result.

Note that at most one of the templates in the `<xsl:choose>` construct will be added to the result tree —

- perhaps none,
- never more than one.

An example of use determining one's current location as the basis for presenting some text:

Example 7–5 Acting on the identity of the current node

```
Line 1  <xsl:choose>
    2     <xsl:when test="self::frame">
```

```
3     <xsl:text>&Frame-word;: </xsl:text>
4     </xsl:when>
5     <xsl:when test="self::lesson">
6       <xsl:text>&Lesson-word;: </xsl:text>
7     </xsl:when>
8     <xsl:otherwise>
9       <xsl:text>&Module-word;: </xsl:text>
10    </xsl:otherwise>
11   </xsl:choose>
12   <xsl:value-of select="title"/>
```

Of note:

- The first test true indicates which named node is on the self axis.

7.1.3 Conditional variable assignment

Conditional constructs can be used in the assignment of a result tree fragment to a variable.

- Calculating the value of a variable is based on criteria.
- Variables can be declared as result tree fragment —
  - and converted to required type when being used.
- Conditional constructs dictate value assigned.

Consider the display of monetary values excerpted from `round.xsl`:

Example 7–6 Binding a conditional value to a variable

```
Line 1  <xsl:template match="fee">
2    <xsl:variable select="ancestor::order/@discounted"
3              name="discount"/>                 <!--get ancestral attribute-->
4    <xsl:variable name="base" select="@base-amount"/>        <!--get base-->
5    <xsl:variable name="use-fee">          <!--based on ancestral attribute-->
6      <xsl:choose>
7        <xsl:when test="$discount='yes'">              <!--not as much-->
8          <xsl:value-of select="$base * .85"/>
9        </xsl:when>
10       <xsl:when test="$discount='internal'">         <!--nothing at all-->
11         <xsl:text>0</xsl:text>
12       </xsl:when>
13       <xsl:otherwise>                                <!--normal amount-->
14         <xsl:value-of select="$base"/>
15       </xsl:otherwise>
16     </xsl:choose>
17   </xsl:variable>
18   <p>
19     <xsl:text>Fee: </xsl:text>                       <!--show information-->
20     <xsl:value-of select="$use-fee"/>
```

```
21    </p>
22   </xsl:template>
```

The intuitive (but incorrect) approach would be to put the variable declaration inside the multiple alternative construct.

- The variable's local scope does not extend beyond the encapsulating construct.
  - Scope is only the declaration's following siblings and their descendants.
- The correct approach is to define the variable at the desired scope and bind as the value the result of the alternative construct.

7.1.4   Node type testing

Examples of using `self::` axis to determine the type of the current node are as follows.

- The following tests can be read "if there are any nodes of the given node type or element node name along the self axis then add the template to the result tree".
- It is useful only for comment, processing instruction, text, and element nodes.
  - The `self::` axis cannot be used for attribute or namespace nodes because the primary node type along the axis is element node.

Example 7–7   Determining a node's identity along the `self::` axis

```
Line 1   <xsl:choose>
     2      <xsl:when test="self::book:fig">                        <!--display caption-->
     3        <xsl:text>book:fig: </xsl:text><xsl:value-of select="."/>
     4      </xsl:when>
     5      <xsl:when test="self::text()">                          <!--show text-->
     6        <xsl:text>Text: </xsl:text><xsl:value-of select="."/>
     7      </xsl:when>
     8      <xsl:when test="self::comment()">                       <!--reveal comment-->
     9        <xsl:text>Comment: </xsl:text><xsl:value-of select="."/>
    10      </xsl:when>
    11      <xsl:when test="self::processing-instruction()">        <!--pi-->
    12        <xsl:text>PI: </xsl:text><xsl:value-of select="."/>
    13      </xsl:when>
    14   </xsl:choose>
```

Using the `self::` axis is safer than `name(.)='string'`.

- The `name(.)` function returns the name with the namespace prefix.

- It is very common for people to use this, but this technique is not namespace aware.
- The `self::` axis accommodates a namespace URI with an arbitrary prefix.

Examples of using the union operator to determine the current node are as follows.

- This technique is useful for identifying root, attribute, and namespace nodes.
- It relies on the count of nodes being one when calculating the union of the current node with the desired node.

Example 7–8   Determining a node's identity along the `namespace::` and `attribute::` axes

```
Line 1   <xsl:choose>
   2       <xsl:when test="count(.|/)=1">                                  <!--root-->
   3         <xsl:text>root </xsl:text>
   4       </xsl:when>
   5                                 <!--specific namespaced-unqualified attribute-->
   6       <xsl:when test="count(.|../@version)=count(../@version)">
   7         <xsl:text>version attribute </xsl:text>
   8       </xsl:when>
   9                                   <!--specific namespace-qualified attribute-->
  10       <xsl:when test="count(.|../@book:ref)=count(../@book:ref)">
  11         <xsl:text>book:ref attribute </xsl:text>
  12       </xsl:when>
  13                                                            <!--any attribute-->
  14       <xsl:when test="count(.|../@*)=count(../@*)">
  15         <xsl:text>attribute </xsl:text>
  16       </xsl:when>
  17                                                     <!--specific namespace-->
  18       <xsl:when test="count(.|../namespace::xsl)=
  19                       count(../namespace::xsl)">
  20         <xsl:text>XSL namespace </xsl:text>
  21       </xsl:when>
  22                                                          <!--any namespace-->
  23       <xsl:when test="count(.|../namespace::*)=
  24                       count(../namespace::*)">
  25         <xsl:text>namespace </xsl:text>
  26       </xsl:when>
  27   </xsl:choose>
```

7.2 Numbering instructions

7.2.1 Source tree numbering

To add text representing numbers to the result tree —

- you can calculate the numeric result of an expression and render the text representation —
  - rounded to an integer value;
- or you can reveal the ordinal position of a source node in various source tree contexts as a number.
- This behavior is determined by the presence of the `value=` attribute.

7.2.1.1   *Non-source-tree-oriented when using* `value=`

- The context is the current node list.
  - It is the *only* time the context for `<xsl:number/>` is the current node list.
- It is useful when `<xsl:value-of select="`*expression*`">` rendering as simple floating point numbers is insufficient.
- `<xsl:number value="`*arbitrary-expression*`" format="`*token*`"/>`
  - renders the calculated rounded integer value of the expression.
- `<xsl:number value="position()" format="i"/>`
  - returns the position of the current node within the current node list,
  - is formatted in lower-case roman numerals.

7.2.1.2   *Source-tree-oriented numbering without using* `value=`

- The context is the source node tree.
- The result is a processor-calculated "identification of quantity".
  - Declarative invocation supplants the need to algorithmically implement counting in the stylesheet.
- The instruction `<xsl:number/>` returns the position of the current node within like-named source tree sibling nodes.

The following attributes defining source tree context are available.

- `count="`*pattern*`"`, `from="`*pattern*`"`, and `level="`*type*`"` characterize the numbering.
- All attributes are evaluated as attribute value templates.

`count="`*pattern*`"`

- determines what nodes are being counted;
  - it may be a simple pattern such as `count="para"`;
  - the current node itself or the first ancestral node that matches the pattern determines whose siblings are used,
- may be used with the union operator;
  - it determines to count nodes of different types or names in the calculation;

- `count="para|fig|list"` indicates all element nodes named either "para", "fig", or "list" are to be considered in the calculation,
- may be omitted for current node,
  - indicates only the type and (if named) name of the current node.

`from="pattern"`

- determines where in the hierarchy to count nodes from;
  - when counting amongst siblings, this pattern represents descendent nodes of a node on the `ancestor::` axis;
  - when counting across sibling boundaries, it represents descendent and following nodes of a node on the `preceding::` and `ancestor-or-self::` axes,
- specifies the point *after* which counting begins,
- may be omitted for the entire document,
  - indicates descendants of the root node (all nodes).

`level="single"`

- determines a single number counted amongst previous siblings,
  - returns a single number of the count of the counted nodes,
  - starts at the closest ancestral node that is a descendant of the node matching the `from="pattern"` pattern,
  - counts amongst that node's `preceding-sibling::` and `self::` axes,
- for example, numbers paragraphs when processing a paragraph using:
  - `<xsl:number/>`
    - to include only the current node type in the count,
  - `<xsl:number count="para|fig" level="single"/>`
    - to include both paragraphs and figures in the count.

`level="any"`

- determines a single number counted amongst previous elements,
  - returns a single number of the count of all counted nodes,
  - counts the current node's `preceding::` and `ancestor-or-self::` axes,
  - starts after the closest node matching `from="pattern"`;
- for example, numbers paragraphs when processing a paragraph using:
  - `<xsl:number level="any"/>`
    - to count document-scope figure number,
  - `<xsl:number level="any" from="sect"/>`
    - to count section-scope figure number.

```
level="multiple"
```

- returns a set of numbers (tumbler) counted at levels of ancestry —
  - amongst siblings of the counted nodes at different levels in the hierarchy,
  - at each level of document hierarchy along the `ancestor-or-self::` axis up to the descendant of the closest ancestral node matching the `from="`*pattern*`"` pattern,
  - amongst each level ancestor's `preceding::` and `ancestor-or-self::` axes,
  - only at levels of ancestry where counted nodes exist (i.e. no tumbler value is ever zero),
- for example, produces a chapter, section, subsection tumbler using:
  - `<xsl:number count="chap|sect|subs" level="multiple"/>`
    - to return Chapter "1", Section "1.1", Subsection "1.1.1", Section "1.2", Subsection "1.2.1", Chapter "2", Section "2.1", Subsection "2.1.1", Section "2.2", etc.
  - `<xsl:number count="sect|subs" from="chap" level="multiple"/>`
    - to return Chapter, Section "1", Subsection "1.1", Section "2", Subsection "2.1", Chapter, Section "1", Subsection "1.1", Section "2", etc.

In each of the `<xsl:number/>` illustrations, the context node is the deepest element node named "e" (shown with a bolded border) and the values calculated differ only by the attributes used.

An illustration of `level="single"` (Figure 7–1):

Figure 7–1   Nodes counted amongst siblings

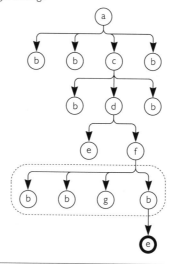

Example 7–9 Counting nodes amongst siblings

```
<xsl:number level="single" count="b"/>
```

- The closest hierarchical element being counted, "b", is the parent of e.
- Only the found ancestor and its preceding siblings are considered in the calculation.
  - Note the scope is the combination of nodes on the preceding-sibling:: and self:: axes.
- The string "3" is added to the result tree.
- Without count=, only nodes of the current type and name would have been counted (in this example "e"), adding the string "1" to the result tree.

Example of use of level="single" to indicate the number of the <module> elements from the ancestral <course> element to the current location in the source node tree (current module number within the current course):

Example 7–10 An example of using level="single"

```
Line 1    <xsl:text>&Module; </xsl:text>
     2    <xsl:number level="single"
     3                from="course"
     4                count="module"/>
     5    <xsl:text>: </xsl:text>
     6    <xsl:value-of select="ancestor-or-self::module/title"/>
```

An illustration of level="any" (Figure 7–2):

Example 7–11 Counting nodes at any level in the hierarchy

```
<xsl:number level="any" count="b"/>
```

- The string "6" is added to the result tree.
- Note the scope is the combination of nodes on the "preceding::" and "ancestor-or-self::" axes after finding the closest ancestor.
- Without count=, only nodes of the current type and name would have been counted (in this example "e"), adding the string "2".

Example of use of `level="any"` to indicate the number of `<figure>` elements from the start of the source node tree (the document-wide figure number):

Example 7–12 An example of using `level="any"`

```
Line 1    <xsl:text>&Figure; </xsl:text>
     2    <xsl:number level="any"
     3               count="figure"
     4               format="i"/>
     5    <xsl:text>: </xsl:text>
     6    <xsl:value-of select="title"/>
```

An illustration of `level="multiple"` (Figure 7–3):

Example 7–13 Counting nodes at all levels in the hierarchy

```
<xsl:number level="multiple" count="b|c|d|g" format="1-1"/>
```

- The string "3-2-4" is added to the result tree.
- A tumbler is included in the string for each level of the `ancestor-or-self::` hierarchy where there are any counted elements at that level (a level of hierarchy is skipped if that level has no members of the `count=` pattern).
- Each element in the hierarchy is counted relative to its `preceding-sibling::` and `self::` axes.

Figure 7–2 Nodes counted at any level in the hierarchy

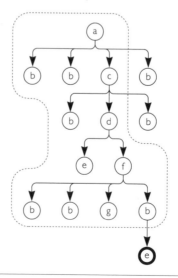

- Note the entire scope is the combination of nodes on the "`preceding::`" and "`ancestor-or-self::`" axes.
- When no `from=` is specified, the counting is from descendants of the root node.
- All members of the `count=` pattern are counted at each level.

Another illustration of `level="multiple"` adding `from=` and using the default formatting (Figure 7–4):

Example 7–14   Counting nodes at some levels of the hierarchy

```
<xsl:number level="multiple" count="b|c|d|g" from="c"/>
```

- The string "`2.4`" is added to the result tree.
- Note the hierarchy examined is along the "`ancestor-or-self::`" axis counting only from the descendants of the closest ancestral element node named with the `from=` attribute.
- Note the scope is the combination of nodes on the "`preceding::`" and "`ancestor-or-self::`" axes that are descendants of the closest ancestral element node named with the `from=` attribute.
- The node being counted from is not included even if it is one of the node names being counted.

Figure 7–3   Nodes counted at all levels in the hierarchy

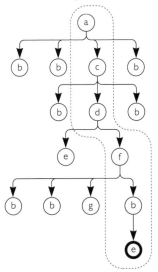

7.2.2   Representing numbers in the result tree

The XSLT processor can format `<xsl:number/>` results.

- Each of the representation of the numbers, the format of the separator sequences between multiple numbers, and the format of the terminator sequence can be specified using attributes allowing attribute value templates.
- The attribute may be omitted to indicate decimal.
  - Default presentation is with the period separator (not terminator) sequence.

`format="token"` specifies the counting scheme to be used when formatting the value.

- `format="1"` counts 1, 2, ..., 9, 10, 11, ..., 99, 100, 101, ...
- `format="01"` counts 01, 02, ..., 09, 10, ..., 99, 100, ...
  - each "0" prefix is a zero-fill indication for number values formatted less than the length of the format string.
  - `grouping-separator=","` specifies the character between groups of digits.
  - `grouping-size="3"` specifies the number of digits in each group (e.g.: 1,000,000).
- `format="a"` counts a, b, ..., z, aa, ab, ac, ...
- `format="A"` counts A, B, ... Z, AA, AB, AC, ...
  - `lang=` specifies the alphabet to be used —

Figure 7–4   Nodes counted at some levels of the hierarchy

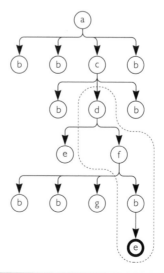

- when numbering with an alphabetic sequence `a`, `b`, ... or `A`, `B`, ...
- using the same range of values as the `xml:lang=` attribute in XML 1.0;
- `format="i"` counts `i`, `ii`, `iii`, `iv`, `v`, ..., `ix`, `x`, `xi`, ...
- `format="I"` counts `I`, `II`, `III`, `IV`, `V`, ..., `IX`, `X`, `XI`, ...
- `format="a-Unicode-character"` specifies a translation;
  - it converts the number into a representation based upon a specific language or character set;
  - the XSLT Recommendation lists a number of examples of Unicode character representing specific conversions such as Katakana (regular and "iroha" orderings), Thai, Hebrew, Greek, Old Slavic, etc.;
  - `letter-value="alphabetic"` and `letter-value="traditional"` may be used for ambiguous distinctions;
    - this attribute distinguishes numbering schemes in those languages where the first character of the sequence is ambiguous —
      - unlike English where the differing first characters of "`a`" and "`i`" distinguish alphabetic and roman numeral formats.

When using `level="multiple"` a number of tokens can be specified.

- Each component (digits and separators) of the resulting string can be formatted differently.
- The digits are formatted by corresponding format tokens.
- The separators used between components are described by sequences appearing before format tokens.
- The period "." is assumed as the separator sequence when no separator sequences are specified.
- The last format token specified is repeated for unspecified format tokens.
- The last separator sequence specified (that which is before the last format token) is repeated for unspecified separator tokens.
- A termination sequence may be specified (that which is after the last format token) and is displayed after the last digits value.

Consider the example where the number "1.4.2" needs to be formatted:

format attribute	resulting string
absent	1.4.2
`format="1.a.i"`	1.d.ii
`format="1.a"`	1.d.b

format attribute	resulting string
`format="A.1"`	`A.4.2`
`format="i"`	`i.iv.ii`
`format="1:a-i"`	`1:d-ii`
`format="1:a"`	`1:d-b`
`format="1---a"`	`1---d---b`
`format="1---a***i"`	`1---d***ii`

7.3 Result tree node instantiation

7.3.1 Building result tree nodes with instructions

Instructions exist to create the following kinds of result tree nodes:

- attribute,
- element,
- comment,
- processing instruction,
- text.

They could be used for validation of the stylesheet.

- By using only these commands and never using literal result elements, the stylesheet XML file can be validated against an XSLT document model (DTD).
- Only a non-normative DTD is supplied in the Recommendation.
- Such validation is not a lot of gain since XSLT processor typically validates much of the input for error recovery.

Adding a single attribute:

Example 7–15 Attributes of the `<xsl:attribute>` instruction

```
Line 1  <xsl:attribute name="attribute-name-AVI"
     2             namespace="optional-namespace-URI-for-name-AVI">
     3    attribute content
     4  </xsl:attribute>
```

- This instruction adds the given attribute to the result node tree for the current element.
  - The name includes namespace prefix, if desired.

Declaring a set of attributes:

- is only allowed as a top level instruction,
- is very useful for creating result trees with the XSL vocabulary due to the plethora of attributes that can be specified,
- declares a number of attributes and their values:

Example 7-16   Attributes of the `<xsl:attribute-set>` instruction

```
Line 1   <xsl:attribute-set name="attribute-set-name">
     2     optional <xsl:attribute> instructions
     3   </xsl:attribute-set>
```

- declares a set of attributes from other sets of attributes:

Example 7-17   Building sets of attributes from other sets of attributes

```
Line 1   <xsl:attribute-set name="attribute-set-name"
     2                   use-attribute-sets="attribute-set-names">
     3     optional <xsl:attribute> instructions
     4   </xsl:attribute-set>
```

Using a set of attributes:

Example 7-18   Including a set of attributes with a literal result element

```
xsl:use-attribute-sets="attribute-set-names"
```

- adds a set or sets of attributes to the result node tree for the literal result element,
- is also available when copying nodes.

Generating attributes:

- works for attributes attached only to an element node of the result node tree,
- is performed before any of the given element's content is added to the result tree,
- is the only way to selectively add an attribute to the result tree:

Example 7–19   Conditionally adding an attribute node to the result tree

```
Line 1   <list intro="no">
   2       <xsl:if test="@type='ol'">
   3         <xsl:attribute name="ordered">yes</xsl:attribute>
   4       </xsl:if>
   5       <xsl:apply-templates/>
   6   </list>
```

which can produce:

Example 7–20   An attribute added conditionally to the result tree

```
Line 1   <list intro="no" ordered="yes">
   2       ...
   3   </list>
```

- can be used for a literal result element or element instruction.
  - Sets are useful for XSL formatting transformations where numerous attributes need to be specified.
  - name= and namespace= are attribute value templates.
  - Specifying an invalid name for a node is an error.
  - One can use <xsl:text> to specify text content —
    - even though a text node is not added to the result tree, because —
    - an attribute node is a leaf of the tree and never has children.

Attribute nodes can be attached from multiple sources. Prioritized handling ensures predictable behavior:

- use-attribute-sets= are processed first;
- attribute specified in a literal result element are added next;
- executed <xsl:attribute> instructions are added last.
- Latter attribute specifications replace former for given element.

Adding element nodes:

Example 7–21   Attributes of the <xsl:element> instruction

```
Line 1   <xsl:element name="element-type-name"
   2                 namespace="optional-namespace-URI-for-name"
   3                 use-attribute-sets="optional-sets-of-attributes">
   4     element-content-template-with-optional-attribute-instructions
   5   </xsl:element>
```

- name= and namespace= are attribute value templates.
  - Name includes namespace prefix, if desired.
- Specifying an invalid name for a node is an error.

Naming an element node with an attribute value template:

Example 7–22   Examples of calculating an element's name

```
Line 1    <xsl:element name="H{count(ancestor-or-self::section) + 1}">
2            <xsl:apply-templates/>
3          </xsl:element>
4
5          <xsl:element name="{local-name(.)}">           <!--strip namespace prefix-->
6            <xsl:apply-templates/>
7          </xsl:element>
```

This provides protection against nuances regarding attached namespace nodes.

- Copying a literal result element node from the stylesheet to the result will copy any namespace nodes not pruned by `exclude-result-prefixes=` attribute.
- Copying an element node using `<xsl:copy/>` from the source tree to the result will copy any attached namespace nodes even if not used by the element node.
- The `<xsl:element>` instruction synthesizes an element node without any unnecessary namespace baggage.

Adding text nodes:

Example 7–23   Using the `<xsl:text>` instruction

```
Line 1   <xsl:text>escaped-text</xsl:text>
2
3        <xsl:text disable-output-escaping="yes">verbatim-text</xsl:text>
```

- `<xsl:text>` cannot have any sub-elements of any kind.
- The XSLT processor is not obliged to respect `disable-output-escaping="yes"`.
- `disable-output-escaping="yes"` can only be used for the text content of an element being added to the result tree,
  - e.g. cannot be used within a result tree fragment variable assignment, or `<xsl:message>` construct.

Stylesheet tree no-operation instruction:

Example 7–24   Using empty `<xsl:text>` instructions to impact on stylesheet node tree construction

```
Line 1    <xsl:for-each select="item">                    <!--with new lines-->
```

```
  2        (<xsl:value-of select="."/>)
  3      </xsl:for-each>
  4
  5      <xsl:for-each select="item">                        <!--without new lines-->
  6        <xsl:text>(</xsl:text>
  7        <xsl:value-of select="."/>
  8        <xsl:text>)</xsl:text>
  9      </xsl:for-each>
 10
 11      <xsl:for-each select="item">                        <!--without new lines-->
 12        <xsl:text/>(<xsl:value-of select="."/>)<xsl:text/>
 13      </xsl:for-each>
```

- Note above the use the empty text instruction to shape the non-whitespace-only text nodes of the stylesheet tree.
- The instruction `<xsl:text/>` adds nothing to the result tree but impacts on the text nodes of the stylesheet tree.

Adding processing instruction and comment nodes:

Example 7–25   Attributes of the `<xsl:processing-instruction>` instruction

```
Line 1  <xsl:processing-instruction name="PI-target-AVI">
  2       processing-instruction-content-template
  3     </xsl:processing-instruction>
```

Example 7–26   Using the `<xsl:comment>` instruction

```
Line 1  <xsl:comment>
  2       comment-content-template
  3     </xsl:comment>
```

- `name=` is an attribute value template.
- Specifying an invalid name for a node is an error.
- One can use `<xsl:text>` to specify text content.
  - A text node is not added to the result tree.
  - The construct is describing a text node in the stylesheet tree.
  - The text from the stylesheet defines the value of the result tree node.
  - These nodes are leaves of the tree and never have children.
- It is error condition when text content contains the same sequence as the lexical delimiter for the construct.
  - Processing instruction text cannot contain "?>".
  - Comment text cannot contain "--".
  - Processor may choose to not report the error.
    - It will inject a space between the characters if no error reported.

7.3.2 Building result tree nodes with literal result elements

Recall that elements in the stylesheet that are in templates and are not XSLT instructions are called "literal result elements."

- When a literal result element is added to the result tree, it is copied as an element node.
- Any attributes present are instantiated in the result tree after being interpreted as attribute value templates.

Literal result element XSLT attributes:

- are allowed in addition to any result vocabulary attributes specified in the literal result element,
- where scoped, influence only descendants of the given literal result element.

`xsl:exclude-result-prefixes="`*`whitespace-separated-prefixes`*`"`

- inhibits the contingent creation of namespace nodes (see Chapter 5),
- does not inhibit the required creation of namespace nodes.

`xsl:extension-element-prefixes=`
`"`*`whitespace-separated-prefixes`*`"`

- declares the namespace prefixes of element instructions available from the XSLT processor (see Chapter 5),
- if missing, results in elements from such prefixes assumed to be literal result elements and not instructions.

`xsl:version="`*`numeric-version`*`"`

- declares the specification level of XSLT required by the stylesheet instructions (see Chapter 5).

`xsl:use-attribute-sets="`*`whitespace-separated-names`*`"`

- adds to the result element all attributes in a previously declared collection of attributes.

You should not use the default namespace for the XSLT instruction namespace.

- This would prevent the above attributes from being used in literal result elements.

- Attributes without namespace prefixes are in no namespace, not in the default namespace.

7.3.3   Copying source tree nodes to the result tree

Copying the current node (shallow copy):

Example 7–27   Using the `<xsl:copy>` instruction

```
Line 1   <xsl:copy>
    2      optional-content-template
    3    </xsl:copy>
```

- The current node (type and, if named, name) is copied to the result node tree.
- The type or name of the source node need not be known.
- Sub-elements and attributes from the source node tree are *not* automatically copied.
    - Any content copying must be explicitly requested in the stylesheet.

Example 7–28   Using the `<xsl:copy>` instruction with attribute sets

```
Line 1   <xsl:copy use-attribute-sets="whitespace-separated-names">
    2      optional-content-template
    3    </xsl:copy>
```

- The current node is copied and sets of attributes are added along the way.

Copying arbitrary nodes and all of their descendants (deep copy):

Example 7–29   Copying a result tree fragment variable

```
<xsl:copy-of select="result-tree-fragment-expression"/>
```

- Fragment is added to the result tree verbatim.

Example 7–30   Copying a source tree node set

```
<xsl:copy-of select="node-set-expression"/>
```

- Nodes from source tree are added to the result tree in document order.
- Template rules are not triggered (this is not a "push").

Example 7–31   Copying other expression values

```
<xsl:copy-of select="other-expression"/>
```

● String value is added as in `<xsl:value-of>`.

7.3.3.1   *Examples*

An example code fragment to copy only the given element and its attributes, but to process its content without blindly copying the content, is as follows:

Example 7–32   Copying only the current node when matching multiple nodes

```
Line I  <xsl:template match="this|that|other">
     2    <xsl:copy>                        <!--copy whatever the matched node is-->
     3      <xsl:copy-of select="@*"/>           <!--copy attached attr nodes-->
     4      <xsl:apply-templates/>                    <!--push child nodes-->
     5    </xsl:copy>
     6  </xsl:template>
```

An example code fragment to copy the entire given element and all its content:

Example 7–33   Copying the sub-tree below the current node when matching multiple nodes

```
Line I  <xsl:template match="this|that|other">
     2    <xsl:copy-of select="."/>            <!--copy the entire current node-->
     3  </xsl:template>
```

Contrast this to the execution of `<xsl:value-of select=".">` on a node of the source node tree that adds to the result tree the concatenation of descendent text nodes as a string of text.

Diagnostic stylesheet example:

● `copyofall.xsl` will copy the entire input XML to the output.
  ○ The entire physical structure of the stylesheet is written into the output as a single file.
    ▪ All external XML markup fragments are consolidated into a single file.
    ▪ Imported and included files are *not* consolidated using this technique.
  ○ All general entities are resolved, thereby revealing what the XSLT processor is seeing as the value of entities that may be parameterized through marked sections.

Example 7–34 A monolithic stylesheet to copy the entire source tree to the result tree

```
Line 1  <?xml version="1.0"?>                                    <!--copyofall.xsl-->
     2  <!--XSLT 1.0 - http://www.CraneSoftwrights.com/training -->
     3  <xsl:stylesheet xmlns:xsl="http://www.w3.org/1999/XSL/Transform"
     4                  version="1.0">
     5
     6  <xsl:template match="/">                            <!--entire copy of root node-->
     7    <xsl:copy-of select="."/>
     8  </xsl:template>
     9
    10  </xsl:stylesheet>
```

Tweaking stylesheet example:

- `copyall.xsl` will copy the entire input XML to the output providing for customization.
  - When imported into another stylesheet, the importing stylesheet can specialize the behavior for specific node template rules.
  - Where it is necessary to copy *most* of a file but change only a few items, this script can be a helpful shell within which to write the customizations.

Example 7–35 A granular stylesheet to copy the entire source tree to the result tree

```
Line 1  <?xml version="1.0"?>                                    <!--copyall.xsl-->
     2  <xsl:stylesheet
     3    xmlns:xsl="http://www.w3.org/1999/XSL/Transform"
     4    xmlns:copyall="http://www.CraneSoftwrights.com/ns/copyall"
     5    exclude-result-prefixes="copyall"
     6    version="1.0">
     7
     8  <!--use the following to copy all of the content of a node-->
     9
    10  <xsl:template name="copyall:copy-content">
    11    <xsl:apply-templates
    12        select="@*|processing-instruction()|comment()|*|text()"/>
    13  </xsl:template>
    14
    15  <!--default behaviours for all nodes-->
    16
    17  <xsl:template match="/|
    18                  processing-instruction()|comment()|*|@*|text()">
    19    <xsl:copy>
    20      <xsl:call-template name="copyall:copy-content"/>
    21    </xsl:copy>
    22  </xsl:template>
    23
    24  </xsl:stylesheet>
```

Importing the `copyall.xsl` stylesheet requires the declaration and exclusion of the stylesheet's namespace:

Example 7–36   Specializing the granular copying stylesheet

```
Line 1  <?xml version="1.0"?>                                    <!--copyalltest.xsl-->
     2  <!--XSLT 1.0 - http://www.CraneSoftwrights.com/training-->
     3  <xsl:stylesheet
     4     xmlns:xsl="http://www.w3.org/1999/XSL/Transform"
     5     xmlns:copystuff="http://www.CraneSoftwrights.com/ns/copyall"
     6     exclude-result-prefixes="copystuff"
     7     version="1.0">
     8
     9  <xsl:import href="copyall.xsl"/>
    10
    11  <xsl:template match="b">                               <!--rename an element -->
    12    <new-b>
    13      <xsl:call-template name="copystuff:copy-content"/>
    14    </new-b>
    15  </xsl:template>
    16
    17  <xsl:template match="d">                               <!--redefine an element -->
    18    <new-d>New d-value here</new-d>
    19  </xsl:template>
    20
    21  <xsl:template match="@a">                              <!--rename an attribute -->
    22    <xsl:attribute name="new-a">
    23      <xsl:value-of select="."/>                         <!--this copies the content-->
    24    </xsl:attribute>
    25  </xsl:template>
    26
    27  <xsl:template match="@c">                              <!--redefine an attribute -->
    28    <xsl:attribute name="{name(.)}">
    29      <xsl:text>new-c</xsl:text>
    30    </xsl:attribute>
    31  </xsl:template>
    32
    33  <xsl:template match="f|@g"/>                   <!--remove an element or attribute-->
    34
    35  </xsl:stylesheet>
```

Note that it is only a convention that the namespace URI also be an addressable.

Consider the following input instance with elements and attributes:

Example 7–37   Sample input to specialized copying

```
Line 1  <?xml version="1.0"?>
     2  <test>
```

```
3     <a a="test">a content</a>
4     <b b="test">b content</b>
5     <c c="test">c content</c>
6     <d d="test">d content</d>
7     <e e="test">e content</e>
8     <f f="test">f content</f>
9     <g g="test">g content</g>
10  </test>
```

The stylesheet above will produce the following output instance:

Example 7–38   Sample result using specialized copying

```
Line 1  <?xml version="1.0" encoding="utf-8"?>
2  <test>
3     <a new-a="test">a content</a>
4     <new-b b="test">b content</new-b>
5     <c c="new-c">c content</c>
6     <new-d>New d-value here</new-d>
7     <e e="test">e content</e>
8
9     <g>g content</g>
10  </test>
```

7.3.4   Escaping text placed in the result tree

XML and HTML serialization ensures well-formed output.

- Characters sensitive to markup processing are protected.
- Processor can choose any method it wishes to ensure characters are escaped —
  - using a CDATA section <![CDATA[...]]>,
  - using a built-in entity reference under processor (not stylesheet) control;
    - any "<", "&", and ">" found in a text node can be emitted as <, &, and > respectively;
    - the HTML output method may recognize HTML built-in entity references for non-ASCII characters,
  - using a numeric entity reference under processor (not stylesheet) control;
    - "<" can be serialized as "<" or "<" or "<";
    - "&" can be serialized as "&" or "&";
    - ">" can be serialized as ">" or ">" or ">";
    - characters outside the serialization encoding can be emitted in decimal or hex.

Stylesheet can only request use of CDATA sections using:

```
<xsl:output  cdata-section-elements="whitespace-separated-
names"/>
```

- This will create a single CDATA section for each element in most cases.
  - The sequence "]]>" in a text node, when be emitted in CDATA in XML, is as follows to ensure the CDATA is not prematurely terminated:

    ```
    <![CDATA[]]]><![CDATA[>]]>
    ```

As a last resort the stylesheet can request no escaping.

- If it is absolutely necessary to actually emit "<" or "&" from the result tree, the desire to do so can be indicated as follows:

  ```
  <xsl:text disable-output-escaping="yes">text</xsl:text>
  <xsl:value-of disable-output-escaping="yes" select="expression"/>
  ```

  - This way it is very easy to produce XML that is not well-formed, or HTML that makes references to entities that do not exist; avoiding this technique ensures all output that is produced is well formed.
  - Note that a conforming XSLT processor is not required to support the disabling of output escaping, so this technique is not guaranteed to be portable across all implementations.
- Output escaping can only be disabled for text generated for element's content —
  - not for the content of `xsl:attribute`, `xsl:comment`, or `xsl:processing-instruction` instructions.

An example use-case where this is required is the emission of ASP code embedded in an HTML file.

Example 7–39   Two examples of generating ASP text

```
Line 1    <xsl:text disable-output-escaping="yes">
   2             &lt;% Method-Call() %></xsl:text>
   3    <xsl:text disable-output-escaping="yes"><![CDATA[
   4             <% Method-Call() %>]]></xsl:text>
```

Both of the above instructions produce the following result (provided the attribute is respected by the processor):

Example 7–40   Example generated ASP text

```
              <% Method-Call() %>
```

For example, the following instruction can be used to coerce the XSLT processor to emit " " in order to reference the entity definition built-in to HTML:

Example 7–41   Synthesizing an entity reference using disabled escaping

```
<xsl:text disable-output-escaping="yes"> </xsl:text>
```

- The two ways to accomplish this in a portable fashion supported by all conforming XSLT processors that support the HTML output method are:
    - to define the entity nbsp as   and reference the entity in the stylesheet,
    - to reference the character entity   directly in the stylesheet.
- In both the above cases, the character is seen to be a non-ASCII character and is recognized by the HTML output method as a known built-in entity, and emitted as the entity reference .

Remember that the input source file still always has to be well-formed XML, hence the stylesheet must escape the characters in the input that are not going to be escaped in the output by —

- using built-in or declared character entity references,
- using numeric character references,
- using CDATA sections.

Consider the need to produce the following result:

Example 7–42   Example HTML use of an entity reference

```
Line 1  <html>
     2  <body>
     3  <p>This is an nbsp reference: ' '.</p>
     4  </body>
     5  </html>
```

The XSLT script disable.xsl disables the output escaping method to emit " ":

Example 7–43   Generating an HTML entity reference using disabled escaping

```
Line 1  <?xml version="1.0"?>                                    <!--disable.xsl-->
     2  <!--XSLT 1.0 - http://www.CraneSoftwrights.com/training -->
     3  <xsl:stylesheet xmlns:xsl="http://www.w3.org/1999/XSL/Transform"
     4                  version="1.0">
     5
```

```
 6  <xsl:output method="html" indent="yes"/>
 7
 8  <xsl:template match="/">                                    <!--root rule-->
 9   <html>
10    <body>
11     <p>
12      <xsl:text>This is an nbsp reference: '</xsl:text>
13      <xsl:text disable-output-escaping="yes"> </xsl:text>
14      <xsl:text>'.</xsl:text>
15     </p>
16    </body>
17   </html>
18  </xsl:template>
19
20  </xsl:stylesheet>
```

The XSLT script `disable-not.xsl` approaches the same problem without circumventing the protection available in XSLT:

Example 7–44 Generating an HTML entity reference without disabling escaping

```
Line 1  <?xml version="1.0"?>                                   <!--disable-not.xsl-->
    2   <!--XSLT 1.0 - http://www.CraneSoftwrights.com/training -->
    3   <!DOCTYPE xsl:stylesheet [
    4   <!ENTITY nbsp " ">                   <!--declare HTML value of the entity-->
    5   ]>
    6   <xsl:stylesheet xmlns:xsl="http://www.w3.org/1999/XSL/Transform"
    7                   version="1.0">
    8
    9   <xsl:output method="html" indent="yes"/>
   10
   11  <xsl:template match="/">                                    <!--root rule-->
   12   <html>
   13    <body>
   14     <p>
   15      <xsl:text>This is an nbsp reference: ' '.</xsl:text>
   16     </p>
   17    </body>
   18   </html>
   19  </xsl:template>
   20
   21  </xsl:stylesheet>
```

Note how the identical output is produced by using an entity reference in the above stylesheet.

- The reference points to the entity declaration in the stylesheet.
  - It could have been included as one of a set of declarations for the entire set utilized by HTML.

- The XML processor in the XSLT processor translates the reference into the entity content and only the character ` ` is stored in the stylesheet tree (not the entity reference).
- The XSLT script adds the character ` ` to the result tree.
- The HTML output method recognizes the ` ` character as matching that value for the ` ` entity and emits the entity reference instead —
  - defined *only* for the HTML output method,
  - not recognized by other output methods.

It may still be necessary to take advantage of this approach:

- to solve problems not solved in a well-behaved fashion for the current implementation of XSLT,
- for a processor that implements output escaping while not supporting emitting the document type declaration,
- to deliver packages of non-well-formed markup from a server process to a browser parsing the output information as markup (e.g. from a database of HTML fragments).

During the processing of the root node (typically, but not necessarily), a block of non-escaped text can be emitted to produce the document type declaration, as in the following example.

- Version 1.0 of XML doesn't support the definition of the output internal declaration subset of the instance.
- The correct method would be to use `doctype-public=` or `doctype-system=`, but these may not be supported by the XSLT processor.
  - If the internal declaration subset is needed, one cannot use these methods since the declaration is ended in order to correctly emit the document element.

Consider the following stylesheet to emit a complete document type declaration by disabling the output escaping on a text node in which the entire prologue is written using a CDATA section to reduce the amount of per-character escaping required in the stylesheet:

Example 7–45   Synthesizing an internal declaration subset for the result

```
Line 1  <?xml version="1.0"?>                                    <!--disable-decl.xsl-->
     2  <!--XSLT 1.0 - http://www.CraneSoftwrights.com/training -->
     3  <xsl:stylesheet xmlns:xsl="http://www.w3.org/1999/XSL/Transform"
     4                  version="1.0">
     5
```

```
6   <xsl:output method="xml" indent="yes" omit-xml-declaration="yes"/>
7
8   <xsl:template match="/">                                    <!--root rule-->
9    <xsl:text disable-output-escaping="yes"><![CDATA[
10  <!DOCTYPE test [
11  <!ENTITY nbsp " ">
12  ]>]]></xsl:text>
13   <test>
14    <xsl:text>This is an nbsp reference: '</xsl:text>
15    <xsl:text disable-output-escaping="yes"> </xsl:text>
16    <xsl:text>'.</xsl:text>
17   </test>
18  </xsl:template>
19
20  </xsl:stylesheet>
```

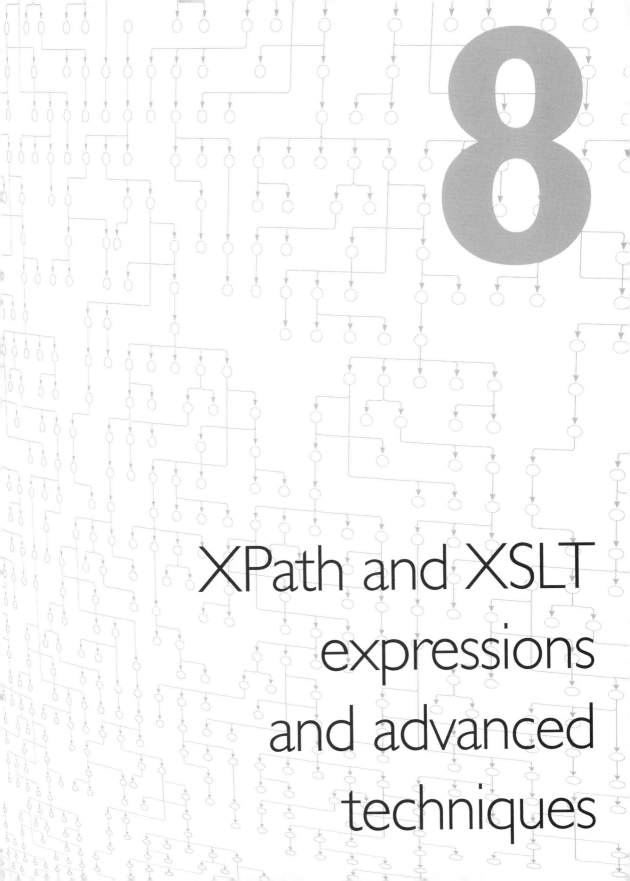

8

XPath and XSLT
expressions
and advanced
techniques

8 XPath and XSLT expressions and advanced techniques

In previous chapters we have reviewed available facilities that operate at a coarse level of granularity, typically dealing with values unmodified from the source node tree. We have been using instructions that build result content with whole portions of source content.

This chapter reviews a number of very useful functions and instructions that give us tremendous control and flexibility when accessing information in our source tree. Also included are some advanced techniques for using some of the previously-described facilities. These techniques are unobvious, and perhaps perceived as unconventional, though they can come in handy.

Powerful functions and expression support. XSLT and XPath provides a number of functions we stylesheet writers need when manipulating our information. We need not be programmers because a number of facilities are implemented by the XSLT processor programmers and made available to us in a declarative fashion. We ask the processor to do a lot of work for us, and we deal with the results without having to know how the routines have been implemented.

For each of the four data types available in XPath, a number of facilities are available:

- boolean operators and functions,
- number operators and functions,
- string functions,
- node set operator and functions.

For additional access to the source node tree, a few specialized functions are available:

- id()
  - returns nodes with unique identifiers;
- key()
  - returns nodes with declared relationships;
- current()
  - returns the current node of the start of expression evaluation.

There is one specialized function defined so far for access to the document model of the source file:

- unparsed-entity-uri()
  - returns URI associated with declared entity.

We can access a number of separate source documents through the use of a specialized function:

- document()
  - returns root nodes of source node trees from external files.

Advanced techniques.   There are some approaches to using XSLT instructions that are not immediately apparent by their definitions in the Recommendation. These approaches do not change the definition of the instructions. Examples of some advanced techniques are narrated to illustrate their utility in meeting certain transformation requirements.

The techniques demonstrated include traversing the source tree incrementally and recursive template invocation.

Included in this chapter.   This chapter includes discussion of the following XSLT advanced instructions.

Instruction related to string formatting is as follows:

- `<xsl:decimal-format>`
  - controls the formatting of numbers when added to the result tree.

Instruction related to advanced access to the source node tree is as follows:

- `<xsl:key>`
  - declares key nodes in the source tree node for bulk processing.

Instruction related to advanced algorithmic techniques is as follows:

- `<xsl:call-template>`
  - uses named templates with subroutine-like control.

8.1 Expression functions

8.1.1 Calculating values using number, string, and boolean expression functions

Formal function prototypes in the Recommendations:

- are only summarized in this material.
  - See Appendix C for indexed list of functions.
    - They are not indexed in the actual Recommendations.
  - Formal language is not copied from the Recommendations into this material.
  - This material does not attempt to be as rigorous as the Recommendations.

Examples of some of the uses of expressions are listed below.

`select="expression"`

- evaluates an arbitrary expression,
- selects nodes for processing.

`test="expression"`

- is used in conditionals,
- converts end result to a boolean and tests for inclusion of a template.

`literal-result-element-attr="{expression}"`

- calculates attribute value template,
- converts end result to a string and injects into result-tree attribute node,

- is not applicable for most stylesheet instruction attributes —
  - patterns,
  - named XSLT constructs,
  - top-level element attributes.

`function-name(function-arguments)`

- calls an XSLT built-in function.

`xmlns:function-namespace="processor-recognized-uri"`
`function-namespace:function-name(function-arguments)`

- calls an extension function supported by the processor.

8.1.2 Calculating values using number functions

The following concerns floating-point number operators and functions in XSLT.

- The range of values is defined by 64-bit IEEE Standard for Binary Floating-Point Arithmetic specification (ANSI/IEEE Std. 754–1985).
  - Special values are "Not-a-Number" (NaN), positive and negative infinity, positive and negative zero.
- An `<xsl:decimal-format>` top-level element for the stylesheet (if available, or one of a number of named ones available) dictates the various visible expressions of numbers in general and the special values `NaN` and infinity`infinity` in particular.
- Radix arithmetic and conversion is not yet available in W3C XSLT.

`number(expression)`

- converts the object argument to a number,
- given a string argument, ignores leading and trailing whitespace and calculates `NaN` if not valid,
- given a node set, converts the value of the first member of the node-set (in document order) to a string before converting to a number,
- without an argument, converts the current node to a string before converting to a number,
- given a boolean argument, converts `true` to 1 and `false` to 0.

Operators "+", "-", "*":

- are traditional arithmetic operations for addition, subtraction and multiplication.

Operators "`div`" and "`mod`":

- are traditional division operations of division and modulus.
  - The slash "/" cannot be used for division as it is a location path separator in the XPath grammar.
  - Modulus is *not* implemented the same as the IEEE remainder operation.

`floor(number)` and `ceiling(number)`

- return closest integer towards negative infinity and positive infinity respectively.

`round(number)`

- returns the closest integer, except in the following situations:
  - the arguments `NaN`, positive infinity, negative infinity, positive zero and negative zero all return the argument as the result;
  - an argument between −0.5 and zero returns negative zero;
  - an argument equidistant to two integers returns the integer closest to positive infinity.

`sum(node-set-expression)`

- takes a node set as an argument,
- converts each node to a string before converting to a number,
- calculates and returns the sum of each of the number values.

Note that when dealing with floating point, sometimes results are not precise; consider the following empirical evidence from `round.xsl`:

```
<xsl:value-of select="format-number(round($use-fee*1.15*100)
                                    div 100,' #0.00] ')"/>
```

- displays a `$use-fee` value of 8.50 with taxes as "9.77",
- should display the value as "9.78" because 8.5 * 1.15 * 100 = 977.5 and the `round()` function rounds a fraction of ".5" towards positive infinity,
- the floating point library calculated 8.5 * 1.15 * 100 = 977.4999999 which, when rounded to the closest integer, rounds to 977.

8.1.3   Calculating values using string functions

Strings are sequences of Unicode (also called the Universal Character Set (UCS)) characters distinguishing fully-formed from composite characters.

`string(expression)`

- converts the argument to a string,
- is used for any function expecting a single string argument to convert that argument to a string,
- returns the empty string when an empty node-set is specified as an argument,
- returns the conversion of the first member of the node set (in document order) when a non-empty node set is specified as an argument,
- converts the number to sequence of characters when a number argument is specified;
  - note that the result of performing arithmetic very rarely results in expected decimal-place rounding;
  - adding two currency amounts with only two digits of significance could produce a floating point number with 20 digits of decimal significance,
- returns a concatenation of all text nodes in the fragment when a result-tree fragment is specified,
- converts the current node to a string when no argument is specified,
- converts `true` to the string "`true`" and `false` to the string "`false`" when a boolean argument is specified.

`concat(string,string,optional-strings)`

- returns the concatenation of each of the arguments' string value,
- requires at least two arguments to be passed to the function.

`substring(first-as-string,second-as-number,optional-third-as-number)`

- returns the sequence of characters of the first argument from the numeric position indicated in the second argument (1 is the origin position) to either the end of the string or the count of characters indicated by the number in the third argument (whichever is less).

`substring-before(`*first,   second*`)` and `substring-after(`*first,*
second`)`

- return the empty string if the first argument doesn't wholly contain
  the second argument, or the portion of the first argument that
  occurs before or after the complete second argument.

`string-length(`*optional-argument*`)`

- returns the count of characters in the supplied string or, if not
  supplied, in the value of the current node.

`contains(`*first,second*`)` and `starts-with(`*first,second*`)`

- return boolean `true` or `false` if the first argument wholly contains,
  or both wholly contains and begins with the complete second
  argument, or not.

`normalize-space(`*optional-expression*`)`

- will act on the value of the current node (if no argument is supplied)
  or on the argument (if one is supplied),
- strips leading and trailing whitespace characters and replaces con-
  tiguous sequences of adjacent whitespace characters with a single
  space character;
  - this mimics the same normalization that XML processors do with tokenized
    attribute values,
- is handy for checking a node's value having only whitespace characters.

`translate(`*first,second,third*`)`

- returns the characters of the first argument translated by replacing
  those characters listed in the second argument with the corresponding characters in the same ordinal position found in the third
  argument,
- removes characters in the second argument positioned beyond the
  length of the third argument from the first argument;
  - for example, `translate(` `"abcDEF"`, `"cDaE"`, `"CdA"` `)` returns "AbCdF".

`format-number(` *first-as-number,   second-as-string,   optional-*
third-as-string `)`

- returns the number represented in the first argument as a string formatted according to the string in the second argument following the decimal format named by the third argument (or the unnamed decimal format if there is no argument),
- for its second argument, accepts a string of characters made up of symbols in one or two patterns that dictate how the digits of the positive or negative values of the number are presented in the resulting string, e.g.:
  - `format-number( .2, "#.00" )` returns ".20";
  - `format-number( .2, "#0.00" )` returns "0.20";
    - the zero-digit indication forces the display of the digit even when it is not significant;
  - `format-number( -12345, "#,###;(#)" )` returns "(12345)";
    - the semi-colon separates the positive value pattern from the negative;
    - some Java-based implementations return "(12.345)" incorrectly,
- uses the format string syntax which is the same as that used in Java and is described in more detail in the next section regarding Decimal Formatting,
- is specific to XSLT and is not part of XPath.

8.1.4   Decimal formatting

The second argument of `format-number()`:

- is a user-specified sequence of formatting characters interpreted by the processor when formatting the numeric value of the first argument to the function,
- may contain one or two format sub-sequences;
  - the first sub-sequence is for positive values and the optional second is for negative values:

    ```
    {p-prefix}p-whole{p-fraction}{p-suffix}
    {pat-sep{n-prefix}n-whole{n-fraction}{n-suffix}}
    ```

  - each sequence is made of up to four components (braces indicate optional components):
    - a prefix that is output verbatim —
      - provided there are no digit or zero-digit characters,
    - the whole number component —
      - is comprised of optional excess digit indicators, followed by leading zero-digit indicators, interspersed with grouping separators,
      - is empirically ignored for negative numbers in Java-based implementations;

- it is sufficient to utilize a single digit indicator;
- whole number component for positive number is utilized for both,
- a fraction number component:
  - is comprised of a decimal separator, followed by optional trailing zero-digit indicators, followed by optional excess digit indicators,
  - is empirically ignored for negative numbers in Java-based implementations;
    - fraction number component for positive number is utilized for both,
- a suffix that is output verbatim and checked for a percent indication —
  - provided there are no digit or zero-digit characters;
- subsequences are separated by the pattern separator character when both are specified;
  - the negative number pattern is not required if the negative number is formatted the same as the positive number.

The third argument of `format-number()`:

- is the name of a declaration of cultural influences on the formatting of numbers,
- may be omitted to specify the default or unnamed decimal format.

`<xsl:decimal-format attributes/>`

- is a top-level instruction describing grammar components and formatting strings,
- may contain the following attributes:
  - `name="description-name"`
    - there cannot be more than one unnamed specification,
    - there cannot be more than one named specification with the same name,
    - there is an exception accommodating external stylesheet fragments:
      - two format declarations with the same name (or unnamed) must have identical effective values,
  - `pattern-separator=` between positive and negative formats ("`;`"),
  - `digit=` for insignificant digits ("`#`"),
  - `zero-digit=` for significant digits ("`0`"),
  - `decimal-separator=` between whole and fraction ("`.`"),
  - `grouping-separator=` between number groups ("`,`"),
  - `percent=` for calculation and display ("`%`"),
  - `per-mille=` for calculation and display ("`&#x2030;`"),
  - `minus-sign=` for presentation of negative numbers ("`-`"),
  - `infinity=` for presentation of infinity values ("`Infinity`"),
  - `NaN=` for presentation of invalid numbers ("`NaN`").

The formal specification of the format string syntax is that used for Java: `http://java.sun.com/products/jdk/1.1/docs/api/java.text.DecimalFormat.html`.

- Each get/set method pair in the documentation is an attribute defined for the `<xsl:decimal-format>` element.
- The currency symbol (0x00a4) cannot be used in a format pattern for portability reasons because this was added after the initial release of JDK 1.1.
- The quote character is not localized.

The following lines are extracted from `dformat.xsl` to illustrate examples of using format patterns:

Example 8–1	Formatting positive and negative numbers into strings

```
Line 1  <xsl:text>1 + '$###,####,##.###0;(########.000#)' </xsl:text>
     2  <xsl:value-of select="format-number(123456789.9876,
     3                         '$###,####,##.###0;(########.000#)')"/>
     4  <xsl:text>&nl;2 - '$######,###.###;($#####,##.####)' </xsl:text>
     5  <xsl:value-of select="format-number(-123456789.9876,
     6                         '$######,###.###;($#####,##.####)')"/>
     7  <xsl:text>&nl;3 + '+#########.##;(##,##,##,##.000#)' </xsl:text>
     8  <xsl:value-of select="format-number(123456789.9876,
     9                         '+#########.##;(##,##,##,##.000#)')"/>
    10  <xsl:text>&nl;4 - '$######,###0.#;$-#'            </xsl:text>
    11  <xsl:value-of select="format-number(-123456789.9876,
    12                              '$######,###0.#;$-#')"/>
    13  <xsl:text>&nl;5 + '$######,#00.####'              </xsl:text>
    14  <xsl:value-of select="format-number(123456789.9876,
    15                              '$######,#00.####')"/>
    16  <xsl:text>&nl;6 - '$#######,##0.000#;(-$#)'       </xsl:text>
    17  <xsl:value-of select="format-number(-123456789.9876,
    18                              '$#######,##0.000#;(-$#)')"/>
    19  <xsl:text>&nl;7 + '###,###.###%;(#)'              </xsl:text>
    20  <xsl:value-of select="format-number(123456789.9876,
    21                              '###,###.###%;(#)')"/>
    22  <xsl:text>&nl;8 - '###,###.###%;(#)'              </xsl:text>
    23  <xsl:value-of select="format-number(-123456789.9876,
    24                              '###,###.###%;(#)')"/>
    25  <xsl:text>&nl;9 + '######,###.###%'              </xsl:text>
    26  <xsl:value-of select="format-number(123456789.9876,
    27                              '######,###.###%')"/>
    28  <xsl:text>&nl;10 - '######,###.###%'             </xsl:text>
    29  <xsl:value-of select="format-number(-123456789.9876,
    30                              '######,###.###%')"/>
```

The following lines are produced when running the stylesheet `dfor-mat.xsl`:

Example 8–2	Rendering of formatted numbers using Java-based XSLT processor

Line 1	+ '$#####,####,###.####0;(#######.000#)'	$1,23,45,67,89.9876
2	- '$######,###.###;($#####,###.####)'	($123,456,789.988)
3	+ '+##########.##;(##,##,##,##.000#)'	+123456789.99
4	- '$######,###0.#;$-#'	$-1,2345,6790
5	+ '$######,#00.####'	$123,456,789.9876
6	- '$######,##0.000#;(-$#)'	(-$123,456,789.9876)
7	+ '###,####.###%;(#)'	12,345,678,998.76%
8	- '###,####.###%;(#)'	(12,345,678,998.76)
9	+ '######,###.###%'	12,345,678,998.76%
10	- '######,###.###%'	-12,345,678,998.76%

Note the following regarding each numbered line above when using a Java-based implementation.

Line 1: The number of digit indicators between the decimal separator and the closest grouping separator dictate the groupings for the entire whole number component (other grouping sizes are ignored).

Line 2: The grouping indications in the negative value pattern are ignored; the whole number and fraction component formatting is dictated by the positive value pattern even when the value is negative.

Line 3: The second digit of the fraction component is the rounded value of the third digit ("8" becomes "9" because of "7").

Line 4: A single digit indicator suffices to delimit the prefix from the suffix in the negative value pattern.

Line 5: Any number of zero digits can lead the decimal separator.

Line 6: Any number of zero digits can follow the decimal separator.

Line 7: The use of the percent indicator in the suffix triggers the value to be multiplied by 100 before being formatted.

Line 8: Illustrating the problem with reliance on the incorrect Java-library, the use of the percent indicator in the positive value triggers the multiplication for the negative value even though the negative value doesn't include the percent indicator; the result should be "–123456789.9876".

Line 9: A complete specification can omit the pattern for negative values.

Line 10: A specification omitting the pattern for negative values defaults to the value being prefixed by the minus sign.

The attributes of the named decimal format declared by an `<xsl:decimal-format>` instruction specify the characters that control the interpretation of a format pattern and/or the formatting of a numeric value.

- Attributes only controlling the interpretation of characters in the grammar of a format pattern (never in the result of formatting a number value) are as follows:
  - `pattern-separator=` (e.g. ";"),
  - `digit=` (e.g. "#"),
  - `zero-digit=` (e.g. "0").
- Attributes both controlling the interpretation of characters in the grammar of a format pattern and specifying the characters that may appear in the resulting string when the function is formatting a number are as follows:
  - `decimal-separator=` (e.g. "." (default) or ","),
  - `grouping-separator=` (e.g. "," (default) or a space),
  - `percent=` (e.g. "%"),
  - `per-mille=` (e.g. Unicode character 0x2030).
- Attributes only specifying the characters and strings that may appear in the result of formatting a number value are as follows:
  - `minus-sign=` (e.g. "-" (hyphen/minus, 0x2d)),
  - `infinity=` (e.g. Unicode character 0x221e; the default value is the string "Infinity"),
  - `NaN=` "Not-a-Number" (e.g. Unicode character 0xfffd; the default value is the string "NaN").

8.1.5   Calculating values using boolean functions

Boolean values are the logical values `true` and `false`.

`boolean(expression)`

- converts the argument to a boolean value,
- converts an empty string to `false` and all other strings to `true`,
- converts an empty node list to `false` and all other node lists to `true`,

- converts `NaN` and positive and negative 0 to `false` and all other values to `true`;
  - to test that a value is `NaN` use:

    ```
    test="number(.)!=0 and not(number(.))"
    ```

- converts any result-tree fragment to `true` as all are considered internally to be comprised of a node-like construct to contain the content.

`true()` and `false()`

- return the values `true` and `false`.

`not(expression)`

- first converts the expression evaluation to boolean using `boolean()`,
- returns the opposite value.

`lang(expression)`

- returns `true` if the inherited `xml:lang=` attribute of the current node represents a language that is the same or a sub-language of the specified argument converted to a string —
  - per XML 1.0 Section 2.12 Language Identification,
- returns `false` if no such inherited attribute is found in the source tree.

Operators `or` and `and`:

- return traditional results of boolean logic,
- when evaluating the `or` operator, terminate evaluation at the first operand evaluating to `true`;
  - note that the "|" operator is the union operator and not the logical `or` as is popular in many programming languages,
- when evaluating the `and` operator, terminate evaluation at the first operand evaluating to `false`.

Operators "<", ">", "<=", ">=", "=" and "!=":

- convert both operands using `number()` if "<" or ">" are used in the operator,
- perform traditional comparison operations on the two operands,
- may have two boolean operands —
  - considered equal if their respective values are equal,

- may have two number operands —
  - considered equal if their respective values are equal,
- may have two string operands —
  - considered equal if their Unicode characters are identical;
    - the full form and composed form of a given character are not identical,
- may have two non-node-set operands;
  - unlike operands are converted to like objects before performing the comparison;
    - `boolean()` is used if either is a boolean, otherwise `number()`,
- may have one or two node-set operands;
  - the comparison deals with values of each individual member of the node set until the `true` value is obtained;
  - the operators performed on two node sets will consider the number values (if greater-than or less-than is used in the operator) or the string values of the members of the node sets and consider the operation `true` if the value of any member of one node set compares as desired to the value of any member of the other node set and `false` if no member of one set compares as desired to all values of the other set;
  - the operators performed on a node set and a non-node-set argument convert the node set member values to like objects (the precedence being number if greater-than or less-than is used in the operator, then boolean if the non-node-set argument is a boolean, then number if it is a number, otherwise string) before performing the comparisons and consider the operation `true` if the value of any member of the node set compares as desired to the value of the other argument;
  - note that this means that the boolean `not()` function applied to a node set comparison will return `true` if all members of the set fail the comparison;
  - examples are:
    - `test='string(switch/@state)="on"'`
      - `true` if *first* of the children named "`switch`" has the attribute equal to "`on`";
      - the `string()` function acts only on the first member of the set and returns a string-typed value, not a node-typed value,
    - `test='switch/@state="on"'`
      - `true` if *any* of the children named "`switch`" have the attribute equal to "`on`";
      - the test checks each of the nodes until the first `true` comparison and only returns `false` if all nodes test `false`,
    - `test='not(switch/@state!="on")'`
      - `true` if *all* of the children named "`switch`" have the attribute equal to "`on`";
      - the inner test checks each of the nodes and only returns `false` if all nodes test `false` (that is that they all have the value "`on`");
      - the outer evaluation changes the inner evaluation from `false` to `true`;

- does *not* test for two nodes as being the same node;
- return `false` when two empty node-sets are compared.

In the order of highest to lowest precedence, the operators are:

- "<", ">", "<=", ">=",
- "=", "!=",
- `and,`
- `or.`

8.1.6 Calculating values using node-set-related expression functions

Node-set operator and functions work on node-sets obtained from source trees.

Operator |

- performs a union of node-sets into a new node-set;
- makes sure the same node is never duplicated in the result set;
- always orders the result set in document order.

`count(`*required-node-set*`)`

- returns the number of nodes in the supplied node-set.

The following functions all optionally use a node-set argument and:

- operate on the current node if no argument supplied
- operate on the first node found in a non-empty node set argument,
- return the empty string for an empty node set argument.

`local-name(`*optional-node-set*`)`

- returns the local part of the namespace-qualified name as a string (see Figure 8–1),
- does not include the namespace prefix if used for the node.

`name(`*optional-node-set*`)`

- returns the fully qualified namespace name as a string,
- includes the namespace prefix if used for the node.
  - Warning: this is not namespace-aware when used in a test against a string value;
  - see Section 7.1.4 for namespace-aware node type testing.

`namespace-uri(`*optional-node-set*`)`

- returns the namespace URI of the namespace-qualified name as a string.

```
generate-id(optional-node-set)
```

- returns an implementation-dependent string that can be used blindly as a unique identifier for the node as a string;
  - it is lexically parsed as a valid XML name, but —
    - not guaranteed to be exclusive of ID/IDREF values;
  - value should always be used in its entirety, as there is no prescribed format,
- returns a value which is persistent through only the given invocation of the XSLT processor, and a given value cannot be relied upon from any other invocation,
- can be used to synthesize hyperlinks where ID/IDREF unavailable:

```
...
<a href="#{generate-id(.)}">
...
<a name="{generate-id(.)}">
...
```

- can be used to compare two nodes as being the same node:

```
test="generate-id($a)=
      generate-id($b)"
```

Below are some examples of using generate-id().

8.1.6.1   *Identification of a node during processing*

- Consider the need to identify the node's position in a different context than the current node list in which the node is being processed.
- Since the node's generated identifier is persistent for the execution of the script (but not after the script has completed), it can be

---

Figure 8–1   Name-related function behavior

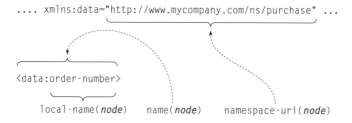

---

assigned to a variable and checked at any time.

- In this example, the template is being called from elsewhere in the script and the location of the current node is evaluated in an arbitrary node list (not the current node list when the template was invoked):

Example 8–3   Using `generate-id()` for node identification

```
Line 1  <xsl:template name="node-position-in-node-and-attr-set">
     2    <xsl:variable name="this-id" select="generate-id(.)"/>
     3                    <!--current node list of parent's children and attributes-->
     4    <xsl:for-each select="../node()|../@*">
     5      <xsl:if test="generate-id(.)=$this-id">            <!--found saved id-->
     6        <xsl:value-of select="position()"/>              <!--using new context-->
     7      </xsl:if>
     8
    10    </xsl:for-each>
    11  </xsl:template>
```

8.1.6.2   *Unique naming of nodes for output stream*

- Consider the need to generate a hyperlinked table of contents where there is no handy XML ID construct to be used to uniquely identify the elements:

Example 8–4   A sample of data without unique identifiers

```
Line 1  <?xml version="1.0"?>
     2  <test>
     3  <section><title>First Section</title>
     4  <para>The content of the section is here.</para></section>
     5  <section><title>Second Section</title>
     6  <para>The content of the section is here.</para></section>
     7  <section><title>Third Section</title>
     8  <para>The content of the section is here.</para></section>
     9  </test>
```

The following script will use the XSLT-processor-generated node identifiers in place of XML ID identifiers:

Example 8–5   Using `generate-id()` to synthesize hyperlinks

```
Line 1  <?xml version="1.0"?>                                      <!--genid.xsl-->
     2  <!--XSLT 1.0 - http://www.CraneSoftwrights.com/training -->
     3  <xsl:stylesheet xmlns:xsl="http://www.w3.org/1999/XSL/Transform"
     4                  version="1.0">
     5
     6  <xsl:template match="/">
```

```
 7    <html>
 8      <h2>Table of Contents</h2>
 9      <xsl:for-each select="//section/title">
10        <a href="#{generate-id(.)}"><xsl:value-of select="."/>
11        </a><br/>
12      </xsl:for-each>
13      <xsl:apply-templates/>
14    </html>
15  </xsl:template>
16
17  <xsl:template match="title">
18    <h2><a name="{generate-id(.)}"><xsl:value-of select="."/>
19        </a></h2>
20  </xsl:template>
21
22  <xsl:template match="para">
23    <p><xsl:apply-templates/></p>
24  </xsl:template>
25
26  </xsl:stylesheet>
```

Note again that the persistence of the values is guaranteed only within the execution of the script and not afterwards to any subsequent execution of the script. The above technique is not appropriate when needing to point into the result from other files in a persistent manner (where using ID would be useful for that purpose).

8.1.7   Node-set intersection and difference

Sometimes it is necessary to determine the intersection or difference of two node-sets selected from the source tree. The following expression, colloquially referred to as the "Kaysian Method" after Mike Kay who first proposed this use of XPath, will select only those nodes that are in both of two node-set variables named set1 and set2:

```
$set1[count(.|$set2)=count($set2)]
```

The above expression takes advantage of the XPath union operator to determine that a given node doesn't impact on the count of nodes of the union of the node and the second node-set. The predicate returns true when the count isn't affected, thus including the member being tested. It is not necessary to test the members of the second set because the intersection would have to include members of the first set, all of which are being tested in the above expression.

The symmetric difference requires an expression involving the union of the determination of those nodes in each set that are not in the other set:

```
(  $set1[count(.|$set2)!=count($set2)]
  | $set2[count(.|$set1)!=count($set1)] )
```

The following script illustrates the assignment of two node-set variables from a common area of the source tree (in this case the stylesheet is also the source tree) and the intersection and symmetric difference of those two variables:

Example 8–6   Sample of calculating node-set intersection and difference

```
Line 1   <?xml version="1.0"?>                               <!--intrdiff.xsl-->
     2   <!--XSLT 1.0 - http://www.CraneSoftwrights.com/training -->
     3   <xsl:stylesheet xmlns:xsl="http://www.w3.org/1999/XSL/Transform"
     4                   xmlns:data="crane"
     5                   version="1.0">
     6
     7   <xsl:output method="text"/>
     8
     9   <data:data>                      <!--data source for testing purposes-->
    10     <item>1</item><item>2</item><item>3</item>
    11     <item>4</item><item>5</item><item>6</item>
    12   </data:data>
    13
    14   <xsl:template match="/">                               <!--root rule-->
    15     <xsl:variable name="ns1" select="//item[position()>1]"/>
    16     <xsl:variable name="ns2" select="//item[position()&lt;5]"/>
    17
    18     <xsl:for-each select="$ns1[count(.|$ns2)=count($ns2)]">
    19       Intersection: <xsl:value-of select="."/>
    20     </xsl:for-each>
    21     <xsl:for-each select="(   $ns1[count(.|$ns2)!=count($ns2)]
    22                             | $ns2[count(.|$ns1)!=count($ns1)] )">
    23       Difference: <xsl:value-of select="."/>
    24     </xsl:for-each>
    25   </xsl:template>
    26
    27   </xsl:stylesheet>
```

When run with itself as input, the following is the result:

Example 8–7   Results of sample calculation of node-set intersection and difference

```
Line 1       Intersection: 2
     2       Intersection: 3
     3       Intersection: 4
```

```
4    Difference: 1
5    Difference: 5
6    Difference: 6
```

8.1.8 ## String variables in location steps

The correct way to use a string variable as a node name in a location step is not intuitive.

- It may be necessary to calculate the name of a node and then access that node from the source node tree.
- The expression syntax does not allow a non-node-set variable reference as a step in a location as in the *incorrect* expression syntax `@$showattr` that one might think would access an attribute whose name is in a variable.
- The expression syntax does allow a variable reference in a predicate, and a predicate can be used in a location step.

Consider markup where the value of one attribute is the name of another attribute:

```
<part useattr="source" source="Source Attr"
                    target="Target Attr"/>
```

By putting the name of the desired attribute in a variable, one can use that variable's value in a predicate selecting by name from a collection of attributes:

Example 8–8   Using `local-name()` in an XPath expression

```
Line 1   <xsl:template match="part">
2     <xsl:variable name="showattr" select="@useattr"/>
3     <xsl:value-of select="@*[local-name(.)=$showattr]"/>
4   </xsl:template>
```

The same technique can be used for any named nodes, but is not namespace-aware.

8.2 Content and document referencing techniques

8.2.1 Element referencing with XML identifiers

Establishing elements with unique identifiers. Recall that element nodes in the source node tree can have unique identifiers defined by the presence of XML attributes of type `ID`. It is a common practice to implement cross referencing from other elements using XML attributes of type `IDREF` or `IDREFS` that point to the unique identifiers of elements with the corresponding `ID` attribute.

- There is a validity constraint that `IDREF` be an XML name.
- There is a validity constraint that `IDREFS` be one or more XML names.

Function `id()` can used to find elements by their unique identifier (see Figure 8–2).

`id(`*non-node-set-value-converted-to-string*`)`

- returns the union of all nodes with identifier equal to *tokenized* string,
- converts the argument into a string as with `normalize-space()`,
- splits the resulting string into set of tokens,
- finds element nodes whose unique identifier is in the set of tokens,
- performs the search in the same document as the current node.

Figure 8–2   Identifying elements with unique identifiers

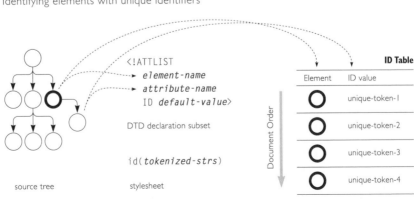

id(*node-set*)

- returns the union of the call to id() with the string value of each of the nodes in the set.
    - Note that the nodes used in the node-set argument need not be attribute nodes, and if any one is an attribute node, it need not be an attribute of XML type IDREF, as the value obtained is just used as a string.
    - Of course the node could, indeed, be an attribute node of type IDREF.

See Section 8.2.5 for an important consideration regarding addressing unique identifiers in multiple source documents.

Here are examples of id() being used stand-alone.

- id("buyer")
    - returns the element whose unique identifier is the string value "buyer".
- id(1)
    - returns the element whose unique identifier is the string value "1".
        - Note it is a validity constraint (XML 3.3.1), but not a well-formedness constraint, that ID values match the Name [XML 5] production.
- id(@where)
    - returns the element whose unique identifier is the same value as the value of any of the space-separated tokens in the where= attribute of the current node.

Here are examples of id() being used as the first step in a multiple-step location path of an expression.

- id(//@where)/phone[2]
    - returns the set of the second phone child elements of all elements referenced by any identifier used in the where= attribute of any element node.
- id(//where)/phone[2]
    - returns the set of the second phone child elements of all elements referenced by any identifier used in any <where> element node in the instance.

8.2.2   Content referencing with XSLT keys

The stylesheet can identify key nodes of the source tree for subsequent fast access by the XSLT processor (Figure 8–3).

- All source tree nodes for each declared key for stylesheet manipulation are identified with a simple name.
- A lookup table of member items is built based on an equality test for the lookup value.

- For example, consider the need to relate all employee records to the employee's respective manager's employee records matching each employee's `ManagedBy` child element value with the corresponding employee record with the same value for its `emp=` attribute.

The XSLT processor can optimize searching in the lookup table.

- All values are fixed after the source tree is processed.
- The processor can index the table for quick retrieval based on lookup value.
- Selected nodes are returned faster than when traversing the axes using XPath expressions and predicates evaluated at the point of reference.

Not all processors support `<xsl:key>`.

8.2.2.1 *Establishing a lookup table of key relationships in a declarative fashion*

When indexing behavior similar to XML `ID`/`IDREF` attribute cross-referencing values is required by either attribute or element content, the stylesheet writer can define and reference key values reflecting the implicit cross-references.

- Keys have three aspects of definition in the `<xsl:key>` top-level instruction:
    - the namespace-qualified name of the key:

        `name="name-of-key-table"`

        - this is what distinguishes the collection of key nodes from other collections of key nodes;

Figure 8–3   Identifying and accessing candidate nodes using a key table

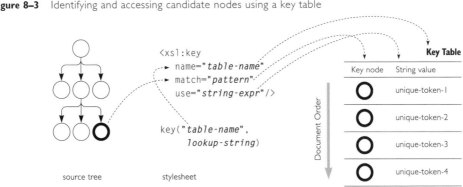

- multiple declarations with the same name cumulatively build the members in the collection of that name,
- the nodes that have the key:

  match="*identifying-pattern-of-nodes-in-key-table*"

  - this is an XPath matching pattern expression;
    - it is similar to count= attribute in <xsl:number/>,
- the lookup values of the keyed nodes:

  use="*expression-evaluating-the-value-of-key-in-the-set*"

  - this is an XPath selection expression;
    - if relative, it is evaluated relative to each keyed node,
  - the expression is evaluated to a string,
  - the string values need not be unique;
    - nodes with like values are ordered in document order.

- The index built for a key is somewhat dissimilar to ID/IDREF.
  - Key values in the set need not be unique.
    - There can be multiple key nodes in a document with the same node, same key name, but different key values.
    - There can be multiple key nodes in a document with the same key name, same key value, but different nodes.
  - A key's value need not be parsed as an XML name token.
    - A node relative to the key node can represent the key's value.
    - A key's value can be the result of an arbitrary expression evaluated with the key node as the current node.
  - A lookup value need not be present in the collection.

Note that a variable reference cannot be used in either the match= or use= expressions.

Using a key

key(*key-name,non-node-set-value-converted-to-string*)

- returns that subset of key nodes whose indexed key value is equal to the given string lookup value.

key(*key-name,node-set*)

- returns the union of the call to key() with the value of each of the nodes in the node set as a lookup value.

Predicates can be applied to the returned node set.

- key('taxes', 'Canada')[1]
  - returns only the first node of all nodes in the "taxes" key table whose lookup value is the string "Canada",

- as like lookup values are returned in document order of the nodes indexed, returns the first such node in document order.
- `key('taxes', 'Canada')[@type='federal'][1]`
  - of all nodes returned by the key function, returns only the first whose `type=` attribute is "`federal`".

Figure 8–4 illustrates how keys can be used to obtain the value of an employee's name indirectly from the value of an attribute (though another model might have the value in a child element's content) used to reference the employee information of a manager.

The following steps correspond to the diagram indicating how the value "John Smith" is obtained as the name of the manager of "Joe Green" indirectly through the `emp=` attribute of the `<ManagedBy>` element.

1: The template rule for `<ManagedBy>` needs to calculate a value from another node based on an attribute value in `emp=` (in another model it could just as well be based on an element node's value rather than an attribute node's value).

Figure 8–4   An illustration of XSLT keys

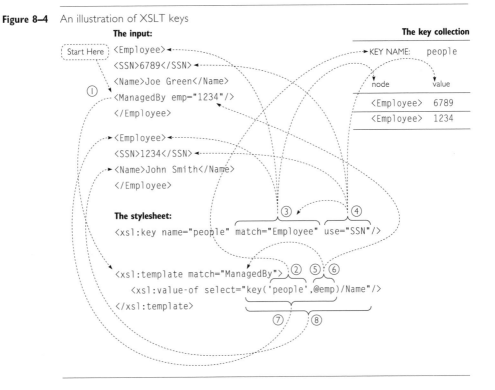

2: The target value calculation begins by first referencing the key named "people", using the first argument to the `key()` function, specifying which of the lookup key tables that were created by the XSLT processor based on values found in the source tree.

3: The key named "people" is declared in a top-level `<xsl:key>` element building a table of nodes matching the given node-set expression indicated with `match=` (all element nodes named "Employee").

4: The `use=` attribute specifies the expression whose evaluated value, relative to each `match=` node, that is used for the lookup comparison value in the key table (the value of the first child element node named "SSN" relative to the element nodes named "Employee").

5: The second argument to `key()` function indicates the node (emp= attribute) relative to the current node (ManagedBy element) whose value is used for the search comparison with the key values (the attribute node for emp=).

6: The example indicates the string value "1234" is what is searched for among the key lookup values.

7: `key()` returns all key nodes (Employee elements) whose lookup value is the string equivalent of the expression value for what is being searched for (only one node in this example).

8: The `<xsl:value-of>` is calculated by then evaluating the complete expression by obtaining the XPath expression (the child element node named "Name") relative to the returned set of key nodes (Employee elements), thus returning the resulting value (the string "John Smith").

Note that the evaluation of `key('people','1234')` would have produced the same result since the lookup value is the supplied string instead of an evaluated expression.

8.2.3 Current node referencing

Remembering how the current node changes during expression evaluation, it is sometimes important in the middle of an expression to reference that node that was the current node before evaluation began.

current()

- re-orients within an XPath expression to the current node in the context in use at the start of the expression.

Consider an example of comparing a remote node's attribute value to the attribute value of the current node. This can be accomplished using a variable to store the value of an attribute relative to the current node at the start of the expression evaluation for the `<xsl:for-each>` below.

- Recall that after the `frame` node test, the context is changed to each `frame` element for the evaluation of the predicate.

Example 8–9   Using a variable to reference the current node

```
Line I  <xsl:template match="module">
     2    <xsl:variable name="mod-label" select="@mod-label"/>
     3    <xsl:for-each select="id(@other-module)//
     4                        frame[@frame-label=$mod-label]">
     5                                                    <!--template-->
     6    </xsl:for-each>
     7  </xsl:template>
```

During the evaluation of the predicate, the expression evaluation can revert to the current node of the start of expression evaluation (the `module` element) as follows, thus producing the equivalent expression without the use of a variable declaration and assignment:

Example 8–10   Using `current()` to reference the current node

```
Line I
     2  <xsl:template match="module">
     3    <xsl:for-each select="id(@other-module)//
     4                        frame[@frame-label=current()/@mod-label]">
     5                                                    <!--template-->
     6    </xsl:for-each>
     7  </xsl:template>
```

`current()` is different than the "." abbreviation.

- "." represents the current node at the point of evaluation in the expression.
- `current()` returns the current node at the start of evaluation of the expression.

8.2.4   Unparsed entity referencing in XSLT

Unparsed entities are general entities declared in the DTD with an NDATA specification of the notation of the entity.

The root node of every document includes a mapping of each unparsed entity to the associated URI.

- The URI may be resolved by the XSLT processor from the public identifier;
- otherwise the URI is the system identifier.
- When the URI is relative, it is resolved to be absolute.

An XSLT stylesheet can obtain the URI for an unparsed entity using:

```
unparsed-entity-uri(entity-name-string-argument)
```

- returns the absolute URI of the specified unparsed entity.
    - The document used is that of the current node.
    - If no such entity exists, the empty string is returned.

The file imgsamp-ent.xml uses an unparsed entity to point to a graphic file name, rather than directly encoding the filename in an attribute:

Example 8–11   Sample of use of unparsed entity declaration

```
Line 1   <?xml version="1.0"?>
     2   <!DOCTYPE imgsamp [
     3   <!NOTATION gif SYSTEM "">
     4   <!ENTITY logo SYSTEM "crane.gif" NDATA gif>
     5   ]>
     6   <imgsamp>
     7   <para>Here is an example:</para>
     8   <fig file="logo">Crane Logo</fig>
     9   <para>End of example</para>
    10   </imgsamp>
```

The stylesheet imgsamp-ent.xsl references the filename to be displayed through the entity declaration found in the DTD of the source file:

Example 8–12   Accessing sample unparsed entity declaration

```
Line 1   <?xml version="1.0"?>                              <!--imgsamp-ent.xsl-->
     2   <!--XSLT 1.0 - http://www.CraneSoftwrights.com/training -->
     3   <!DOCTYPE xsl:stylesheet [
     4   <!ENTITY dark-green "#004400">
```

```
 5   ]>
 6   <xsl:stylesheet xmlns:xsl="http://www.w3.org/1999/XSL/Transform"
 7               version="1.0"
 8               xmlns="http://www.w3.org/TR/REC-html40">
 9
10   <xsl:output method="html"
11           doctype-public="-//W3C//DTD HTML 4.0 Transitional//EN"/>
12
13   <xsl:template match="/">                              <!-- root rule -->
14     <html>
15       <head><title>Image Sample</title></head>
16       <body><xsl:apply-templates/></body>
17     </html>
18   </xsl:template>
19
20   <xsl:template match="fig">
21     <div style="font-size:10pt;text-align:center">
22       <img src="{unparsed-entity-uri(@file)}" alt="{.}"/>
23       <div>
24         <xsl:apply-templates/>
25       </div>
26     </div>
27   </xsl:template>
28
29   <xsl:template match="para">
30     <div style="font-size:15pt;color=&dark-green;">
31       <xsl:apply-templates/>
32     </div>
33   </xsl:template>
34
35   </xsl:stylesheet>
```

8.2.5   Document referencing in XSLT

document(*non-node-set-URI-string*, *optional-base-URI-node*)

- returns the root node of the document addressed by the URI as a string converted from the argument;
  - the URI may include a fragment identifier thus qualifying the node set to be a particular subset of the remote document resource,
- resolves relative URI values using the base URI of the node value second argument;
  - if absent, the stylesheet instruction's Base URI is used;
  - typically it is the source file;
  - it may be a node from an external parsed entity.

```
document(node-set, optional-base-URI-node)
```

- returns the union of calling `document()` with the string value of each of the nodes in the set,
- uses the supplied second argument for each call,
- when the second argument is absent, uses the Base URI of the node from which the string of the first argument is calculated.

```
document("")
```

- returns the root node of the stylesheet fragment in which the instruction resides that uses the function call.

Once the root nodes are obtained from each of the remote documents —

- they can be processed as one would process any node set —
  - as either a stand-alone step of a complete location path,
  - or the first step in a multiple-step location path,
- node values can be pulled for inclusion in the result:

Example 8–13   Sample of pulling information from another document

```
Line 1   <xsl:value-of select="document('infofile.xml',..)
     2                         //figure[position()=last()]"/>
```

- nodes can be pushed through the stylesheet for template rule processing:

Example 8–14   Sample of pushing information from another document

```
Line 1   <xsl:apply-templates select="document('infofile.xml',..)
     2                               //table"/>
```

In a file system there are four possible sources of a relatively addressed URI (see Figure 8–5):

- the directory in which the invoked stylesheet file (e.g. `purchase.xsl`) is found,
- the directory in which the stylesheet fragment executing the `document()` function (e.g. `addr.xsl`) is found,
- the directory in which the invoked source file (e.g. `purch1.xml`) is found,

- the directory in which an external parsed general entity including the current node (e.g. `info.xml`) is found.

Note that the stylesheet itself is accessible with this function, therefore —

- the stylesheet can contain top-level, non-XSLT constructs containing rich markup that can be accessed as a source node tree (thus providing a location for stylesheet data that is not separated from the stylesheet file itself);
  - note that the container element for such data must have its own namespace as it cannot have the XSLT namespace and it cannot use the default namespace;
  - the contents of the container element can use any namespace;
  - it may be necessary to use `exclude-element-prefixes=` to keep the data's namespace from being declared in the emitted result tree;
- the stylesheet can process result tree fragment top-level variable declarations as a node set as follows:

Example 8–15   Sample of pushing information from the stylesheet

```
Line 1   <xsl:apply-templates
     2       select="document('')/*/xsl:variable[@name='variable-name']"/>
```

Figure 8–5   Possible uses of the document function with a relative URI

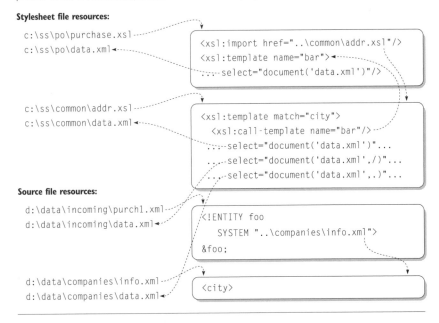

process `d:\data\incoming\purch1.xml` with `c:\ss\po\purchase.xsl`

Stylesheet file resources:

`c:\ss\po\purchase.xsl`
`c:\ss\po\data.xml`

```
<xsl:import href="..\common\addr.xsl"/>
<xsl:template name="bar">
    select="document('data.xml')"/>
```

`c:\ss\common\addr.xsl`
`c:\ss\common\data.xml`

```
<xsl:template match="city">
  <xsl:call-template name="bar"/>
    select="document('data.xml')"...
    select="document('data.xml',/)"...
    select="document('data.xml',..)"...
```

Source file resources:

`d:\data\incoming\purch1.xml`
`d:\data\incoming\data.xml`

```
<!ENTITY foo
    SYSTEM "..\companies\info.xml">
&foo;
```

`d:\data\companies\info.xml`
`d:\data\companies\data.xml`

```
<city>
```

Consider the following example:

Example 8–16   Illustration of accessing information from multiple XML documents

```
Line 1  <?xml version="1.0"?>                                  <!--document.xsl-->
     2  <!--XSLT 1.0 - http://www.CraneSoftwrights.com/training -->
     3  <!DOCTYPE xsl:stylesheet [<!ENTITY nl "&#xd;&#xa;">]>
     4  <xsl:stylesheet xmlns:xsl="http://www.w3.org/1999/XSL/Transform"
     5                  version="1.0">
     6
     7  <xsl:output method="text"/>
     8
     9  <xsl:template match="/">
    10    <xsl:text>Processing refs for each document:&nl;</xsl:text>
    11
    12                       <!--using document() as a stand-alone location path-->
    13    <xsl:for-each select="document(//doc/@loc)">
    14      <xsl:text>&nl;Resource: </xsl:text>
    15      <xsl:value-of select="resource/title"/>
    16      <xsl:for-each select="//ref">
    17        <xsl:sort/>
    18        <xsl:text>&nl;</xsl:text><xsl:value-of select="title"/>
    19      </xsl:for-each>
    20    </xsl:for-each>
    21    <xsl:text>&nl;&nl;</xsl:text>
    22    <xsl:text>Processing references in all documents:</xsl:text>
    23    <xsl:text>&nl;</xsl:text>
    24
    25                       <!--using document() as the first step in a location path-->
    26    <xsl:for-each select="document(//doc/@loc)//ref/title">
    27      <xsl:sort/>
    28      <xsl:value-of select="."/><xsl:text>&nl;</xsl:text>
    29    </xsl:for-each>
    30  </xsl:template>
    31
    32  </xsl:stylesheet>
```

With the control data file `document.xml`:

Example 8–17   Sample control file referring to other XML instances

```
Line 1  <?xml version="1.0"?>
     2  <set>
     3    <doc loc="doc1.xml"/>
     4    <doc loc="doc2.xml"/>
     5  </set>
```

The data file `doc1.xml` with unsorted references:

Example 8–18   First sample XML instance being referenced

```
Line 1   <?xml version="1.0"?>
     2   <resource>
     3     <title>First Resource</title>
     4     <ref><title>D - First ref in First resource</title></ref>
     5     <ref><title>B - Second ref in First resource</title></ref>
     6     <ref><title>E - Third ref in First resource</title></ref>
     7   </resource>
```

And the data file doc2.xml with unsorted references:

Example 8–19   Second sample XML instance being referenced

```
Line 1   <?xml version="1.0"?>
     2   <resource>
     3     <title>Second Resource</title>
     4     <ref><title>C - First ref in Second resource</title></ref>
     5     <ref><title>A - Second ref in Second resource</title></ref>
     6   </resource>
```

The following result is produced:

Example 8–20   Result of reporting information from multiple XML documents

```
Line 1   Processing refs for each document:
     2
     3   Resource: First Resource
     4   B - Second ref in First resource
     5   D - First ref in First resource
     6   E - Third ref in First resource
     7   Resource: Second Resource
     8   A - Second ref in Second resource
     9   C - First ref in Second resource
    10
    11   Processing references in all documents:
    12   A - Second ref in Second resource
    13   B - Second ref in First resource
    14   C - First ref in Second resource
    15   D - First ref in First resource
    16   E - Third ref in First resource
```

Note that the id() and key() functions cannot be used as anything other than the first step in a location path as in the need to reference a unique identifier in another document.

- *It is invalid syntax* to use "document(*argument*)/id(*argument*)" as a location path.

- The context must be changed to the document before locating the context of the unique identifier.
- The `<xsl:for-each>` construct effects such a "temporary" change during the instantiation of its template, even when there is only one document to be referenced.
- Consider the example where one is trying to obtain the value of the "`label`" attribute associated with the element with the unique identifier "`start`" in the document "`otherdoc.xml`".
  - *The incorrect syntax* is:

Example 8–21   Incorrect XPath expression for accessing an identifier in another document

```
<xsl:value-of select=" document('otherdoc.xml')/id('start')/@label"/>
```

- The correct syntax is:

Example 8–22   Correct XPath expression for accessing an identifier in another document

```
Line 1    <xsl:for-each select="document('otherdoc.xml')">
     2      <xsl:value-of select="id('start')/@label"/>
     3    </xsl:for-each>
```

8.3 Traversing the source tree

8.3.1 Inferring structure when there is none

An XPath location step addresses all nodes along an axis before being filtered by a predicate.

Consider the need to infer nested structure from a flat structure when formatting lists and list items from the instance `bullet.xml`:

Example 8–23   An XML instance with flat bulleted information

```
Line 1    <?xml version="1.0"?>
     2    <doc>
     3    <listhead>The first list of information:</listhead>
     4    <bullet>first member of first list</bullet>
     5    <bullet>second member of first list</bullet>
     6    <bullet>third member of first list</bullet>
     7    <listhead>The second list of information:</listhead>
     8    <bullet>first member of second list</bullet>
     9    <bullet>second member of second list</bullet>
    10    </doc>
```

The desired output is:

Example 8–24   A rendering of bulleted information in properly nested lists

```
Line 1  <!DOCTYPE html PUBLIC "-//W3C//DTD HTML 4.0 Transitional//EN">
     2  <html>
     3  <p>The first list of information:</p>
     4  <ul>
     5  <li>first member of first list</li>
     6  <li>second member of first list</li>
     7  <li>third member of first list</li>
     8  </ul>
     9
    10
    11  <p>The second list of information:</p>
    12  <ul>
    13  <li>first member of second list</li>
    14  <li>second member of second list</li>
    15  </ul>
    16
    17  </html>
```

It is necessary to deal with sibling elements in order to place adjacent siblings into the inferred structure, but XPath expressions do not distinguish adjacent siblings from siblings that are separated from each other.

Note the differences between the following expressions available with XPath.

- `following-sibling::bullet`
  - refers to all following sibling element nodes named "`bullet`".
- `following-sibling::*[self::bullet]`
  - refers to all following sibling element nodes named "`bullet`".
- `following-sibling::bullet[1]`
  - refers to the first following sibling element nodes named "`bullet`", not considering that there may or may not be any intervening sibling elements of other types.
- `following-sibling::*[1]`
  - refers to the immediately following sibling element node, regardless that node's name.
- `following-sibling::*[1][self::bullet]`
  - refers to the immediately following sibling element node *only* if it is named "`bullet`", otherwise the empty node set is returned.

The following `bullet.xsl` accomplishes the desired result:

Example 8–25   Transforming flat bulleted information to hierarchical bulleted information

```
Line 1  <?xml version="1.0"?>                                    <!--bullet.xsl-->
     2  <!--XSLT 1.0 - http://www.CraneSoftwrights.com/training -->
     3  <xsl:stylesheet xmlns:xsl="http://www.w3.org/1999/XSL/Transform"
     4                  version="1.0">
     5
     6  <xsl:output indent="yes"/>
     7
     8  <xsl:template match="doc">
     9    <html><xsl:apply-templates/></html>
    10  </xsl:template>
    11
    12  <xsl:template match="bullet">               <!--handle every bullet in turn-->
    13    <xsl:choose>                  <!--don't always act on *every* bullet there is-->
    14                         <!--when there is an immediate previous sibling of the
    15                             same name, then assume this node has already been
    16                             addressed by the first of the contiguous siblings-->
    17      <xsl:when test="preceding-sibling::*[1][self::bullet]"/>
    18      <xsl:otherwise>                  <!--at the first of a group of siblings-->
    19        <ul>            <!--"walk" along all sibling bullets for list items-->
    20          <xsl:apply-templates select="." mode="sibling-bullets"/>
    21        </ul>
    22      </xsl:otherwise>
    23    </xsl:choose>
    24  </xsl:template>
    25
    26                              <!--place each of a group of adjacent siblings-->
    27  <xsl:template match="bullet" mode="sibling-bullets">
    28    <li><xsl:apply-templates/></li>                     <!--put out this one-->
    29                                                        <!--go to next one-->
    30    <xsl:apply-templates mode="sibling-bullets"
    31          select="following-sibling::*[1][self::bullet]"/>
    32  </xsl:template>
    33
    34  <xsl:template match="listhead">                      <!--other stuff-->
    35    <p><xsl:apply-templates/></p>
    36  </xsl:template>
    37
    38  </xsl:stylesheet>
```

8.3.2   Templates as pseudo-subroutines

Some algorithms required for transformation are not met by simple pattern matching and node set selection when —

- sibling elements are indistinguishable to pattern matching;
- ancestral elements are indistinguishable to pattern matching;

- it is sometimes necessary to "walk" along the source node tree to find or process information.

By passing control to another template rule, opportunities exist to:

- add to the result tree before passing control again,
- add to the result tree after control is passed back,
- pass values to bind to parameterized variables.

Consider the (contrived) need to process the following instance:

Example 8–26   A deeply nested example

```
Line 1  <?xml version="1.0"?>
     2  <test val="a">
     3   <test val="b">
     4    <test val="c">
     5     <test val="d">
     6      <test>
     7       <greeting>Greeting in the middle of the file.</greeting>
     8      </test>
     9     </test>
    10    </test>
    11   </test>
    12  </test>
```

Note how the innermost `test` element has no attribute, has no `test` element as a child, and is contained within elements that are nested back to the document element, each uniquely identified by an attribute value for reporting purposes (but not used in this contrived example for pattern matching).

The following result echoes the instance with typical template rules and then inverts the instance inside-out, translating the innermost element, and then inverting the wrapping elements by walking the node tree towards the root (note the attributes are copied into both the mock start and end tags to illustrate where in the node tree processing is being executed):

Example 8–27   Illustration of inverting information inside out

```
Line 1  <result>
     2  Non-inverted Structure (translated):
     3  {test val="a"}
     4  {test val="b"}
     5  {test val="c"}
```

```
 6  {test val="d"}
 7  {test}
 8  <greeting>Greeting in the middle of the file.</greeting>
 9  {/test}
10  {/test val="d"}
11  {/test val="c"}
12  {/test val="b"}
13  {/test val="a"}
14
15  Inverted Structure:
16  {/test}
17  {/test val="d"}
18  {/test val="c"}
19  {/test val="b"}
20  {/test val="a"}
21
22  {test val="a"}
23  {test val="b"}
24  {test val="c"}
25  {test val="d"}
26  {test}
27  </result>
```

Note how in the resulting inverted structure:

- the mock end tags precede the mock start tags;
- the innermost test mock element (with attribute "a") is the original document element.

This translation cannot be accomplished using only match patterns.

The following stylesheet invert-simple.xsl walks the input structure:

Example 8–28   Transforming information inside out

```
Line 1  <?xml version="1.0"?>                               <!--invert-simple.xsl-->
     2  <!--XSLT 1.0 - http://www.CraneSoftwrights.com/training -->
     3  <!DOCTYPE xsl:stylesheet [
     4  <!ENTITY nl "&#xA;">
     5  ]>
     6  <xsl:stylesheet xmlns:xsl="http://www.w3.org/1999/XSL/Transform"
     7                  version="1.0">
     8
     9  <xsl:output omit-xml-declaration="yes"/>
    10
    11  <xsl:template match="/">
    12    <result>
    13  <xsl:text>&nl;Non-inverted Structure (translated):</xsl:text>
    14  <xsl:apply-templates/>
    15  <xsl:text>&nl;Inverted Structure:&nl;</xsl:text>
    16                          <!-- start from the test node that has no children-->
```

```
17    <xsl:apply-templates mode="walk-up" select="//test[not(test)]"/>
18    <xsl:text>&nl;</xsl:text>
19    </result>
20    </xsl:template>
21
22    <xsl:template match="test">                          <!--walking down the tree-->
23      <xsl:text>&nl;{test</xsl:text>
24      <xsl:call-template name="showattrs"/>                    <!--echo attrs-->
25      <xsl:text>}</xsl:text>
26      <xsl:apply-templates select="*"/>            <!--walk down to children-->
27      <xsl:text>{/test</xsl:text>
28      <xsl:call-template name="showattrs"/>                    <!--echo attrs-->
29      <xsl:text>}&nl;</xsl:text>
30    </xsl:template>
31
32    <xsl:template match="greeting">                      <!--preserve greeting-->
33      <xsl:text>&nl;</xsl:text>
34      <xsl:copy-of select="."/>
35      <xsl:text>&nl;</xsl:text>
36    </xsl:template>
37
38    <xsl:template mode="walk-up" match="*">          <!--walking up the tree-->
39                              <!--processing before the "subroutine call"-->
40      <xsl:text>{/test</xsl:text>
41      <xsl:call-template name="showattrs"/>                    <!--echo attrs-->
42      <xsl:text>}&nl;</xsl:text>
43      <xsl:if test="parent::*">
44                                  <!--the pseudo "subroutine call" itself-->
45        <xsl:apply-templates mode="walk-up" select="parent::*"/>
46      </xsl:if>
47                              <!--processing after the "subroutine call"-->
48      <xsl:text>&nl;{test</xsl:text>
49      <xsl:call-template name="showattrs"/>                    <!--echo attrs-->
50      <xsl:text>}</xsl:text>
51    </xsl:template>
52
53    <xsl:template name="showattrs">                  <!--display the attributes-->
54      <xsl:for-each select="@*">
55        <xsl:text> </xsl:text>
56        <xsl:value-of select="name(.)"/>="<xsl:value-of
57                    select="."/>"</xsl:for-each>
58    </xsl:template>
59
60    </xsl:stylesheet>
```

8.3.3 Passing variables to pseudo-subroutines

The following result from the same data can be achieved by passing
information when treating templates as pseudo-subroutines:

Example 8–29   Illustration of inverting information inside out with passed parameters

```
Line 1  <result>
     2  Non-inverted Structure (translated):
     3  {test val="a"}
     4  {test val="b"}
     5  {test val="c"}
     6  {test val="d"}
     7  {test}<hello>Greeting in the middle of the file.</hello>{/test}
     8  {/test val="d"}
     9  {/test val="c"}
    10  {/test val="b"}
    11  {/test val="a"}
    12
    13  Inverted Structure:
    14  {/test}
    15  {/test val="d"}
    16  {/test val="c"}
    17  {/test val="b"}
    18  {/test val="a"}
    19  <hello>Greeting in the middle of the file.</hello>
    20  <greeting>Greeting in the middle of the file.</greeting>
    21  {test val="a"}
    22  {test val="b"}
    23  {test val="c"}
    24  {test val="d"}
    25  {test}
    26  </result>
```

Information is passed from being generated in the innermost-nested source tree element, to be displayed in the outermost-nested source tree element that is the innermost result tree element. Both result tree fragments and node sets are shown to compare how their processing differs.

The stylesheet invert-parm.xsl illustrates this technique of passing information:

Example 8–30   Transforming information inside out while using parameters

```
Line 1  <?xml version="1.0"?>                              <!--invert-parm.xsl-->
     2  <!--XSLT 1.0 - http://www.CraneSoftwrights.com/training -->
     3  <!DOCTYPE xsl:stylesheet [<!ENTITY nl "&#xA;">]>
     4  <xsl:stylesheet xmlns:xsl="http://www.w3.org/1999/XSL/Transform"
     5                  version="1.0">
     6
     7  <xsl:output omit-xml-declaration="yes"/>
     8
     9  <xsl:template match="/">
    10    <result>
```

```
11    <xsl:text>&nl;Non-inverted Structure (translated):</xsl:text>
12    <xsl:apply-templates/>
13    <xsl:text>&nl;Inverted Structure:&nl;</xsl:text>
14                        <!-- start from the test node that has no children-->
15    <xsl:apply-templates mode="walk-up" select="//test[not(test)]">
16
18      <xsl:with-param name="middle-rtf">
19        <xsl:apply-templates select="//test[not(test)]/*"/>
20      </xsl:with-param>
21      <xsl:with-param name="middle-node"
22                  select="//test[not(test)]/*"/>
23    </xsl:apply-templates>
24    <xsl:text>&nl;</xsl:text>
25    </result></xsl:template>
26
27  <xsl:template match="test">                    <!--walking down the tree-->
28    <xsl:text>&nl;{test</xsl:text>
29    <xsl:call-template name="showattrs"/>              <!--echo attrs-->
30    <xsl:text>}</xsl:text>
31    <xsl:apply-templates select="*"/>              <!--walk down to children-->
32    <xsl:text>{/test</xsl:text>
33    <xsl:call-template name="showattrs"/>              <!--echo attrs-->
34    <xsl:text>}&nl;</xsl:text></xsl:template>
35
36  <xsl:template match="greeting">                <!--transform greeting-->
37    <hello><xsl:apply-templates/></hello></xsl:template>
38  <xsl:template mode="walk-up" match="*">        <!--walking up the tree-->
39    <xsl:param name="middle-rtf"/>                  <!--"called" variables-->
40    <xsl:param name="middle-node"/>
41                            <!--processing before the "subroutine call"-->
42    <xsl:text>{/test</xsl:text>
43    <xsl:call-template name="showattrs"/>              <!--echo attrs-->
44    <xsl:text>}&nl;</xsl:text>
45    <xsl:choose>
46      <xsl:when test="parent::*">
47                            <!--the pseudo "subroutine call" itself-->
48      <xsl:apply-templates mode="walk-up" select="parent::*">
49                            <!--"calling" vars-->
50        <xsl:with-param name="middle-rtf" select="$middle-rtf"/>
51        <xsl:with-param name="middle-node" select="$middle-node"/>
52      </xsl:apply-templates>
53      </xsl:when>
54      <xsl:otherwise>            <!--illustrate both types of variables-->
55        <xsl:copy-of select="$middle-rtf"/>          <!--tree fragment-->
56        <xsl:text>&nl;</xsl:text>
57        <xsl:copy-of select="$middle-node"/>          <!--node set-->
58      </xsl:otherwise>
59    </xsl:choose>
60                            <!--processing after the "subroutine call"-->
61    <xsl:text>&nl;{test</xsl:text>
62    <xsl:call-template name="showattrs"/>              <!--echo attrs-->
63    <xsl:text>}</xsl:text>
```

8 XPath and XSLT expressions and advanced techniques **257**

```
64  </xsl:template>
65
66  <xsl:template name="showattrs">                    <!--display the attributes-->
67    <xsl:for-each select="@*">
68      <xsl:text> </xsl:text>
69      <xsl:value-of select="name(.)"/>="<xsl:value-of
70                    select="."/>"</xsl:for-each>
71  </xsl:template>
72
73  </xsl:stylesheet>
```

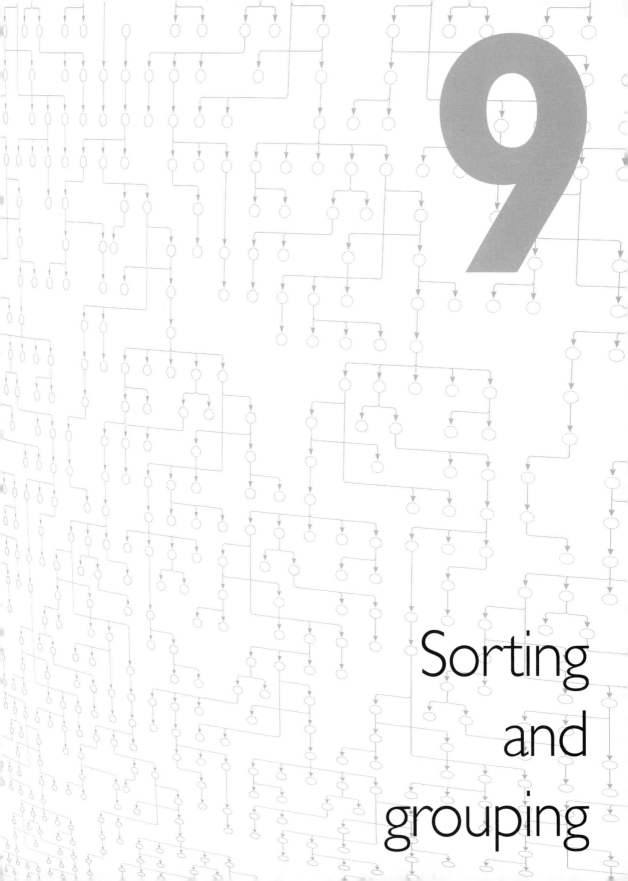

9

Sorting
and
grouping

9 Sorting and grouping

Presenting information in a sorted and/or grouped fashion is often essential to effective presentation and transformation. XSLT processors implement sorting algorithms for us to access, as usual using declarative mechanisms.

However, the XSLT language does *not* provide built-in facilities for grouping unsorted or sorted information. The common requirements we have that are best fulfilled by grouping information according to common values must be met by algorithmic means rather than by integral functionality.

This chapter has examples illustrating both simple sorting and the approach to grouping information.

Sorting. This chapter details the use of a single sort criterion or multiple sort criteria when processing source information. These measures can be based on language values, numeric values or custom semantics available from the XSLT processor.

Grouping and uniqueness. Without integral grouping facilities it is necessary to effect grouping results by explicit algorithmic traversal of the source information. This chapter overviews the basics of the algorithm that must be implemented by the stylesheet writer using explicit template processing:

Included in this chapter.   This chapter includes discussion of the following XSLT sorting instruction:

- `<xsl:sort>`
  - specifies a criterion with which to sort a set of nodes.

9.1   **Sorting source nodes to make result nodes**

9.1.1   The sort instruction

This instruction is available only when creating a node list for processing, by using:

- `<xsl:apply-templates>` for push,
- `<xsl:for-each>` for pull,
- `select="node-set-expression"` (implicit or explicit) for selecting the nodes to make up the node set.

```
<xsl:sort select="optional-expression"/>
```

- One instruction must be provided for each sort key.
  - Typically `select="relative-node-set-expression"` is used.
    - The expression is evaluated relative to each node of the node set.
    - When absent, the value of each node is assumed:
      ```
      select="."
      ```
- Multiple keys can be specified in order —
  - primary, secondary, tertiary, etc.
- All sorting instructions must appear before any template content.
  - They do not need to appear before `<xsl:with-param>`.
- Equal sort values are sorted in document order.

The sorted node set becomes the current node list.

- This defines the XPath context of current node list and current node.
- The current node list is processed after being sorted.
  - Sorting does not rearrange the source node tree, only the current node list.
- The `position()` function reflects the sorted position.

- References through the axes are *not* affected.
  - Nodes along axes are always regarded in proximity order in expressions.
  - Sets of nodes from axes are always regarded in document order.

The `<xsl:sort>` instruction is not considered part of the template;

- syntactically it is included within the template of the instruction,
- but is consumed by the instruction interpretation and ignored when processing individual nodes.

Sort key evaluation criteria attributes are as follows.

- The sort order is defined by —
  - either `order="ascending"` (the default),
  - or `order="descending"`.
- The sort nature is defined by —
  - `data-type="text"` (the default):
    - indicates the sort order is lexicographic, based on the text of the sort keys,
    - with `lang="language-code"`:
      - takes into account the language of the sort keys,
      - complies to XML 1.0 Recommendation for the `xml:lang` attribute,
        - which is the same as IETF RFC–1766 "Tags for the Identification of Languages,"
    - uses case order and default which are language dependent;
      - with `case-order="upper-first"`,
        - the sort order is A a B b C c;
      - with `case-order="lower-first"`,
        - the sort order is a A b B c C.
    - is related to the work of the W3C I18N Working Group who:
      - is responsible for the issues of internationalization,
      - will have the results of its work incorporated into XSLT,
  - `data-type="number"`:
    - indicates the sort order is numeric based on the text of the sort keys being converted to numeric values (the `lang=` attribute is ignored),
  - `data-type="prefix:processor-recognized-sort-scheme-name"`:
    - requires the prefix to be defined by `xmlns:prefix="processor-recognized-URI-reference"`,
    - indicates the sort order is according to an algorithm recognized by the XSLT processor for the specified scheme.

An example with one sort key:

- shows the generation of HTML for external links in a presentation.

Example 9–1   Applying a single sort instruction when pushing nodes

```
Line 1  <table summary="&ext-title;" border="1">
     2    <xsl:apply-templates mode="extlink-creation"
     3                         select="//ext-link
     4                              [not(ancestor::module/exception
     5                                   [@presence='exclude'])
     6                              or  ancestor::module/exception
     7                                   [@presence='include']]">
     8      <xsl:sort select="@href"/>
     9    </xsl:apply-templates>
    10  </table>
```

The above creates a table element where —

- the nodes that are sorted are all `ext-link` element nodes in the document that do not have a `module` ancestor where `module` has an `exception` child whose `presence` attribute is "`exclude`", or, if it does have such an ancestor, the ancestor also has an `exception` child whose `presence` attribute is "`include`";
- the criteria by which the `ext-link` nodes are sorted is in ascending order of the attached `href` attribute node value for each node;
- the resulting ordered node list is processed by the XSLT processor, pushing the nodes through to the template rules in the stylesheet or built-in template rules to indicate which templates define the nodes that are added to the result tree.

Here is an example with multiple sort keys.

- People's names are composite (given name and surname), but treated as a whole;
  - both parts of the name are always displayed when the name is displayed.
- We need to first report the names unsorted,
- then sorted by the surname,
- then sorted by the surname and then by the given name.

The example XML source `sorttest.xml` is as follows:

Example 9–2   A list of names to be sorted

```
Line 1  <?xml version="1.0"?>
     2  <names>
     3  <name><given>Julie</given><surname>Holman</surname></name>
     4  <name><given>Margaret</given><surname>Mahoney</surname></name>
     5  <name><given>Ted</given><surname>Holman</surname></name>
     6  <name><given>John</given><surname>Mahoney</surname></name>
```

```
7    <name><given>Kathryn</given><surname>Holman</surname></name>
8    <name><given>Ken</given><surname>Holman</surname></name>
9    </names>
```

The desired result is as follows:

Example 9–3   Names sorted with zero, one and two sort keys (respectively)

```
Line 1   Holman,Julie
2        Mahoney,Margaret
3        Holman,Ted
4        Mahoney,John
5        Holman,Kathryn
6        Holman,Ken
7        ---
8        Holman,Julie
9        Holman,Ted
10       Holman,Kathryn
11       Holman,Ken
12       Mahoney,Margaret
13       Mahoney,John
14       ---
15       Holman,Julie
16       Holman,Kathryn
17       Holman,Ken
18       Holman,Ted
19       Mahoney,John
20       Mahoney,Margaret
```

The following stylesheet `sorttest.xsl` will produce the desired results:

Example 9–4   Sorting names with zero, one and two sort keys

```
Line 1   <?xml version="1.0"?>                                    <!--sorttest.xsl-->
2        <!--XSLT 1.0 - http://www.CraneSoftwrights.com/training -->
3        <!DOCTYPE xsl:stylesheet [<!ENTITY nl "&#xd;&#xa;">]>
4        <xsl:stylesheet xmlns:xsl="http://www.w3.org/1999/XSL/Transform"
5                        version="1.0">
6        <xsl:output method="text"/>
7
8        <xsl:template match="/">                                 <!--root rule-->
9          <xsl:apply-templates select="//name"/>                 <!--unsorted-->
10         <xsl:text>---&nl;</xsl:text>
11         <xsl:apply-templates select="//name">          <!--sort with one key-->
12           <xsl:sort select="surname"/>
13         </xsl:apply-templates>
14         <xsl:text>---&nl;</xsl:text>
15         <xsl:for-each select="//name">                 <!--sort with two keys-->
16           <xsl:sort select="surname"/>
17           <xsl:sort select="given"/>
18           <xsl:call-template name="name"/>             <!--show the name-->
```

```
19    </xsl:for-each>
20   </xsl:template>
21
22                        <!--both direct and indirect application of template-->
23   <xsl:template name="name" match="name">
24    <xsl:value-of select="surname"/>,<xsl:value-of select="given"/>
25    <xsl:text>&nl;</xsl:text>
26   </xsl:template>
27
28   </xsl:stylesheet>
```

Of note:

- The name display template is used for both push and pull operations on the tree.
- The program illustrates pushing with one sort key and pulling with two sort keys.

9.2   Grouping constructs found in the source node tree

9.2.1   Grouping and uniqueness using axes

You may need to report composite information grouped by components with equal values.

- It is often difficult to characterize a problem to be solved as being a grouping problem.
- Simple sorting obliges the reporting of all information in the component;
- grouping requires identifying all items with a common component and reporting under each unique value of that component —
  - identifying unique values of grouping component,
  - reporting other components of all items with same grouping value.

Grouping and uniqueness can be achieved by traversing axes.

- Unsorted grouping involves:
  - suppression of common adjacent values;
- Sorted grouping (uniqueness) involves:
  - identifying unique values in a set of nodes,
  - grouping the set of nodes according to unique values,
    - showing the common use of the unique value as a heading of the members of the set,

- listing the sub-constructs under the unique values as distinguishers.

To test preceding sibling values, use:

- `preceding-sibling::`*`test`*`[1]`
  - It *always* uses reverse document order of nodes;
    - axes are source node tree proximity oriented;
    - the first item on prior axes is the closest such item;
      - if there are no such first items, then the current node must be the first item;
  - it *does not* act on resulting sort order of nodes;
    - there are no functions to work on or address members of a sorted set of nodes.

To test preceding values when not dealing with siblings, use:

- `preceding::`*`test`*`[1]`

The essence of grouping is to utilize a test on all values that is true only once for each unique value.

- Recall that sorting does not rearrange the source node tree and that axes always relate to the order in the source node tree.
- You could check along an axis in either document order to check following values or reverse document order to find preceding values.
- For example purposes, the following will check the set of nodes in reverse document order to be empty to determine a given value is the first in document order.

For each key, starting with the primary key, find unique values of the key as follows:

- Visit all values of the data in sorted order (not in the order of the source node tree).
  - Determine for each given value whether it is the first such value in document order in the source node tree.
    - The source tree can be tested for any preceding nodes of the same calculated comparison value.
- If there are no preceding nodes in the source node tree of the same value —
  - assume the given value has not been processed yet;
  - process the given value;
    - revisit data selecting only those nodes matching the given value;
    - process the resulting current node set that represents the key's value set;

- for example, do next level sort given the value found at this level;
- for example, do the final result tree building based on key value.

- If there are preceding nodes in the source node tree of the same value —
    - assume the given value has already been processed;
    - ignore the node and value.

Consider the need to produce the following result, the original plus both adjacent and sorted summaries, each grouped according to surname:

Example 9–5   Unsorted and sorted groupings of names by surname

```
Line 1   Holman, Julie
     2   Mahoney, Margaret
     3   Holman, Ted
     4   Mahoney, John
     5   Holman, Kathryn
     6   Holman, Ken
     7   ---
     8   Holman     Julie
     9   Mahoney    Margaret
    10   Holman     Ted
    11   Mahoney    John
    12   Holman     Kathryn
    13              Ken
    14   ---
    15   Holman:
    16              Julie
    17              Kathryn
    18              Ken
    19              Ted
    20   Mahoney:
    21              John
    22              Margaret
```

Note in the second section above how only the last prefix is omitted because the only adjacent common surnames are at the end of the original list of names.

The following script group.xsl accomplishes the desired result:

Example 9–6   Grouping names unsorted and sorted

```
Line 1   <?xml version="1.0"?>                                    <!--group.xsl-->
     2   <!--XSLT 1.0 - http://www.CraneSoftwrights.com/training -->
     3   <!DOCTYPE xsl:stylesheet [
     4   <!ENTITY nl "&#xd;&#xa;">
```

```
 5  <!ENTITY pad "           ">
 6  ]>
 7  <xsl:stylesheet xmlns:xsl="http://www.w3.org/1999/XSL/Transform"
 8                  version="1.0">
 9  <xsl:output method="text"/>
10
11  <xsl:template match="/">                                 <!--root rule-->
12    <xsl:for-each select="//name">                         <!--unsorted-->
13      <xsl:value-of select="surname"/><xsl:text>, </xsl:text>
14      <xsl:value-of select="given"/>
15      <xsl:text>&nl;</xsl:text></xsl:for-each>
16    <xsl:text>---&nl;</xsl:text>
17
18    <xsl:for-each select="//name">                     <!--group unsorted-->
19      <xsl:choose>
20        <xsl:when test="not( preceding-sibling::name )
21                  or surname!=preceding-sibling::name[1]/surname">
22          <xsl:value-of select="surname"/>
23          <xsl:value-of select="substring( '&pad;', 1,
24            string-length('&pad;') - string-length( surname ) )"/>
25        </xsl:when>
26        <xsl:otherwise><xsl:text>&pad;</xsl:text></xsl:otherwise>
27      </xsl:choose>
28      <xsl:value-of select="given"/>
29      <xsl:text>&nl;</xsl:text></xsl:for-each>
30    <xsl:text>---&nl;</xsl:text>
31
32    <xsl:for-each select="//name">                        <!--group sorted-->
33      <xsl:sort select="surname"/>                        <!--by primary key-->
34      <xsl:variable name="surname" select="surname"/>
35
37      <xsl:if test="not( preceding-sibling::name
38                                        [surname=$surname] )">
39        <xsl:value-of select="$surname"/>
40        <xsl:text>:&nl;</xsl:text>
41                        <!--reselect only nodes with current primary key-->
42        <xsl:for-each select="//name[surname=$surname]">
43          <xsl:sort select="given"/>                      <!--by secondary key-->
44          <xsl:text>&pad;</xsl:text>
45          <xsl:value-of select="given"/>
46          <xsl:text>&nl;</xsl:text>
47        </xsl:for-each>
48      </xsl:if>
49    </xsl:for-each>
50  </xsl:template>
51
52  </xsl:stylesheet>
```

Of note:

- When checking for like surnames when unsorted —

- the test first checks if the node is the first node of the set by looking for any preceding sibling element nodes of the same name;
- if there are preceding sibling element nodes, then the presence of any preceding sibling element nodes with the same value of the surname element child is checked.

- When checking for like surnames when sorted —
  - each node in the data is visited twice,
    - once to establish order of the primary key,
    - once to establish order of the secondary key within all elements matching the primary key.

9.2.2   Grouping and uniqueness using keys

Grouping can be achieved by identifying key nodes.

- Group a set of nodes according to a node's presence in an `<xsl:key>` table;
  - find the first member in the table with each unique value;
- show the unique value of the construct as a heading;
- reselect the members from the table using that construct's value, displaying distinguishing values separately.
  - Selecting from the table is faster than selecting from the tree.

This technique is colloquially referred to as the "Muenchian Method" after Steve Muench who first proposed the use of `<xsl:key>` for grouping.

For each key, starting with the primary key:

- find unique values of the key;
  - find the generated id of the first entry of a given key's value in the `<xsl:key>` table:

    ```
    generate-id(key(key-name,lookup-value))
    ```

    - recall that the generated identifier for a node is persistent through the execution of a given stylesheet and that it operates on the first member of a given node set;
      - two nodes can be checked as being the same node by comparing their respective generated identifiers:

        ```
        generate-id(.)=
        generate-id(key(key-name,lookup-value))
        ```

  - find each node in the tree that is the first node of the key's unique value;

- when used as a predicate, the following expression finds all first matching members of a location step resulting from the node test:

```
select="axis-and-node-test[generate-id(.)=
              generate-id(key(key-name,lookup-value))]"
```

  - the found nodes can be sorted if desired;
  - group-oriented processing can occur for each node selected as it represents each unique value from the key table;

- reselect all nodes in the tree matching the particular value:

```
select="key(key-name,lookup-value)"
```

- process the resulting current node set that represents the key's value set;
  - for example, do next level sort given the value found at this level;
  - for example, do the final result tree building based on key value.

Consider again the need to produce the following result, the original plus a sorted summary grouped according to surname:

Example 9–7 Ungrouped and grouped names

```
Line 1   Holman, Julie
     2   Mahoney, Margaret
     3   Holman, Ted
     4   Mahoney, John
     5   Holman, Kathryn
     6   Holman, Ken
     7   - - -
     8   Holman:
     9           Julie
    10           Kathryn
    11           Ken
    12           Ted
    13   Mahoney:
    14           John
    15           Margaret
```

The following script `group2.xsl` accomplishes the desired result:

Example 9–8 Transforming to ungrouped and grouped names

```
Line 1   <?xml version="1.0"?>                              <!--group2.xsl-->
     2   <!--XSLT 1.0 - http://www.CraneSoftwrights.com/training -->
     3   <!DOCTYPE xsl:stylesheet [
     4   <!ENTITY nl "&#xd;&#xa;">
     5   <!ENTITY pad "          ">
     6   ]>
     7   <xsl:stylesheet xmlns:xsl="http://www.w3.org/1999/XSL/Transform"
     8                   version="1.0">
```

```
 9  <xsl:output method="text"/>
10
11  <xsl:key name="names" match="name" use="surname"/>
12
13  <xsl:template match="/">                              <!--root rule-->
14    <xsl:for-each select="//name">                     <!--unsorted-->
15      <xsl:value-of select="surname"/><xsl:text>, </xsl:text>
16      <xsl:value-of select="given"/>
17      <xsl:text>&nl;</xsl:text></xsl:for-each>
18    <xsl:text>---&nl;</xsl:text>
19                                                  <!--group sorted-->
20                                 <!--get the first node of each surname-->
21    <xsl:for-each select="//name
22            [generate-id(.)=generate-id(key('names',surname))]">
23      <xsl:sort select="surname"/>                  <!--by primary key-->
24      <xsl:value-of select="surname"/>
25      <xsl:text>&nl;</xsl:text>
26                            <!--get all nodes for the given surname-->
27      <xsl:for-each select="key('names',surname)">
28        <xsl:sort select="given"/>                <!--by secondary key-->
29        <xsl:text>&pad;</xsl:text>
30        <xsl:value-of select="given"/>
31        <xsl:text>&nl;</xsl:text>
32      </xsl:for-each>
33    </xsl:for-each>
34  </xsl:template>
35
36  </xsl:stylesheet>
```

9.2.3   Grouping and uniqueness within sub-trees using keys

Typical use of the key table scopes key values across the entire document.

Consider the following data in `grpsub.xml`:

- course contains lessons;
- lessons contain frames;
- frames are distinguished by their applicability as stated in an attribute;
- lessons and frames have titles authored by hand (note the whitespace).

Example 9–9   Sample of applicability attributes in instructional information

```
Line 1  <?xml version="1.0"?>
     2  <course>
     3  <lesson>
```

```
 4  <title>
 5  The XML family of Recommendations</title>
 6  <frame id="xml-info" appl="a">
 7  <title>
 8  Extensible Markup Language (XML)</title>
 9  </frame>
10  <frame id="xml-links" appl="b">
11  <title>
12  XML information links</title>
13  </frame>
14  ...
15  </lesson>
16  <lesson>
17  <title>
18  Transformation data flows</title>
19  <frame id="x2xml" appl="a">
20  <title>
21  Transformation from XML to XML</title>
22  </frame>
23  ...
```

The information grouped across the document, alphabetically by applicability, is as follows:

Example 9–10   Grouping of all frames in course by applicability attribute

```
Line 1   a
 2         Extensible Markup Language (XML) 1.1
 3         Some simple examples 3.1
 4         Stylesheet association 1.10
 5         Stylesheet requirements 4.1
 6         Styling structured information 1.4
 7         Templates and template rules 4.3
 8         Three-tiered architectures 2.5
 9         Transformation from XML to XML 2.1
10       b
11         Extensible Stylesheet Language Transformations (XSLT) 1.6
12         Historical development of the XSL and XSLT Recommendations 1.7
13         Instructions and literal result elements 4.2
14         Transformation from XML to XSL formatting semantics 2.2
15         XML information links 1.2
16         XML Path Language (XPath) 1.3
17         XSL information links 1.8
18         XSLT as an application front-end 2.4
19       c
20         Approaches to stylesheet design 4.6
21         Explicitly declared stylesheets 4.5
22         Extensible Stylesheet Language (XSL) 1.5
23         Implicitly declared stylesheets 4.4
24         Namespaces 1.9
25         Transformation from XML to non-XML 2.3
```

To group across the document, the key value is a simple value calculated from relative node content.

- Use the applicability attribute value as grouping criterion.

Example 9–11   Grouping all frames in course by applicability attribute

```
Line 1  <?xml version="1.0"?>                                        <!--grpsub.xsl-->
     2  <!--XSLT 1.0 - http://www.CraneSoftwrights.com/training -->
     3  <!DOCTYPE xsl:stylesheet [<!ENTITY nl "&#xd;&#xa;">]>
     4  <xsl:stylesheet xmlns:xsl="http://www.w3.org/1999/XSL/Transform"
     5                  version="1.0">
     6  <xsl:output method="text"/>
     7
     8  <xsl:key name="appls" match="frame" use="@appl"/>
     9
    10  <xsl:template match="/">                                        <!--root rule-->
    11    <xsl:for-each select=
    12      "//frame[generate-id(.)=generate-id(key('appls',@appl))]">
    13      <xsl:sort select="@appl"/>                    <!--alphabetical group order-->
    14      <xsl:text> </xsl:text>
    15      <xsl:value-of select="@appl"/>                      <!--show group title-->
    16      <xsl:text>&nl;</xsl:text>
    17      <xsl:for-each select="key('appls',@appl)">            <!--all in group-->
    18        <xsl:sort select="normalize-space(title)"/>
    19        <xsl:text>    </xsl:text>
    20        <xsl:value-of select="normalize-space(title)"/>
    21        <xsl:text> </xsl:text>
    22        <xsl:number count="lesson|frame" level="multiple"/>
    23        <xsl:text>&nl;</xsl:text>
    24      </xsl:for-each>
    25    </xsl:for-each>
    26  </xsl:template>
    27
    28  </xsl:stylesheet>
```

Key table values need not be solely constructed from node content.

- The values can be concatenated from other sources relative to the
  node or generated from the node.
- Care must be taken to prevent ambiguous value calculations;
  - the resulting concatenation of two values must not conflict with a third value.
- generate-id() produces a lexical name token that cannot have
  spaces;
  - therefore a space is a viable delimiter of generated identifier values.
- Build a table entry as a concatenation of three values:
  - generated identifier of the ancestral point in the hierarchy,

- the space —
  - guaranteed to not be in the generated identifier,
- distinguishing node value.
- You must look up the table with the ancestral generated identifier, or node value will not be found.

Use of internal general entities can help work with complex code.

- The algorithm for generating a key table node entry's value can be declared once and reused, which improves the stylesheet's —
  - readability,
  - maintainability.

The information grouped under each lesson, alphabetically by lesson and then alphabetically by applicability, is as follows:

- the lesson information is not composite, so grouping isn't needed;
- the applicability information is composite, so grouping is needed.

Example 9–12   Grouping of frames within lessons by applicability attribute

```
Line 1   Stylesheet examples
   2       a
   3         Some simple examples 3.1
   4     Syntax basics - stylesheets, templates, instructions
   5       a
   6         Stylesheet requirements 4.1
   7         Templates and template rules 4.3
   8       b
   9         Instructions and literal result elements 4.2
  10       c
  11         Approaches to stylesheet design 4.6
  12         Explicitly declared stylesheets 4.5
  13         Implicitly declared stylesheets 4.4
  14     The XML family of Recommendations
  15       a
  16         Extensible Markup Language (XML) 1.1
  17         Stylesheet association 1.10
  18         Styling structured information 1.4
  19       b
  20         Extensible Stylesheet Language Transformations (XSLT) 1.6
  21         Historical development of the XSL and XSLT Recommendations 1.7
  22         XML information links 1.2
  23         XML Path Language (XPath) 1.3
  24         XSL information links 1.8
  25       c
  26         Extensible Stylesheet Language (XSL) 1.5
  27         Namespaces 1.9
  28     Transformation data flows
```

```
29   a
30      Three-tiered architectures 2.5
31      Transformation from XML to XML 2.1
32   b
33      Transformation from XML to XSL formatting semantics 2.2
34      XSLT as an application front-end 2.4
35   c
36      Transformation from XML to non-XML 2.3
```

To group under a sub-tree, the key value is a calculated from the identifier of the apex node combined with the relative node content (note the use of internal parsed general entities to promote consistency):

Example 9–13   Grouping frames within lessons by applicability attribute

```
Line 1  <?xml version="1.0"?>                                      <!--grpsub2.xsl-->
     2  <!--XSLT 1.0 - http://www.CraneSoftwrights.com/training -->
     3  <!DOCTYPE xsl:stylesheet [<!ENTITY nl "&#xd;&#xa;">
     4                  <!--group under ancestral lesson by applicability attribute-->
     5  <!ENTITY frame-lookup
     6      "concat( generate-id(ancestor::lesson),' ',@appl )">
     7  <!ENTITY frame-group "key('appls', &frame-lookup;)">
     8  <!ENTITY frame-group-first
     9              "frame[generate-id(.)=generate-id(&frame-group;)]"> ]>
    10  <xsl:stylesheet xmlns:xsl="http://www.w3.org/1999/XSL/Transform"
    11                  version="1.0">
    12  <xsl:output method="text"/>
    13
    14  <xsl:key name="appls" match="frame" use="&frame-lookup;"/>
    15
    16  <xsl:template match="/">                                        <!--root rule-->
    17    <xsl:for-each select="//lesson">              <!--group under each lesson-->
    18      <xsl:sort select="normalize-space(title)"/>
    19      <xsl:value-of select="normalize-space(title)"/>
    20      <xsl:text>&nl;</xsl:text>
    21      <xsl:for-each select="&frame-group-first;">           <!--each group-->
    22        <xsl:sort select="@appl"/>                 <!--alphabetical group order-->
    23        <xsl:text>  </xsl:text>
    24        <xsl:value-of select="@appl"/>                     <!--show group title-->
    25        <xsl:text>&nl;</xsl:text>
    26        <xsl:for-each select="&frame-group;">              <!--all in group-->
    27          <xsl:sort select="normalize-space(title)"/>
    28          <xsl:text>    </xsl:text>
    29          <xsl:value-of select="normalize-space(title)"/>
    30          <xsl:text> </xsl:text>
    31          <xsl:number count="lesson|frame" level="multiple"/>
    32          <xsl:text>&nl;</xsl:text>
    33        </xsl:for-each>
    34      </xsl:for-each>
```

```
35        </xsl:for-each>
36    </xsl:template>
37
38    </xsl:stylesheet>
```

9.3 Other uses of sorting

9.3.1 Finding the minimum and maximum values

Sometimes it is necessary to identify nodes that have a minimum or maximum value from a set of values.

- Recall that a node-set comparison continues as long as the evaluation is false and stops once the evaluation is true;
  - when used in a predicate as in the example below, the comparison only evaluates true for those nodes that are either largest or smallest based on the comparison.
- Recall that `<xsl:sort>` reorders the current node list (not the source node tree) and that `position()` reflects the sorted order (not the tree order);
  - the first item in the list is the first in sorted order.

Example 9–14   Calculation of minimum and maximum values from nodes and values

```
Line 1   <?xml version="1.0"?>                                       <!--minmax.xsl-->
     2   <!--XSLT 1.0 - http://www.CraneSoftwrights.com/training -->
     3   <!DOCTYPE xsl:stylesheet [
     4   <!ENTITY nl "&#xd;&#xa;">
     5   ]>
     6   <xsl:stylesheet xmlns:xsl="http://www.w3.org/1999/XSL/Transform"
     7                   version="1.0">
     8   <xsl:output method="text"/>
     9
    10   <xsl:template match="/">
    11     <xsl:variable name="itemnodes" select="//item"/>
    12     <xsl:text>Minimum nodes:&nl;</xsl:text>                      <!--get nodes-->
    13     <xsl:for-each
    14         select="$itemnodes[ not( $itemnodes/@val &lt; @val ) ]">
    15       <xsl:value-of select="."/><xsl:text>&nl;</xsl:text>
    16     </xsl:for-each>
    17
    18     <xsl:text>Maximum value: </xsl:text>                         <!--get single value-->
    19     <xsl:for-each select="$itemnodes">                           <!--sort all in order-->
    20       <xsl:sort data-type="number" order="descending"
    21               select="@val"/>
    22       <xsl:if test="position() = 1">                             <!--first in list is max-->
    23         <xsl:value-of select="@val"/>
    24       </xsl:if>
    25     </xsl:for-each>
```

```
26    <xsl:text>&nl;</xsl:text>
27  </xsl:template>
28
29  </xsl:stylesheet>
```

A

XML
to HTML
transformation

A XML to HTML transformation

Many of us need to transform our XML into presentations appropriate for display on web browsers. To this end, the serialization facilities accommodate our need to support older browsers at the markup convention level. As described earlier we can choose to output arbitrary XML following XML markup conventions, or we can request the XSLT processor to serialize the tree distinguishing components of the HTML vocabulary and following SGML markup conventions.

The markup we choose to use in this environment can be influenced by a number of related W3C Recommendations. This markup constitutes our rendering vocabulary, and as such we are obliged to transform instances of our XML vocabularies into instances recognizable to the web browsers being used to consume our information visually.

Hypertext Markup Language (HTML). The HTML Recommendation is an SGML application describing a markup language for text, multimedia and hyperlinking. Using the semantics of HTML we can present, associate and relate pages of information for display in a web user agent (typically a web browser). User agents have built-in assumptions regarding the presentation of HTML constructs on the canvas.

Extensible Hypertext Markup Language (XHTML). The XHTML Recommendation is the HTML vocabulary recast as a conforming XML application rather than as a conforming SGML application.

Cascading Stylesheets (CSS). The CSS Recommendation gives us the tools to specify how we want to override the built-in presentation assumptions regarding HTML constructs. We can also use CSS to associate formatting properties for elements of arbitrary XML vocabularies. In both cases we are decorating the structured information represented by an HTML or XML instance with presentation-related rendering information.

User Agent Screen Painting. HTML has semantic-free constructs with which we can paint the user agent canvas with our information. This prevents overloading the semantic constructs defined by HTML for purposes other than as intended by the language semantics.

Included in this annex. This annex overviews considerations for producing different flavors of HTML to support different user agents. As well, stylesheet fragments illustrating common requirements to mark up images and links are described.

Issues of compatibility between different user agent implementations and recommended markup practices are not reviewed in this material. A discussion of such issues can be found at:

- `http://www.w3.org/TR/xhtml1/#guidelines`

A.1 **The W3C web presentation standards context**

A.1.1 Hypertext Markup Language (HTML)

HTML was initially developed as a markup language for sharing information at the European Center for Nuclear Research (CERN) using a protocol called the Hypertext Transfer Protocol (HTTP) based on a vision of Tim Berners-Lee.

- Project proposal within CERN (March 1989):
  - is at `http://www.w3.org/History/1989/proposal.html`.

- First published version of HTML representing initial practice in 1992:
  - is at `http://www.w3.org/History/19921103-hypertext/hypertext/WWW/Mark-Up/MarkUp.html`.
- First W3C version (HTML 2.0) which came from HTML Working Group representing current practice in 1994:
  - is at `http://www.w3.org/MarkUp/html-spec/` (edited by Dan Connolly).
- Widely adopted version (HTML 3.2) representing current practice in 1996:
  - is at `http://www.w3.org/TR/REC-html32.html` (edited by Dave Raggett).
- Current W3C version (HTML 4.01) which became a final recommendation in April 1998:
  - is at `http://www.w3.org/TR/REC-html40/`,
  - was revised in August 1999 and is at `http://www.w3.org/TR/1999/PR-html40-19990824`,
  - introduces semantic-free constructs for browser canvas painting,
  - introduces a document model manipulated by scripting for Dynamic HTML (DHTML).

A.1.2 Extensible HyperText Markup Language (XHTML)

Extensible HyperText Markup Language (XHTML):

- is at `http://www.w3.org/TR/xhtml1`;
  - `http://www.w3.org/TR/xhtml-roadmap`
    - presents future plans for XHTML;
  - `http://www.w3.org/TR/xhtml-events`
    - uniformly integrates behaviors of user agents,
- is a reformulation of HTML using XML 1.0,
- reproduces, subsets and extends HTML 4 vocabulary,
- is XML-conforming and operates in HTML 4 conforming user agents,
- is devised so that XHTML files are acceptable input to XML processing tools:
  - stylesheets,
  - applications.

IBTWSH:

- is at `http://home.ccil.org/~cowan/XML/ibtwsh6.dtd`,
- means Itsy Bitsy Teeny Weeny Simple Hypertext DTD —

- written by John Cowan,
- is a minimized document model of XHTML constructs useful for inclusion in other document models.

WAI:

- is at `http://www.w3.org/WAI/`,
- means Web Accessibility Initiative,
- provides important guidelines for designing accessible HTML documents.

A.1.3   Cascading Stylesheets (CSS)

HTML was not initially designed to be used as a general purpose browser canvas painting language.

- It is a hypertext markup language describing links to information.
- It is very difficult to flexibly paint the browser screen using the element types available.
  - The built-in rendering semantics implemented in the browsers dictate the appearance.

Vendors implemented incompatible extensions without sticking to Recommendations.

- The Recommendations didn't provide the desired formatting at the time.
- Users wanted control of the canvas.

Cascading style sheets were introduced to:

- target for both page designers and users (page readers),
- override built-in rendering semantics of browsers and achieve more of an artistic effect on the screen,
- get influence the presentation of documents without sacrificing device independence or adding new HTML element types,
- decorate the document tree without modifying the structure of the document's hierarchy,

CSS–1 (December 1996):

- is at `http://www.w3.org/pub/WWW/TR/REC-CSS1`,
- adds style to web documents,

- has rules describing facets of style; a collection of rules is a stylesheet,
- allows mixing and overriding of stylesheets by cascading.

CSS–2 (May 1998):

- is at `http://www.w3.org/TR/REC-CSS2/`,
- provides for media-specific stylesheets (e.g. printers and aural devices),
- supports downloadable fonts,
- supports element positioning,
- supports tables,
- supports XML documents.

A.1.4 Browser screen painting

HTML 4.0 introduces the concept of Grouping Elements with no stand-alone presentational idioms (thus the groups are semantic free, see Figure A–1).

- `<DIV>`
  - is a block-level construct (breaks the line flow).

Figure A–1 Using semantic-free constructs for rendering

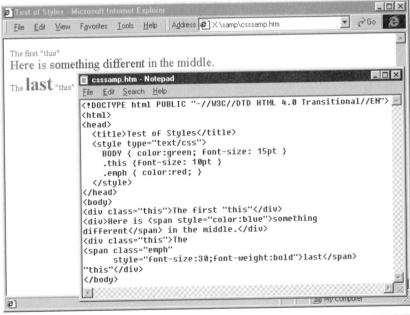

- `<SPAN>`
  - is an inline-level construct (doesn't break the line flow).
- When used in conjunction with `id=` and `class=` attributes, this concept adds generic method for adding structure to HTML presentation.
- When used in conjunction with CSS style rule specifications, this concept adds generic method for painting the browser screen with formatting properties.
- The "cascade" is the priority of applying properties from different sources (e.g.: markup, identifier value, class value, element type property set, external stylesheet).

A.2 Well-formed HTML

A.2.1 What makes well-formed and valid HTML?

There are differences in the markup of empty elements in HTML, XML, and XHTML:

- `<hr>`
  - according to HTML rules, an empty element cannot be distinguished from a non-empty element by just the start tag;
- `<hr/>`
  - according to XML rules, an empty element is distinguished by just the start tag;
  - some older user agents assume the "/" is part of the element type and do not recognize or act on XML well-formed empty HTML elements;
- `<hr />`
  - according to XHTML rules, an empty element's name is followed by a space;
  - it satisfies those older user agents that assume the "/" is part of the element type;
  - this is well-formed XML, but is not typically what is serialized by processors for the XML method.

When the output method is HTML, the XSLT processor must serialize using HTML conventions:

```
<xsl:output method="html"/>
```

- note also that the HTML output method is assumed when the output method is not specified and the document element of the result tree is "html" (in upper or lower case);

- this method makes use of known empty element types, attribute minimizations, built-in Latin–1 character entity references, etc.

HTML completeness is important with respect to rigor.

- Older user agents cannot all accommodate a well-formed or valid HTML file.
- `<!DOCTYPE`
  - An HTML file should have declaration (though some older user agents incorrectly display this on the canvas);
  - note it is the responsibility of the stylesheet writer to use the `doctype-public=` attribute of `<xsl:output>` to ensure this;
  - some user agents will accept incomplete HTML without a `<!DOCTYPE` declaration but will not accept incomplete HTML when there is a `<!DOCTYPE` declaration.
- `<head>` and `<title>`
  - Some older user agents require the content of the `<head><style>` element to be an HTML comment `<!-- -->` to prevent display on the canvas.

A.3 HTML markup generation techniques

A.3.1 Image elements

`<img>`

- is an empty element with two required attributes:
  - `src=`
    - points to the image storage location;
  - `alt=`
    - contains a short text description (important for accessibility; some user agents will display a pop-up of the text when the pointer hovers over the image),
- may contain optional attributes:
  - `longdesc=`
    - complements `alt=` by pointing to the Universal Resource Identifier (URI) of more information;
  - `height=` and `width=`
    - override the image parameters;
  - `usemap=` and `ismap=`
    - define client-side and server-side image maps (deprecated).

Note that while the HTML convention for displaying images is to point to the filename directly in the attribute value, and this can be done in XML, it is a common design practice to point to image files indirectly through unparsed entity declarations. An example of doing so is included in Chapter 8.

Consider the XML instance imgsamp.xml encoding the logo's filename directly in an attribute value:

Example A–1   Sample graphic and caption information

```
Line 1   <?xml version="1.0"?>
     2   <?xml-stylesheet type="text/xsl" href="imgsamp.xsl"?>
     3   <imgsamp>
     4   <para>Here is an example:</para>
     5   <fig file="crane.gif">Crane Logo</fig>
     6   <para>End of example</para>
     7   </imgsamp>
```

A possible rendering reveals the caption below the image itself as it is shown in Figure A–2.

Of note:

• The fig element type is not empty, the content is the figure caption.

Figure A–2   Rendering of sample graphic and caption information

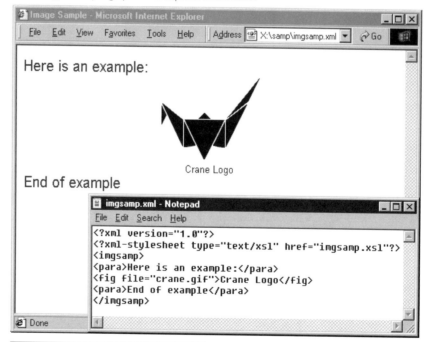

- The caption is being used both for the image alternate text and for the canvas.

One possible XSLT stylesheet, `imgsamp.xsl`, would be as follows:

Example A–2   Sample stylesheet for transforming graphic and caption information

```
Line 1  <?xml version="1.0"?>                                          <!--imgsamp.xsl-->
     2  <!--XSLT 1.0 - http://www.CraneSoftwrights.com/training -->
     3  <!DOCTYPE xsl:stylesheet [ <!ENTITY dark-green "#004400"> ]>
     4  <xsl:stylesheet xmlns:xsl="http://www.w3.org/1999/XSL/Transform"
     5                  version="1.0" xmlns="http://www.w3.org/TR/REC-html40">
     6  <xsl:output method="html"
     7              doctype-public="-//W3C//DTD HTML 4.0 Transitional//EN"/>
     8
     9  <xsl:template match="/">                                        <!-- root rule -->
    10    <html>
    11      <head><title>Image Sample</title></head>
    12      <body><xsl:apply-templates/></body>
    13    </html>
    14  </xsl:template>
    15
    16  <xsl:template match="fig">
    17    <div style="font-size:10pt;text-align:center">
    18      <img src="{@file}" alt="{.}"/>
    19      <div>
    20        <xsl:apply-templates/>
    21      </div>
    22    </div>
    23  </xsl:template>
    24
    25  <xsl:template match="para">
    26    <div style="font-size:15pt;color=&dark-green;">
    27      <xsl:apply-templates/>
    28    </div>
    29  </xsl:template>
    30
    31  </xsl:stylesheet>
```

A.3.2 HTML meta-data

Consider the XML instance `metasamp.xml` encoding page title information in the instance:

Example A–3   Sample meta data information

```
Line 1  <?xml version="1.0"?>
     2  <?xml-stylesheet type="text/xsl" href="metasamp.xsl"?>
     3  <metasamp>
     4  <banner>The Sample Title</banner>
```

```
     5   <para>Here is a paragraph</para>
     6   <para>End of example</para>
     7   </metasamp>
```

The rendering in Figure A–3 reuses the meta data for the HTML file in two places, in each of the title bar of the window and on the canvas.

The XSL stylesheet `metasamp.xsl` renders the example:

Example A–4   Sample stylesheet for transforming meta data information

```
Line 1   <?xml version="1.0"?>                                    <!--metasamp.xsl-->
     2   <!--XSLT 1.0 - http://www.CraneSoftwrights.com/training -->
     3   <!DOCTYPE xsl:stylesheet [
     4   <!ENTITY dark-green "#004400">
     5   ]>
     6   <xsl:stylesheet xmlns:xsl="http://www.w3.org/1999/XSL/Transform"
     7                   version="1.0">
     8
     9   <xsl:template match="/">                                    <!-- root rule -->
    10     <html>
    11       <head>
    12         <title><xsl:value-of select="//banner"/></title>
    13       </head>
    14       <body>
    15         <xsl:apply-templates/>
    16       </body>
    17     </html>
    18   </xsl:template>
    19
    20   <xsl:template match="banner">
    21     <div style="font-size:15pt;color=red;text-align:center">
    22       <xsl:apply-templates/>
    23     </div>
    24   </xsl:template>
    25
    26   <xsl:template match="para">
    27     <div style="font-size:15pt;color=&dark-green;">
    28       <xsl:apply-templates/>
    29     </div>
    30   </xsl:template>
    31
    32   </xsl:stylesheet>
```

A.3.3   Anchor elements

Consider the need to de-reference use of the XML concepts of ID and IDREF pointers (XML 1.0 Recommendation production [56]) as in `asamp.xml`:

Example A–5 Sample cross-referenced information

```
Line 1   <?xml version="1.0"?>
    2    <?xml-stylesheet type="text/xsl" href="asamp.xsl"?>
    3    <!DOCTYPE asamp [
    4    <!ELEMENT asamp    ( section+ )>
    5    <!ELEMENT section ( title, para+ )>
    6    <!ATTLIST section id ID #REQUIRED>
    7    <!ELEMENT title    ( #PCDATA )>
    8    <!ELEMENT para     ( #PCDATA | sectref )*>
    9    <!ELEMENT sectref EMPTY>
   10    <!ATTLIST sectref idref IDREF #REQUIRED>
   11    ]>
   12    <asamp>
   13    <section id="s1">
   14    <title>Section One</title>
   15    <para>First paragraph of section one.</para>
   16    <para>Second paragraph of section one.</para>
   17    </section>
   18    <section id="s2">
   19    <title>Section Two</title>
   20    <para>First paragraph of section two.</para>
   21    <para>Second paragraph of section two
   22    with reference to <sectref idref="s1"/> embedded.</para>
   23    </section>
   24    </asamp>
```

With the desired result replacing the empty section reference elements with a hyperlink pointing to the section itself and the displayed content of the hyperlink being the title of the section to which it points:

Figure A–3 Rendering of sample meta data information

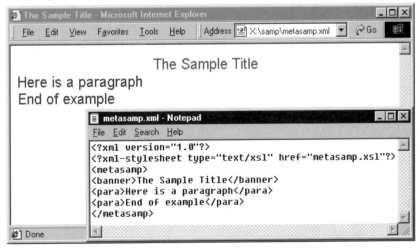

Example A–6   Transformation of the sample cross-referenced information

```
Line 1  <!DOCTYPE html PUBLIC "-//W3C//DTD HTML 4.0 Transitional//EN">
     2  <html>
     3  <head>
     4  <title>Anchor Example</title>
     5  </head>
     6  <body>
     7
     8  <a name="s1">
     9  <p style="font-size:15pt;color=red;text-align:center">Section One</p>
    10  </a>
    11  <p style="font-size:15pt;color=#004400">First paragraph of section one.</p>
    12  <p style="font-size:15pt;color=#004400">Second paragraph of section one.</p>
    13
    14
    15  <a name="s2">
    16  <p style="font-size:15pt;color=red;text-align:center">Section Two</p>
    17  </a>
    18  <p style="font-size:15pt;color=#004400">First paragraph of section two.</p>
    19  <p style="font-size:15pt;color=#004400">Second paragraph of section two
    20  with reference to <a href="#s1">Section One</a> embedded.</p>
    21
    22  </body>
    23  </html>
```

The XSLT stylesheet `asamp.xsl` effects this transformation as follows, utilizing the XSLT `id()` function described in Chapter 8:

Example A–7   Sample stylesheet for transforming cross-referenced information

```
Line 1  <?xml version="1.0"?>                                        <!--asamp.xsl-->
     2  <!--XSLT 1.0 - http://www.CraneSoftwrights.com/training -->
     3  <!DOCTYPE xsl:stylesheet [ <!ENTITY dark-green "#004400"> ]>
     4  <xsl:stylesheet xmlns:xsl="http://www.w3.org/1999/XSL/Transform"
     5                  version="1.0">
     6
     7  <xsl:output method="html"
     8          doctype-public="-//W3C//DTD HTML 4.0 Transitional//EN"/>
     9
    10  <xsl:template match="/">                                    <!-- root rule -->
    11    <html>
    12      <head><title>Anchor Example</title></head>
    13      <body><xsl:apply-templates/></body></html></xsl:template>
    14
    15  <xsl:template match="section/title">
    16    <a name="{../@id}">
    17      <p style="font-size:15pt;color=red;text-align:center">
    18        <xsl:apply-templates/>
    19      </p></a></xsl:template>
    20
```

```
21  <xsl:template match="para">
22    <p style="font-size:15pt;color=#004400">
23      <xsl:apply-templates/></p></xsl:template>
24
25  <xsl:template match="sectref">
26    <a href="#{@idref}">
27      <xsl:value-of select="id(@idref)/title"/></a></xsl:template>
28
29  </xsl:stylesheet>
```

B

XSL formatting
semantics
introduction

B XSL formatting semantics introduction

A very common requirement we all share is the need to render our information to some medium: typically a print device, though some of us render information aurally to a sound device or visually to a display device. The same W3C working group responsible for XSLT is also responsible for the Extensible Stylesheet Language (XSL), a vocabulary representing formatting and flow concepts useful for rendering.

The XSL vocabulary is used with an XSL rendering agent much the same way the HTML vocabulary is used to present information in a web browser. We transform instances of our own XML vocabularies to use the XSL vocabulary in a rendering agent, as these agents have no awareness of the presentation semantics associated with the arbitrary elements and attributes we choose for ourselves in our own vocabularies.

Accordingly, the XSL Recommendation normatively references the XSLT Recommendation. XSL processors incorporating XSLT processors need only interpret the formatting and flow vocabulary to produce an end result, hence, the rendering vocabulary may or may not be made available as elements and attributes in an actual XML instance. This was depicted earlier in Figure 1–6.

With XSL, as with HTML or any rendering vocabulary, our XSLT transformation specifications are stylesheets incorporating both the rearrangement and the presentation of our information.

The Extensible Stylesheet Language (XSL). The XSL Recommendation defines a catalog of formatting objects and flow objects, each with their own properties influencing behavior, for rendering information to a target device. The emphasis here (no pun intended) is the formatting or presentation of our information in a medium intended for human consumption.

The first version of the Recommendation includes concepts that address basic word-processing-level pagination. These concepts are incorporated in a semantic model for formatting. The formatting and flow objects of XSL make up the semantic model and are expressed in terms of a vocabulary. Though this vocabulary is documented and serialized as XML markup, an instance of the hierarchical model can be acted upon as the end result of transformation (the result tree) without necessitating serialization.

Sophisticated pagination and support for layout-driven documents. The pagination and formatting support is oriented to the layout of information in the target medium. Established Recommendations and International Standards form the rich heritage of XSL concepts. Indeed, the members of XSL working group include active participants of International Organization for Standardization (ISO) committees for document description and processing and active members of W3C working group on a common formatting model.

The Document Style Semantics and Specification Language (DSSSL) ISO–10179 is an International Standard addressing many of the objectives addressed by XSL. This Standard includes semantics for both simple and complex page geometries and writing-direction-less formatting. The specification language is a LISP-like derivative of the Scheme language.

Cascading Stylesheets (CSS) is a W3C Recommendation allowing the attachment of formatting properties to structured documents. The properties support some media-specific stylesheets so authors can tailor the formatting to specialized devices. The CSS and Formatting Properties working group is responsible for the developments in this area.

While the XSL working group is distinct from the CSS working group, the stated general aim of the two groups is to keep their respective formatting models compatible and the properties the same where there are overlapping areas of functionality. Pagination imposes arbitrary boundaries on the content, such as pages or regions of a page, that are not present on a scrolling screen window of infinite length or stretchable width. These concepts are only supported with formatting properties beyond that found in CSS, thus requiring a dedicated focus as found in XSL.

Note: Here we have the meeting of the "doc heads" (from the ISO document world) and the "web heads" (from the W3C web world). Two groups with distinctly different backgrounds, both working together to accomplish a common view of formatting. We mostly benefit from this merging of perspectives and objectives that has created the XSL definition, however, there are some places were duplication has been preserved to accommodate members of both camps.

Though I actively contribute to both communities, my personal background is as a "doc head," having been involved with international standardization much longer than with the W3C.

Well-defined constructs.   The semantics are described according to the documented XSL formatting model of nested areas stacked on top of each other in a hierarchical fashion. The page itself represents an area upon which other areas are placed, and then areas within those areas are created by specifications found in the stylesheet.

We use the XSL vocabulary representing the semantics in order to express our formatting intent. Our stylesheets are declarative, and not procedural, in that this intent is a static description of the spirit of our desired end result.

This specification of our intent is managed and interpreted by a formatter, which is some software or device that is actually responsible for the rendering processes to get dots on a page, pixels on a screen, or sound out of a speaker. This rendering agent flows our information according to our flow specifications into areas we describe with formatting specifications, thus producing the end result.

This arms-length relationship between our rendering specifications and the rendering device means there is no feedback loop; no querying of the rendering process in the middle of specifying the rendering results. We are obliged to declare all aspects of our intended result *before* passing on the result to be acted upon.

Page fidelity is, therefore, not guaranteed between two conforming XSL rendering agents if we do not declare our formatting intent at a fine-enough granularity to accommodate differences in interpretation of our specifications. If we do not specify, for example, low-level hyphenation and justification rules, then two rendering agents could implement differing rules. Two conforming agents would then produce results of different lengths and differing page images.

Effecting the formatting of XML with XSL formatting semantics.
Our objective as XSL stylesheet writers is to create a transformation of instances of our vocabularies into instances using only the XSL vocabulary. An XSL rendering agent doesn't know how to render an element of type `<customer-number>` or what to do with an attribute named `display="indented"` as these represent semantics that we have divined for ourselves.

If the textual content of our `<customer-number>` element is to be rendered as a stand-alone paragraph with a boilerplate prefix and using italicized text of a given font size, we transform the element into an XSL construct such as would be serialized as `<block font-size="20pt" font-style="italic">` with the content of that block being a combination of the boilerplate and our source text.

The XSL rendering agent implements the XSL formatting semantics by recognizing our use of the XSL vocabulary. Any constructs of our own vocabulary would be nonsensical to the rendering agent. This is quite unlike CSS where we adorn our document tree with formatting properties a rendering agent finds attached to our own elements from our own vocabulary. A CSS rendering agent formats our decorated document trees according to the ornamental properties found for each element.

Intermediate result of rendering. Remembering that XSLT is primarily designed for use with XSL, we can now see why the normative result of XSLT transformation is merely the abstract result tree and not a physical XML entity of some kind. An XSL rendering agent with an integral XSLT processor can act on the result tree created by transformation, without needing to serialize that result tree as actual markup. The result tree is an intermediate result of the rendering process.

Nonetheless, serialization of the result tree as XML markup is *very* useful, particularly for diagnostic purposes. For those of us who do not write perfect results the first time, our results may not clearly indicate the problems we have in our transformations. Formatting and flow objects of the he XSL vocabulary are serialized as XML elements. Properties are reified as attribute/value pairs. By examining exactly what we have asked the rendering agent to act upon, we can determine how it differs from what we actually wanted.

Included in this annex. This annex briefly introduces the concepts and basic constructs used in an XSL Candidate Recommendation, without going into the details of the vocabulary or markup required to support these concepts. The topic of formatting objects and their semantics and markup warrants an entire book on its own and is thus separate from this material.

An end-to-end example illustrates the transformation of arbitrary XML to the XSL vocabulary.

B.1 Formatting model

B.1.1 Summary of formatting model components

XSL incorporates *most* of the formatting objects and properties of CSS.

- 90% of the XSL properties are properties already defined in CSS.
  - Some old CSS properties now represent a shorthand definition of a collection of properties offering finer control.
- New properties are introduced for a model for pagination and layout.

- They will be extended to page structures beyond the simple page models of the first version of the Recommendation.

Some properties are direction-independent.

- Some constructs can be specified with adjectives that are writing mode relative:
  - "before", "after", "start", and "end" vs. "top", "bottom", "left", and "right".
- Stylesheets need not change to accommodate different writing directions.
  - Resulting rendering is relative to writing direction.

The formatting model basics include:

- rectangular areas of content;
  - the content is flowed into the layout description;
  - future extensions to the model may include non-rectangular areas,
- spaces around and between content areas;
  - the spaces make adjustments to the layout and do not have content.

Area behavior:

- is specified by the stylesheet writer;
  - the stylesheet writer specifies areas and their traits using formatting objects and their properties,
- is managed by the formatter tasked with rendering the areas to the target device;
  - areas may be filled explicitly by the stylesheet writer;
    - traits are explicitly specified in the stylesheet properties;
  - areas may be filled implicitly by the formatter;
    - some traits are implicitly derived;
    - for example, if the stylesheet writer specifies a block that is filled with text, then the resulting line areas that comprise the block are synthesized by the formatter to accommodate the block;
    - the formatter manages inheritance when creating areas and must derive certain properties when synthesizing areas not specified explicitly by the stylesheet writer;
  - default values are included in the inheritance hierarchy.

Important notes:

- This design does not ensure page fidelity between two conforming implementations.

- The declarative nature gives implementations leeway in certain aspects of rendering not specified by the stylesheet writer.

There is a hierarchy of rectangular areas managed by the stylesheet writer and the formatter.

- An area container:
  - may contain block areas, display spaces, or nested area containers,
  - may be placed at a specific position within a containing area,
  - may be attached to the inside of any edge of a containing area.
- A block area:
  - is filled (perpendicular to the writing direction) with line areas (that are in the writing direction), display spaces, a graphic element, or nested block areas,
  - stacks nested block areas within the containing area without the ability to span across a container boundary.
- A line area:
  - is filled with inline areas and inline spaces,
  - is stacked in the block area with other line areas or display spaces.
- An inline area:
  - may contain other inline areas,
  - may have complex content (e.g.: an inline mathematical expression),
  - at its lowest level contains a single glyph area.

Each rectangular area has —

- a border surrounding the content of the area,
- padding defining the open space between the inside of the border and the content.

There are two kinds of space managed by the stylesheet writer and the formatter.

- A display space:
  - is assigned preceding and following line areas and block areas to control placement,
  - coalesces with adjacent display spaces according to resolution rules.
- An inline space:
  - is assigned preceding and following inline areas,
  - coalesces with adjacent inline spaces according to resolution rules.
- Resolution rules include:
  - the concept of conditionality — whether or not a space is to exist,
  - the concept of precedence — which aspect of space definition overrides others.

A simple illustration of rectangular areas is shown in Figure B–1.

B.2 Formatting objects

B.2.1 Formatting object vocabulary

Formatting and flow object vocabulary:

- are identified by namespace URI and version —

  `http://www.w3.org/1999/XSL/Format`

  - 56 different objects are defined:
    - pagination and layout,
    - block,
    - inline,
    - table,
    - list,
    - link and multi,
    - out-of-line,
    - other,

- may have attributes specified in stylesheet control properties of objects;

  - not all properties apply to all objects;

Figure B–1   Rectangular areas in XSL

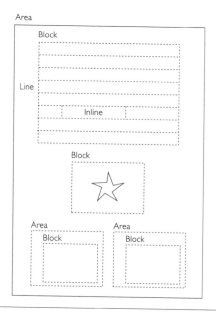

- 246 different properties are defined:
  - common accessibility properties,
  - common absolute position properties,
  - common aural properties,
  - common border, padding and background properties,
  - common font properties,
  - common hyphenation properties,
  - common keeps and breaks properties,
  - common margin properties — block,
  - common margin properties — inline,
  - pagination and layout properties,
  - table properties,
  - character properties,
  - rule and leader properties,
  - page-related properties,
  - float-related properties,
  - number to string conversion properties,
  - link properties,
  - miscellaneous properties.

B.3   Example stylesheet with formatting constructs

B.3.1   Example stylesheet with formatting constructs

The stylesheet `fmtsamp.xsl` illustrates an example of a stylesheet using the XSL formatting constructs for the result tree:

Example B–1   Sample stylesheet producing XSL result

```
Line 1  <?xml version="1.0"?>                                       <!--fmtsamp.xsl-->
     2  <!--XSLT 1.0 - http://www.CraneSoftwrights.com/training -->
     3  <xsl:stylesheet xmlns:xsl="http://www.w3.org/1999/XSL/Transform"
     4                  xmlns:fo="http://www.w3.org/1999/XSL/Format"
     5                  version="1.0">
     6  <xsl:output method="xml"/>
     7
     8              <!--Important note: http://www.w3.org/TR/2000/CR-xsl-20001121/
     9                  ... works with http://xml.apache.org/fop/ Version 0.15 -->
    10
    11  <xsl:param name="font-size" select="'20pt'"/>
    12
    13  <xsl:template match="/">                   <!--put all on in one page sequence-->
    14    <fo:root><fo:layout-master-set>
    15      <fo:simple-page-master master-name="crane"
    16                     margin-top=".5in" margin-bottom=".5in"
    17                     margin-left=".75in" margin-right=".75in"
    18                     page-width="8.5in" page-height="11in">
```

```
19        <fo:region-body region-name="crane-content"/>
20       </fo:simple-page-master></fo:layout-master-set>
21       <fo:page-sequence master-name="crane">
22       <fo:flow flow-name="crane-content" font-size="{$font-size}">
23         <xsl:apply-templates/>
24       </fo:flow></fo:page-sequence></fo:root></xsl:template>
25
26  <xsl:template match="para">                         <!--a standard paragraph-->
27    <fo:block space-before.optimum="{$font-size}">
28      <xsl:apply-templates/></fo:block></xsl:template>
29
30  <xsl:template match="emph">                         <!--emphasize some information-->
31    <fo:inline font-weight="bold">
32      <xsl:apply-templates/></fo:inline></xsl:template>
33
34  </xsl:stylesheet>
```

When processing the source file `fmtsamp.xml`:

Example B–2   Sample data file for XSL rendering

```
Line 1  <?xml version="1.0"?>
    2   <doc>
    3   <para>First paragraph.</para>
    4   <para>Second para <emph>with emphasis</emph> embedded.</para>
    5   <para>Last paragraph.</para>
    6   </doc>
```

Figure B–2   FOP rendering of sample XSL

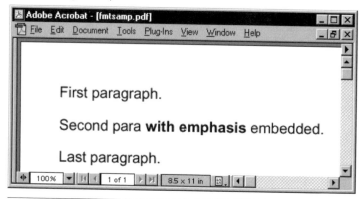

Produces the result file `fmtsamp.fo`:

Example B–3 XSL produced from sample data file

```
Line 1  <?xml version="1.0" encoding="utf-8"?>
     2  <fo:root xmlns:fo="http://www.w3.org/1999/XSL/Format">
     3  <fo:layout-master-set><fo:simple-page-master master-name="crane"
     4  margin-top=".5in" margin-bottom=".5in" margin-left=".75in"
     5  margin-right=".75in" page-width="8.5in" page-height="11in">
     6  <fo:region-body region-name="crane-content"/>
     7  </fo:simple-page-master></fo:layout-master-set>
     8  <fo:page-sequence master-name="crane">
     9  <fo:flow flow-name="crane-content" font-size="20pt">
    10  <fo:block space-before.optimum="20pt">First paragraph.</fo:block>
    11  <fo:block space-before.optimum="20pt">Second para <fo:inline
    12  font-weight="bold">with emphasis</fo:inline> embedded.</fo:block>
    13  <fo:block space-before.optimum="20pt">Last paragraph.</fo:block>
    14  </fo:flow></fo:page-sequence></fo:root>
```

Rendering to PDF using FOP `http://xml.apache.org/fop/` is shown in Figure B–2.

C

Instruction,
function,
and grammar
summaries

C   Instruction, function, and grammar summaries

The XSLT 1.0 Recommendation at `http://www.w3.org/TR/1999/REC-xslt-19991116` and XPath 1.0 Recommendation at `http://www.w3.org/TR/1999/REC-xpath-19991116` are excellent and rigorous references to the facilities and function of these two Recommendations.

This annex lists alphabetized references to the XSLT instruction elements and the XSLT and XPath built-in functions. Each entry notes the chapter in this book where the construct is primarily described.

Also included is a summary of the grammars for patterns and string expressions from XSLT and XPath, rendered with cross-references not found in the recommendations themselves.

C.1   Vocabulary and functions

C.1.1   XSLT instruction element summary

All elements in the XSLT vocabulary are listed below in alphabetical order, listing the specification section and the chapter in this book where the element is described:

- xsl:apply-imports
  - 5.6 Overriding Template Rules,
  - Chapter 6;
- xsl:apply-templates
  - 5.4 Applying Template Rules,
  - Chapter 4;
- xsl:attribute
  - 7.1.3 Creating Attributes with xsl:attribute,
  - Chapter 7;
- xsl:attribute-set
  - 7.1.4 Named Attribute Sets,
  - Chapter 7;
- xsl:call-template
  - 6 Named Templates,
  - Chapter 6,
  - Chapter 8;
- xsl:choose
  - 9.2 Conditional Processing with xsl:choose,
  - Chapter 7;
- xsl:comment
  - 7.4 Creating Comments,
  - Chapter 7;
- xsl:copy
  - 7.5 Copying,
  - Chapter 7;
- xsl:copy-of
  - 11.3 Using Values of Variables and Parameters with xsl:copy-of,
  - Chapter 7;
- xsl:decimal-format
  - 12.3 Number Formatting,
  - Chapter 8;
- xsl:element
  - 7.1.2 Creating Elements with xsl:element,
  - Chapter 7;
- xsl:fallback
  - 15 Fallback,
  - Chapter 6;
- xsl:for-each
  - 8 Repetition,

- Chapter 4;
- `xsl:if`
  - 9.1 Conditional Processing with `xsl:ifm`
  - Chapter 7;
- `xsl:import`
  - 2.6.2 Stylesheet Import,
  - Chapter 6;
- `xsl:include`
  - 2.6.1 Stylesheet Inclusion,
  - Chapter 6;
- `xsl:key`
  - 12.2 Keys,
  - Chapter 8;
- `xsl:message`
  - 13 Messages,
  - Chapter 5;
- `xsl:namespace-alias`
  - 7.1.1 Literal Result Elements,
  - Chapter 5;
- `xsl:number`
  - 7.7 Numbering,
  - Chapter 7;
- `xsl:otherwise`
  - 9.2 Conditional Processing with `xsl:choose`,
  - Chapter 7;
- `xsl:output`
  - 16 Output,
  - Chapter 5;
- `xsl:param`
  - 11 Variables and Parameters,
  - Chapter 6;
- `xsl:preserve-space`
  - 3.4 Whitespace Stripping,
  - Chapter 3;
- `xsl:processing-instruction`
  - 7.3 Creating Processing Instructions,
  - Chapter 7;
- `xsl:sort`
  - 10 Sorting,

C.1.2 XPath and XSLT function summary

All functions of both XPath and XSLT in alphabetical order, listing the Recommendation, the section, and the chapter in this book where the function is described (unless it is described in Chapter 8 as are most functions):

- XPath 4.4 Number Functions;
- concat()
  - XPath 4.2 String Functions;
- contains()
  - XPath 4.2 String Functions;
- count()
  - XPath 4.1 Node Set Functions;
- current()
  - XSLT 12.4 Miscellaneous Additional Functions;
- document()
  - XSLT 12.1 Multiple Source Documents;
- element-available()
  - XSLT 15 Fallback,
  - Chapter 6;
- false()
  - XPath 4.3 Boolean Functions;
- floor()
  - XPath 4.4 Number Functions;
- format-number()
  - XSLT 12.3 Number Formatting;
- function-available()
  - XSLT 15 Fallback
  - Chapter 6;
- generate-id()
  - XSLT 12.4 Miscellaneous Additional Functions;
- id()
  - XPath 4.1 Node Set Functions;
- key()
  - XSLT 12.2 Keys;
- lang()
  - XPath 4.3 Boolean Functions;
- last()
  - XPath 4.1 Node Set Functions,
  - Chapter 3;
- local-name()
  - XPath 4.1 Node Set Functions;
- name()

- XPath 4.1 Node Set Functions;
- `namespace-uri()`
  - XPath 4.1 Node Set Functions;
- `normalize-space()`
  - XPath 4.2 String Functions;
- `not()`
  - XPath 4.3 Boolean Functions;
- `number()`
  - XPath 4.4 Number Functions;
- `position()`
  - XPath 4.1 Node Set Functions;
  - Chapter 3
- `round()`
  - XPath 4.4 Number Functions;
- `starts-with()`
  - XPath 4.2 String Functions;
- `string()`
  - XPath 4.2 String Functions;
- `string-length()`
  - XPath 4.2 String Functions;
- `substring-after()`
  - XPath 4.2 String Functions;
- `substring-before()`
  - XPath 4.2 String Functions;
- `substring()`
  - XPath 4.2 String Functions;
- `sum()`
  - XPath 4.4 Number Functions;
- `system-property()`
  - XSLT 12.4 Miscellaneous Additional Functions,
  - Chapter 2;
- `translate()`
  - XPath 4.2 String Functions;
- `true()`
  - XPath 4.3 Boolean Functions;
- `unparsed-entity-uri()`
  - XSLT 12.4 Miscellaneous Additional Functions.

C.2 Grammars

Unlike the web-based published Recommendations, the following summaries of the two grammars include the numeric references of the productions being referenced in the right hand slide of each production.

C.2.1 XPath grammar productions

Location paths (2):

```
[1] LocationPath          ::= RelativeLocationPath[3]
                            | AbsoluteLocationPath[2]

[2] AbsoluteLocationPath ::= '/' RelativeLocationPath[3]?
                            | AbbreviatedAbsoluteLocationPath[10]

[3] RelativeLocationPath ::= Step[4]
                            | RelativeLocationPath[3] '/' Step[4]
                            | AbbreviatedRelativeLocationPath[11]
```

Location steps (2.1):

```
[4] Step          ::= AxisSpecifier[5] NodeTest[7] Predicate[8]*
                    | AbbreviatedStep[12]

[5] AxisSpecifier ::= AxisName[6] '::'
                    | AbbreviatedAxisSpecifier[13]
```

Axes (2.2):

```
[6] AxisName    ::= 'ancestor'
                  | 'ancestor-or-self'
                  | 'attribute'
                  | 'child'
                  | 'descendant'
                  | 'descendant-or-self'
                  | 'following'
                  | 'following-sibling'
                  | 'namespace'
                  | 'parent'
                  | 'preceding'
```

```
                        | 'preceding-sibling'
                        | 'self'
```

Node tests (2.3):

```
[7] NodeTest      ::= NameTest[37]
                    | NodeType[38] '(' ')'
                    | 'processing-instruction' '(' Literal[29] ')'
```

Predicates (2.4):

```
[8] Predicate     ::= '[' PredicateExpr[9] ']'

[9] PredicateExpr ::= Expr[14]
```

Abbreviated syntax (2.5):

```
[10] AbbreviatedAbsoluteLocationPath ::= '//' RelativeLocationPath[3]

[11] AbbreviatedRelativeLocationPath ::= RelativeLocationPath[3] '//'
                                         Step[4]

[12] AbbreviatedStep               ::= '.'
                                     | '..'

[13] AbbreviatedAxisSpecifier      ::= '@'?
```

Expression basics (3.1):

```
[14] Expr         ::= OrExpr[21]

[15] PrimaryExpr  ::= VariableReference[36]
                    | '(' Expr[14] ')'
                    | Literal[29]
                    | Number[30]
                    | FunctionCall[16]
```

Function calls (3.2):

```
[16] FunctionCall ::= FunctionName[35] '(' ( Argument[17] ( ','
                      Argument[17] )* )? ')'

[17] Argument     ::= Expr[14]
```

Node-sets (3.3):

[18] UnionExpr	::=	PathExpr[19]
		| UnionExpr[18] '|' PathExpr[19]

[19] PathExpr	::=	LocationPath[1]
		| FilterExpr[20]
		| FilterExpr[20] '/' RelativeLocationPath[3]
		| FilterExpr[20] '//' RelativeLocationPath[3]

[20] FilterExpr	::=	PrimaryExpr[15]
		| FilterExpr[20] Predicate[8]

Boolean expressions (3.4):

[21] OrExpr	::=	AndExpr[22]
		| OrExpr[21] 'or' AndExpr[22]

[22] AndExpr	::=	EqualityExpr[23]
		| AndExpr[22] 'and' EqualityExpr[23]

[23] EqualityExpr	::=	RelationalExpr[24]
		| EqualityExpr[23] '=' RelationalExpr[24]
		| EqualityExpr[23] '!=' RelationalExpr[24]

[24] RelationalExpr	::=	AdditiveExpr[25]
		| RelationalExpr[24] '<' AdditiveExpr[25]
		| RelationalExpr[24] '>' AdditiveExpr[25]
		| RelationalExpr[24] '<=' AdditiveExpr[25]
		| RelationalExpr[24] '>=' AdditiveExpr[25]

Numeric expressions (3.5):

[25] AdditiveExpr	::=	MultiplicativeExpr[26]
		| AdditiveExpr[25] '+' MultiplicativeExpr[26]
		| AdditiveExpr[25] '-' MultiplicativeExpr[26]

[26] MultiplicativeExpr	::=	UnaryExpr[27]
		| MultiplicativeExpr[26] MultiplyOperator[34] UnaryExpr[27]
		| MultiplicativeExpr[26] 'div' UnaryExpr[27]
		| MultiplicativeExpr[26] 'mod' UnaryExpr[27]

[27] UnaryExpr	::=	UnionExpr[18]
		| '-' UnaryExpr[27]

Lexical structure (3.7):

[28] ExprToken	::=	`'(' | ')'	'['	']'	'.'	'..'	'@'`
		`	','	'::'`
		`| NameTest[37]`
		`| NodeType[38]`
		`| Operator[32]`
		`| FunctionName[35]`
		`| AxisName[6]`
		`| Literal[29]`
		`| Number[30]`
		`| VariableReference[36]`
[29] Literal	::=	`'"' [^"]* '"'`
		`| "'" [^']* "'"`
[30] Number	::=	`Digits[31] ('.' Digits[31]?)?`
		`| '.' Digits[31]`
[31] Digits	::=	`[0-9]+`
[32] Operator	::=	`OperatorName[33]`
		`| MultiplyOperator[34]`
		`| '/'	'//'	'|'	'+'	'-'	'=' |`
		`'!='	'<'	'<='	'>'	'>='`
[33] OperatorName	::=	`'and'	'or'	'mod'	'div'`
[34] MultiplyOperator	::=	`'*'`
[35] FunctionName	::=	`QName[XML-Names-6] - NodeType[38]`
[36] VariableReference	::=	`'$' QName[XML-Names-6]`
[37] NameTest	::=	`'*'`
		`| NCName[XML-Names-4] ':' '*'`
		`| QName[XML-Names-6]`
[38] NodeType	::=	`'comment'`
		`| 'text'`
		`| 'processing-instruction'`
		`| 'node'`
[39] ExprWhitespace	::=	`S[XML-3]`

C.2.2 XSLT grammar productions

Patterns (5.2):

[1] Pattern	::=	LocationPathPattern[2] | Pattern[1] '|' LocationPathPattern[2]
[2] LocationPathPattern	::=	'/' RelativePathPattern[4]? | IdKeyPattern[3] (('/' | '//') RelativePathPattern[4])? | '//'? RelativePathPattern[4]
[3] IdKeyPattern	::=	'id' '(' Literal[XPath-29] ')' | 'key' '(' Literal[XPath-29] ',' Literal[XPath-29] ')'
[4] RelativePathPattern	::=	StepPattern[5] | RelativePathPattern[4] '/' StepPattern[5] | RelativePathPattern[4] '//' StepPattern[5]
[5] StepPattern	::=	ChildOrAttributeAxisSpecifier[6] NodeTest[XPath-7] Predicate[XPath-8]*
[6] ChildOrAttributeAxisSpecifier	::=	AbbreviatedAxisSpecifier[XPath-13] | ('child' | 'attribute') '::'

D

Sample
tool
information

D Sample tool information

For those who are new to XSLT, choosing a particular processor tool or product may seem a daunting task. There are a number of areas of interpretation or choice where an XSLT processor can behave in different fashions.

Answers to the following questions may prove useful when trying to better understand an XSLT product offering from a vendor. The specific questions are grouped under topical questions. This by no means makes up a complete list of questions as you may have your own criteria to add, nonetheless, they do cover aspects of XSLT that may impact on the stylesheets and transformation specifications you write.

- How is the product identified?
    - What is the name of the XSLT processor in product literature?
    - What value is returned by the `xsl:vendor` system property?
    - What value is returned by the `xsl:vendor-url` system property?
    - What version of XSLT is supported (also returned by the `xsl:version` system property)?
    - To which email address or URL are questions forwarded for more information in general?

- To which email address or URL are questions forwarded for more information specific to the answers to these technical questions?
- What output serialization methods are supported for the result node tree?
  - XML?
  - HTML?
  - Text?
  - XSL formatting and flow objects?
    - In what ways are the formatting objects interpreted (direct to screen? HTML? PostScript? PDF? TEX? etc.)?
  - Other non-XML text-oriented methods different than the standard text method (e.g. NXML by XT)?
    - What are the semantics and vocabulary for each such environment?
  - Other custom serialization methods?
    - What are the semantics and vocabulary for each such environment?
  - What customization is available to implement one's own interpretation of result tree semantics?
    - Is there access to the result tree as either a DOM tree or SAX events?
    - Does such access still oblige serialization to an external file?
- How does the processor differ from the W3C working drafts or recommendations?
  - Upon which dated W3C documents describing XSL, XSLT and XPath is the software based?
  - Which constructs or functions are not implemented at all?
  - Which constructs or functions are implemented differently than in the W3C description?
  - What namespace URI values are used for those available constructs or functions described differently or not described in W3C version?
  - Is the W3C recommended stylesheet association technique implemented for the direct processing XML instances?
    - If so, can it be selectively engaged and disengaged?
- Are any extension functions or extension elements implemented?
  - What is the recognized extension namespace and the utility of the extension functions and elements implemented?
    - Is there an extension function for the conversion of a result tree fragment to a node-set?
    - Are there any built-in extension functions or extension elements for the writing of templates to an output URL?
      - Is the XT-defined extension element `<document>` and associated namespace explicitly supported?
  - Can additional extension functions or extension elements (beyond those supplied by the vendor) be added by the user?
    - How so?

- ## How are particular XSLT facilities implemented?
  - What is the implementation in the processor of `indent="yes"` for `<xsl:output>`?
  - Is a method provided for defining top-level `<xsl:param>` constructs?
  - What are the lexical patterns implemented for the `generate-id()` function?
    - Does the processor accommodate explicit `ID` values that would otherwise conflict with generated values?
  - How is the `<xsl:message>` construct implemented?
  - Which UCS/Unicode format tokens are supported for `<xsl:number>`?
  - Which `lang=` values are supported for `<xsl:sort>`?

- ## How are XSLT errors handled?
  - Are the errors reported or gracefully handled —
    - regarding template conflict resolution?
    - regarding improper content of result tree nodes (e.g. comments, processing instructions)?
    - regarding invocation of unimplemented functions or features?
    - regarding any other areas?
  - Can fatal error reporting (e.g. template conflict resolution or other errors) be selectively turned on to diagnose stylesheets targeted for use with other XSLT processors that fail on an error?

- ## What are the details of the implementation and invocation of the XSLT processor?
  - Which hardware/operating system platforms support the processor?
  - Which character sets are supported for the input file encoding and output serialization?
  - What is the XML processor used within the XSLT processor?
    - Does the XML processor support minimally declared internal declaration subsets with only attribute list declarations of `ID`-typed attributes?
    - Does the XML processor support XML Inclusions (Xinclude)?
    - Does the XML processor support catalogues for public identifiers?
    - Does the XML processor validate the source file?
      - Can this be turned on and off?
  - Can the processor be embedded in other applications?
    - Can the processor be configured as a servlet in a web server?
    - Is there access to the result tree as either a DOM tree or SAX events?
  - Is the source code of the processor available?
    - In what language is the processor written?
  - For Windows-based environments:
    - Can the processor be invoked from the MS DOS command-line box?
    - Can the processor be invoked from a GUI interface?
    - What other methods of invocation can be triggered (DLL, RPC, etc.)?
    - Can error messages be explicitly redirected to a file using an invocation parameter (since, for example, Windows 95 does not allow for redirection of the standard error port to a file)?

- Does the processor take advantage of parallelism when executing the stylesheet, or is the stylesheet always processed serially?
- Does the processor implement tail recursion for called named templates?

Included in this annex. The first XSLT processor publicly available is written by James Clark, the editor of the XSLT Recommendation and co-editor of the XPath Recommendation. This annex includes installation and invocation information for XT, and overviews how James provides extensibility in implementations of extension elements (instructions), functions, and serialization methods.

The first browser-based XSLT processor publicly available is Internet Explorer 5 by Microsoft. Very early releases support only an archaic dialect of XSLT/XPath working drafts, while later releases support the mature Recommendations much more closely. To date, releases have provided little or no access to the intermediate result of transformation when rendering using HTML. This annex includes Windows-based scripts for stand-alone XSLT processing useful both for diagnostics and for static page generation compatible with the browser-based transformations. Also included is an example ASP script illustrating server-side delivery of the result of transforming an XML document with an XSLT stylesheet.

D.1 James Clark's XT

Mr. James Clark has long been one of the most, of not *the* most, generous contributors of time, effort and free software related to markup technologies and publishing. He is the editor of the XSLT 1.0 Recommendation and co-editor of the XPath 1.0 Recommendation. His test bed for XSLT concepts, written in numerous releases during the development of the Recommendation, is named XT.

D.1.1   XT differences from W3C XSLT/XPath Recommendations

This is a Java-based implementation of XSLT and XPath that:

- is described in detail in the information file:
    `http://www.jclark.com/xml/xt.html`
- follows the XSL Transformations Recommendation very closely with few exceptions (noted in detail in the information file);

- notably, there is no implementation of `<xsl:key>`,
- does not interpret the XSL Formatting Object vocabulary,
- does not report very many kinds of errors and will recover silently in many areas,
- is acknowledged by the author to be only a beta release,
- is documented regarding how to be used as a servlet,
- is available with full source code,
- is available as a Windows executable dependent only on the Microsoft Java Virtual Machine.

Although a few of the more esoteric features are not implemented, the tool can be used for most typical uses of the XSLT Recommendation.

XT includes implementations of element, function and serialization method extensions illustrating the extensibility of the XSLT language.

A support site dedicated to XT is at `http://www.4xt.org/`.

D.1.2 Extension element: Multiple output documents

An extension element in an XSLT stylesheet attempts to invoke an extension instruction supported by the XSLT processor executing the stylesheet. Extension elements are distinguished from literal result elements by the declaration in the stylesheet that the namespace used for the element is an extension (see Chapter 5).

XT supports an extension instruction named `<prefix:document>` in stylesheets to direct the instruction's template to a specific output document's result tree for serialization. We can execute as many of these instructions as we need output files, each file created contains the instruction's template as its content.

In the instruction or somewhere earlier in the hierarchy, the namespace prefix to XT must be declared as an extension element prefix. The following assertions must, therefore, be made for the instruction to be recognized:

Example D–1   The use of XT's `<document>` element

Line 1 `xmlns:prefix="http://www.jclark.com/xt"`
2 `extension-element-prefixes="prefix"`

```
3    <prefix:document href="output-URL-location">
4      template_serialized_to_output_location
5    </prefix:document>
```

Comment   The attributes on lines 1 and 2 must be declared either in the `<document>` element or in one of its ancestors.

The other attributes allowed in `<prefix:document>` are the same attributes allowed in `<xsl:output>` (see Chapter 5 again) and have the same semantics and level of support implemented in XT. Only the `href=` attribute is required; all other attributes are optional.

Consider the need to create a number of inter-linked HTML documents from a single XML source as in this following example.

- The content of each HTML file comes from portions of the source tree.
- The XML use of `ID` and `IDREF` typed attributes ensure self-referentially correct linking in the source.
  - `<link idref="doc2"/>` is a link to document 2 found in the content portion of document 1.
  - `<linkend id="doc2"/>` is the target of the link and is found in document 2.
- The corresponding emission of the links must create HTML hyperlink (anchor) markup utilizing the document identifiers from ancestral elements.
  - `<a href="multhtm2.htm#doc2">` is needed in the generated `multhtml.htm` as the source.
  - `<a name="doc2">` is needed in `multhtm2.htm` as the target.

Example D–2   A file describing multiple files

```
Line 1   <?xml version="1.0"?>
2   <!DOCTYPE test [
3   <!ATTLIST linkend id ID #REQUIRED>
4   ]>
5   <test>
6   <doc file="multhtml.htm">
7   <head><title>Test Output 1</title></head>
8   <body><linkend id="doc1"/>
9   <p>This is a link to <link idref="doc2"/>
10  from document 1.</p>
11  </body>
12  </doc>
13  <doc file="multhtm2.htm">
14  <head><title>Test Output 2</title></head>
15  <body><linkend id="doc2"/>
16  <p>This is a link to <link idref="doc1"/>
```

```
17   from document 2.</p>
18   </body>
19   </doc>
20   </test>
```

Line 3 is an internal declaration subset informing the XSLT processor that the id= attribute of the element <linkend> is of XML type ID. This ensures the node for the element is assigned a unique identifier for referencing purposes in the source node tree.

The two document descriptions are contained, respectively, in the elements starting on lines 6 and 13. Each container element specifies the filename to be created in the file= attribute. The content of each container element is the HTML vocabulary to be used in the result, with the exception of the customized linking elements.

Two <link> elements are on lines 9 and 16. These links make reference to, respectively, the <linkend> elements on lines 15 and 8. These links make the one input file referentially complete. Though more than one output file is described, our links in this input file are properly and fully described.

The following XSL source multhtm.xsl utilizes XT's extension instruction and creates the described hyperlinked files:

Example D–3 A stylesheet using an extension element

```
Line 1  <?xml version="1.0"?>                                    <!--multhtm.xsl-->
2   <!--XSLT 1.0 - http://www.CraneSoftwrights.com/training -->
3   <xsl:stylesheet xmlns:xsl="http://www.w3.org/1999/XSL/Transform"
4                   version="1.0"
5                   xmlns:xt="http://www.jclark.com/xt"
6                   extension-element-prefixes="xt">
7
8   <xsl:template match="/">
9     <xsl:for-each select="//doc">                <!--copy documents out as HTML-->
10      <xt:document method="html" href="{@file}">
11        <html>
12          <xsl:apply-templates select="*"/>
13        </html>
14      </xt:document>
15    </xsl:for-each>
16  </xsl:template>
17
18  <xsl:template match="link">                    <!--create link to other document-->
19    <a href="{id(@idref)/ancestor::doc/@file}#{@idref}">
```

```
20        <xsl:value-of select="@idref"/>
21      </a>
22    </xsl:template>
23
24    <xsl:template match="linkend">                    <!--create anchor for links-->
25      <a name="{@id}"/>
26    </xsl:template>
27                                                      <!--all other elements just copied-->
28    <xsl:template match="*|@*">
29      <xsl:copy>
30        <xsl:apply-templates select="*|@*|text()"/>
31      </xsl:copy>
32    </xsl:template>
33
34    </xsl:stylesheet>
```

The XSLT container element informs the processor of a number of items: the namespace for XSLT instructions on line 3, the version of XSLT required on line 4, the prefix and namespace for XT extension instructions on line 5, and the indication on line 6 that the XT prefix is to be interpreted as an instruction because it is used for extension elements.

Lines 8 through 16 describe the template rule for the root node. Each of the document descriptions in the input file are accessed with the `<xsl:for-each>` on line 9. The first element in the template is an instruction from the XT extension namespace, thus the XSLT processor is asked to execute the instruction for each of the `<doc>` nodes of the source tree.

The `<document>` instruction on line 10 writes the enclosed template to the resource named in the `href=` attribute. This is obtained from the `file=` attribute of the `<doc>` element (the current focus of the `<xsl:for-each>`). The enclosed template in lines 11 through 13 describes an HTML file whose contents are the processed contents of the `<doc>` source node.

The following two template rules accommodate the presence of `<link>` and `<linkend>` elements in the source node tree. The start of a link becomes a hyperlinking `<a>` anchor with an `href=` attribute specified on line 19. This expression is two attribute value templates with an octothorp in between. The left expression evaluates to the file name of the target by navigating first to the node of the target, then to the ancestor named "doc", then from there to the attribute named "file". The right expression evaluates to the attribute named "idref". The three components together make up the complete URI for the named HTML anchor of the target in the target file. The displayed content of the linking anchor is the content of the <link> element itself.

The template rule in lines 24 through 25 is for the end of the link. The template adds to the result tree the empty named <a> anchor that is the target for the hyperlink. Note that this is added regardless of whether or not there is a hyperlinking construct pointing to it.

The "catch-all" template rule in lines 28 through 32 copies to the result tree all other element and attribute nodes found in the source tree, thus copying the source node tree to the result node tree. Processing instructions and comments, if they existed in the source, would not be copied to the result.

Each output file is produced containing the link to the other, as in the first document:

Example D–4   The first output file produced

```
Line 1   <html>
     2   <head>
     3   <title>Test Output 1</title>
     4   </head>
     5   <body>
     6   <a name="doc1"></a>
     7   <p>This is a link to <a href="multhtm2.htm#doc2">doc2</a>
     8   from document 1.</p>
     9   </body>
    10   </html>
```

And as in the second document:

Example D–5   The second output file produced

```
Line 1   <html>
     2   <head>
     3   <title>Test Output 2</title>
     4   </head>
     5   <body>
     6   <a name="doc2"></a>
     7   <p>This is a link to <a href="multhtml.htm#doc1">doc1</a>
     8   from document 2.</p>
```

```
 9   </body>
10   </html>
```

D.1.3   Extension functions: Node set manipulation

An extension function in an XSLT stylesheet attempts to invoke functionality supported by the XSLT processor executing the stylesheet. Extension functions are identified by the use of a namespace to name the function uniquely (see Chapter 6). Extension functions can be used in an XPath expression anywhere where XPath and XSLT functions are allowed.

XSLT does not support operations on result tree fragments; such expressions can only be added to the result tree as created. Result tree fragments may contain references to source tree nodes as well. XT supports three extension functions to generate and manipulate node-sets:

Example D–6   XT's node manipulation extension functions

```
Line 1   xmlns:prefix="http://www.jclark.com/xt"
     2   prefix:node-set(result-tree-fragment-or-node-set)
     3   prefix:intersection(first-node-set,second-node-set)
     4   prefix:difference(first-node-set,second-node-set)
```

Comment   the attribute on line 1 must be in the element or the hierarchy of the element that uses the functions described in lines 2, 3 and 4

The `node-set()` function shown on line 2 converts a result tree fragment into an unnamed singleton node (quite like a root node) created as if the nodes of the result tree were source nodes existing as children of the unnamed node. This singleton node can be processed by the stylesheet as can any node from the source tree.

The `intersection()` function on line 3 returns a node set whose members are found in *both* the first node set argument and the second node set argument.

The `difference()` function on line 4 returns a node set whose members are those from the first node set argument that are *not* also in the second node set argument.

The members of the return sets are in document order, as is true with all sets of source tree nodes.

The stylesheet xtnodes.xsl illustrates the use of all three:

Example D–7 An illustration of using XT's node extension functions

```
Line 1  <?xml version="1.0"?>                                        <!--xtnodes.xsl-->
     2  <!--XSLT 1.0 - http://www.CraneSoftwrights.com/training -->
     3  <!DOCTYPE xsl:stylesheet [
     4  <!ENTITY nl "&#xd;&#xa;">
     5  ]>
     6  <xsl:stylesheet xmlns:xsl="http://www.w3.org/1999/XSL/Transform"
     7                  xmlns:xt="http://www.jclark.com/xt"
     8                  version="1.0">
     9  <xsl:output method="text"/>
    10
    11  <xsl:template match="/">                                        <!--root rule-->
    12    <xsl:variable name="data">                      <!--a fragment with 4 elements-->
    13      <a>The A element</a><b>The B element</b>
    14      <c>The C element</c><d>The D element</d>
    15    </xsl:variable>
    16                 <!--process children of the node returned by the function-->
    17    <xsl:for-each select="xt:node-set($data)/*">
    18      <xsl:value-of select="."/><xsl:text>&nl;</xsl:text>
    19    </xsl:for-each>
    20              <!--determine intersection and difference using two children-->
    21    <xsl:text>Intersection:</xsl:text><xsl:text>&nl;</xsl:text>
    22    <xsl:for-each select="xt:intersection(xt:node-set($data)/*,
    23                          xt:node-set($data)/b|
    24                          xt:node-set($data)/c)">
    25      <xsl:value-of select="."/><xsl:text>&nl;</xsl:text>
    26    </xsl:for-each>
    27    <xsl:text>Difference:</xsl:text><xsl:text>&nl;</xsl:text>
    28    <xsl:for-each select="xt:difference(xt:node-set($data)/*,
    29                          xt:node-set($data)/b|
    30                          xt:node-set($data)/c)">
    31      <xsl:value-of select="."/><xsl:text>&nl;</xsl:text>
    32    </xsl:for-each>
    33  </xsl:template>
    34
    35  </xsl:stylesheet>
```

Line 4 is an internal declaration subset defining a useful entity for indicating a new line in an MSDOS window. For non-MSDOS environments, a simple
 should be sufficient for indicating a new line.

The extension namespace is declared on line 7 and need not be declared specifically as an extension namespace as is required for extension elements. It is sufficient just to use the namespace as a qualified name for function invocation.

The result tree fragment being manipulated is defined in lines 13 and 14 and assigned to the $data variable. The first operation performed on the result tree fragment is on line 17 where the variable is converted to a node set using *prefix*:node-set(): the result is an unnamed node with the result tree fragment elements as children of that node. To display each of the nodes, the <xsl:for-each> renders the value of each node on a new line.

The second operation performed on the tree is the intersection of two node sets using *prefix*:intersection() on lines 22 through 24. The first argument supplied is all of the children of the node set. The second argument is the union of the <b> child and <c> child of the node set. The intersection of these two are the <b> and <c> children and they are each displayed on a new line.

The third operation is the difference of two node sets using *prefix*:difference() on lines 28 through 30. The first argument supplied is all of the children of the node set. The second argument is the union of the <b> child and <c> child of the node set. The difference of these two are the <a> and <d> children and they are each displayed on a new line.

The listing above indicates the successful outcome of the expectations described for the stylesheet.

D.1.4 Extension functions: Java library access

Many programmers are familiar with the Java runtime library and the facilities available therein to return and manipulate information. XT offers access to the Java library through namespace URI values that are patterned to reference the packages of Java classes.

The Java platform has a number of packages of classes that are formally described at:

- http://java.sun.com/products/jdk/1.2/docs/api/index.html
  - each package has a name, e.g.: "io";
  - each class in each package has a name, e.g.: "File".

XT provides access to the methods in a class by declaring a namespace prefix whose associated URI points to the class; access to the functions then uses the method names within that namespace as in the following example for the class above:

- xmlns:*prefix*="http://www.jclark.com/xt/java/java.io.File"
  - points to the File class in the io package;
- *prefix*:new(*string*)
  - returns a File object with the given string as the file name;
- *prefix*:exists(*File-object*)
  - returns true or false if the file exists or not.

Consider a stylesheet that reads an instance of file names and reports whether or not the given files exist:

Example D-8   An illustration of XT access to Java functions

```
                                                          <!--exists.xsl-->
Line 1  <?xml version="1.0"?>
2  <!--XSLT 1.0 - http://www.CraneSoftwrights.com/training -->
3  <!DOCTYPE xsl:stylesheet [ <!ENTITY nl "&#xd;&#xa;"> ]>
4  <xsl:stylesheet version="1.0"
5          xmlns:xsl="http://www.w3.org/1999/XSL/Transform"
6          xmlns:file="http://www.jclark.com/xt/java/java.io.File">
7
8  <xsl:output method="text"/>
9
10  <xsl:template match="/">
11    <xsl:if test="not( function-available('file:exists') and
12                       function-available('file:new') )">
13      <xsl:message terminate="yes">
14        <xsl:text>Required Java file facilities </xsl:text>
15        <xsl:text>are not available</xsl:text>
16      </xsl:message>
17    </xsl:if>
18    <xsl:for-each select="//file">              <!--process each file-->
19      <xsl:text>File </xsl:text><xsl:value-of select="."/>
20      <xsl:text>: </xsl:text>                   <!--display file name-->
21      <xsl:choose>                              <!--report existence-->
22        <xsl:when test="file:exists(file:new(string(.)))">
23          <xsl:text>exists&nl;</xsl:text>
24        </xsl:when>
25        <xsl:otherwise>
26          <xsl:text>does not exist&nl;</xsl:text>
27        </xsl:otherwise>
28      </xsl:choose>
29    </xsl:for-each>
30  </xsl:template>
```

```
31
32  </xsl:stylesheet>
```

Line 3 contains an internal declaration subset defining a useful entity for indicating a new line in an MSDOS window. For non-MSDOS environments, a simple
 should be sufficient for indicating a new line.

The namespace prefix for functions from the `File` class of the `io` package is declared on line 6. The prefix `file:` can now be used to reference any of the methods in that class.

Lines 11 and 12 check the existence of the required functions. The message on lines 13 through 16 will be displayed and the stylesheet will halt (according to the attribute on line 13) if the functions are not available.

This stylesheet calls the *prefix*:`exists()` function and *prefix*:`new()` function on line 22, determining whether or not the file name obtained from the source file exists or not. Note that the file name in the source tree is the value of the current node: the node itself cannot be passed to the `new()` function, only a string, thus the XSLT `string(.)` function returns the string value of the current node (or the first of whatever nodes are described in the XPath expression argument).

Consider executing the stylesheet on the `exists.xml` source file:

Example D–9   Sample input data for Example D–8

```
Line 1  <?xml version="1.0"?>
2  <files>
3  <file>exists.xml</file>
4  <file>exists.junk</file>
5  <file>exists.xsl</file>
6  </files>
```

The following is the result of executing the stylesheet:

Example D–10   Executing Example D–8 on Example D–9

```
Line 1  X:\samp>xt exists.xml exists.xsl
2  File exists.xml: exists
3  File exists.junk: does not exist
4  File exists.xsl: exists
```

```
5
6   X:\samp>
```

This execution reveals that the file `exists.junk` does not exist in the directory where the files `exists.xml` and `exists.xsl` reside.

D.1.5   Extension method: Non-XML serialization

An XSLT stylesheet using an extension serialization method requests that the result tree be emitted following conventions programmed into the XSLT processor. One uses a namespace-qualified name to identify the extension method uniquely (see Chapter 5).

- A method named "nxml" is requested using the extension namespace URI for XT:

  - `xmlns:prefix="http://www.jclark.com/xt"`
  - `method="prefix:nxml"`

- This method creates the result tree which conforms to a simple document model:

Example D–11   Document model for NXML vocabulary

```
Line 1   <!ELEMENT nxml (escape*, (control | data)*)>           <!--document elem.-->
     2                  <!--tell XT which characters to escape when found in <data>-->
     3   <!ELEMENT escape (#PCDATA | char)*>
     4   <!ATTLIST escape char CDATA #REQUIRED>                 <!--character value-->
     5                  <!--information in <data> is escaped by XT when necessary-->
     6   <!ELEMENT data    (#PCDATA | data | control)*>
     7                  <!--all information in <control> is passed untouched by XT-->
     8   <!ELEMENT control (#PCDATA | char | data | control)*>
     9   <!ELEMENT char EMPTY>                        <!--emit a single character by XT-->
    10   <!ATTLIST char number NMTOKEN #REQUIRED>               <!--character value-->
```

To create raw text output from an XML file source, transform the source into a result tree instance according to the Non-XML document model and XT will interpret that instance into a stream of text characters using the character set indicated by the `encoding=` attribute (if present) used in the `<xsl:output>` element.

This is different than the raw `method="text"` output method that is part of XSLT in that it provides a customizable escaping mechanism for characters the stylesheet writer deems to be sensitive, the control over which content is subject to escaping, and the ability to emit arbitrary code points.

- Element type `nxml` (line 1).

  - This is the required document element of the result tree. The output method will not serialize a result tree that uses any other document element type.

- Element type `escape` (lines 2–4).

  - The writer of the instance must declare all "sensitive" characters, those being the ones the NXML serialization software must check for when serializing certain text nodes. One declaration is made using a single `<escape>` element for each such character. There can be as many sensitive characters as desired, but they must all be declared at the start of the document element's content, before any other content of the result.

    The serialization software will check for sensitive characters in the text content of `<data>` elements in the result tree. The text content of `<control>` elements in the result tree is not checked for such characters.

    Each declaration identifies in the `char=` attribute the character considered to be sensitive. When sensitive characters are being checked, the text content of the `<escape>` element is the sequence to be emitted by the serialization software in place of the declared character.

- Element type `data` (lines 5–6).

  - The text content of all `<data>` elements is checked for sensitive characters. Any character not declared at the start of the result to be sensitive is emitted in clear text. Even when a character sensitive to XML (such as the built-in character general entities) is part of the content, the rules for escaping are as declared in the result, not as defined in XML.

    Of course the source documents must still use built-in character general entities for sensitive XML characters because all inputs are well-formed XML.

- Element type `control` (lines 7–8).

  - The text content of all `<control>` elements is emitted in clear text, regardless of the sensitive nature of the characters contained therein.

- Element type `char` (lines 9–10)

  - The `<char>` empty element is used to emit a single character to the output. The code-point value of the character is the number expressed in the `number=` attribute. This attribute is an attribute value template, thus it is possible to algorithmically calculate the character code.

    This is most useful for emitting characters that are *not* valid XML characters, since it is impossible to instantiate these characters in the source documents. For example, the line feed character (hex 0a) is a valid XML character, but the form feed character (hex 0c) is not. Indeed, most of the control characters defined below hex 20 are not valid in an XML file, so they cannot be specified in either a source file or a stylesheet file.

Consider the following stylesheet using the XT NXML serialization method:

Example D–12   An illustration of using NXML

```
Line 1  <?xml version="1.0"?>                                      <!--nxml.xsl-->
   2    <!--XSLT 1.0 - http://www.CraneSoftwrights.com/training -->
   3    <!--XT (see http://www.jclark.com/xml/xt.html)-->
   4    <xsl:stylesheet xmlns:xsl="http://www.w3.org/1999/XSL/Transform"
   5                    version="1.0">
   6
   7                  <!--encoding attribute from suffix of sun.io.ByteToCharLatin1-->
   8    <xsl:output method="xt:nxml"
   9               encoding="Latin1"
  10               xmlns:xt="http://www.jclark.com/xt"/>
  11
  12    <xsl:template match="/">                            <!--kind of text being produced-->
  13      <nxml>
  14        <escape char="\">\\</escape>                        <!--escape any back slashes-->
  15        <data><xsl:apply-templates/></data>                   <!--translate <data>-->
  16      </nxml>
  17    </xsl:template>
  18
  19    <xsl:template match="Name|Address">                       <!--prefix information-->
  20      <xsl:value-of select="name(.)"/>: <xsl:value-of select="."/>
  21    </xsl:template>
  22
  23    <xsl:template match="charValue">                  <!--don't translate <control>-->
  24      <control><xsl:text>\</xsl:text>
  25            <xsl:value-of select="@val"/>-<char number="{@val}"/>
  26            <xsl:text>\</xsl:text>
  27      </control>
  28    </xsl:template>
  29
  30    </xsl:stylesheet>
```

Lines 8 and 10 engage the use of the customized serialization environment. Note that the declaration on line 9 asks the processor to serialize using a particular character set (see Section D.1.6 for the discussion on XT's use of character sets for output serialization).

Lines 13 and 16 satisfy the method's requirement that the document element of the result be <nxml>. Line 14 declares that only one character is a sensitive character that needs escaping. Line 15 packages the processing of the source document inside of a `<data>` element, thus assuming that all input data is subject to being escaped.

Name and address information is reported using the template in lines 19 to 21.

The source file's `<charValue>` element puts out a string of text representing the given character value. This string is not to be escaped on output, thus, the string is added to the result tree inside a `<control>` element. The string emitted for each such input character is the numeric value as passed in the argument, followed by a dash, followed by the character whose code point is the given value.

Line 5 of this source file includes a number of characters of interest. Two of the characters are "<" and "&", entered using XML built-in general entities. A single backslash character is between these, and since it is the escaped character, it must be handled accordingly by the output method. An explicit character value defined by its numeric attribute is also included on the line.

Here we see line 5 of the source file output to line 3 of the result. The XML-sensitive characters are emitted in clear text, while the `<charValue>` element produces the required string.

D.1.6   Character encoding for the serialized result

For output serialization methods other than XML, XT supports the user specification of `encoding=` in `<xsl:output>` (as described in Chapter 5). However, XT can only use a set of values described by the Java environment in which XT is being run; thus, the same XT code will behave differently depending on the Java virtual machine the operator is using.

When the user does not specify a value, the assumption is that the default character set for the Java virtual machine.

A specified value is assumed to be a suffix to the string `sun.io.ByteToChar` that represents the name of a Java class in the virtual machine. The classes with this prefix are responsible for converting abstract characters into a string of bytes according to the particular character set supported by the class. Two examples of such classes, which happen to reference the same character set encoding using two different names, are `sun.io.ByteToCharISO8859_1.class` and `sun.io.ByteToChar-Latin1.class`.

The presence of these example classes dictates the ability to support, respectively, `encoding="ISO8859_1"` and `encoding="Latin1"`. XT will exit with an error if the encoding requested is not supported. On Microsoft Windows NT, both Sun's Java Runtime Environment (JRE) and Microsoft's Java Virtual Machine support "`Latin1`", but only the JRE supports "`ISO8859_1`".

To determine which encoding values are supported by a particular Java virtual machine, review a listing of the methods in the class libraries in alphabetical order to group all available classes contiguously. This may be found under either the name "`sun.io.ByteToChar`" or the name `ByteToChar` in the class subdirectory "`/sun/io`".

D.1.7 Invoking XT

Using XT as a Java program. The complete source and invocation documentation for XT is available at:

- `http://www.jclark.com/xml/xt.html`

One can use any Simple API for XML (SAX) driver, though such a driver is supplied for use with the XP processor (XP itself is not supplied with XT); for example, the following files would need to be found on the class path:

- `xt.jar`
  - from `http://www.jclark.com/xml/xt.html`
- `xp.jar`
  - from `http://www.jclark.com/xml/xp/index.html`
- `sax.jar`
  - from `http://www.megginson.com/SAX/SAX1/index.html`

A sample invocation batch file using the Java runtime environment JRE is as follows (this file can be found in the `/prog` directory of the sample files):

Example D–13   An example invocation batch file for XT

```
Line 1   @echo off
     2   REM xsljavaxt.bat
     3   REM check arguments: %1=source XML, %2=script XSL, %3=result XML
     4   REM environment: SET jclark=p:\jclark\
     5   jre -cp "%jclark%xt.jar;%jclark%sax.jar;%jclark%xp.jar" ^
     6       com.jclark.xsl.sax.Driver %1 %2 %3
     7   REM post-process results
```

Comment   Line 6 is a continuation of line 5; Windows'NT supports the line continuation character '^' but on other versions of Windows the character must be removed and the two lines joined to make one.

Note how on line 5 in the above example, the invocation file is expecting the environment variable named `jclark` to be set to the directory in which the required `.jar` files are found (commented out in line 4):

```
set jclark=directory-with-.jar-files
```

- Note the trailing directory separator character must be included in the value.
- This is not obligatory as the invocation file can be changed to specify the locations of the `.jar` files explicitly.

Note also that the invocation file is not complete with respect to passing top-level parameter binding values.

Using XT as a Windows executable.   A Windows executable version of the tool named `xt.exe` and using the Microsoft Java Virtual Machine is available through links in the web-based documentation. A batch file can wrap the invocation of XT with preprocessing and post-processing commands, rather than invoking XT directly:

Example D–14   A simple customizable invocation batch file

```
Line 1   @echo off
     2   REM xslxt.bat
     3   REM check arguments: %1=source XML, %2=script XSL, %3=result XML
     4   xt %1 %2 %3
     5   REM post-process results
```

Note: In my own system I often use this apparently redundant batch file invocation because it allows me to "swap out" the different brands of XSLT processor by changing the contents of the batch files without changing the scripts that invoke the XSLT process. I have created a number of batch files for different processors and I copy the batch file

I wish to use to the name "xsl.bat", which allows me to then always invoke "xsl.bat" when using XSLT.

This indirect invocation appears to behave the same way as direct invocation:

Example D–15 A simple invocation of the simple batch file

```
Line 1  X:\samp>..\prog\xslxt hello.xml hello.xsl hello.htm
    2
    3  X:\samp>type hello.htm
    4  <b><i><u>Hello world.</u></i></b>
    5  X:\samp>
```

Not shown above are two aspects of invocation not engaged by the example batch file:

- additional command line parameters following the source, stylesheet and output provide binding values for top-level parameters:

  `parameter-name=parameter-value`

- the source and output arguments can specify directories instead of files to process all of the source files in the source directory with the specified stylesheet to produce correspondingly named output files in the output directory:

  `xt input-directory stylesheet-file output-directory`

D.2 Microsoft Internet Explorer 5

The XSLT processor found in the Internet Explorer 5 (IE5) product is part of the MSXML subsystem. At this time of writing, intermediate releases of MSXML support more XSLT functionality than production releases of IE5.

D.2.1 Invoking the Microsoft MSXML processor

Installing the latest web release of MSXML. The latest MSXML `msxml3.exe` is installed and engaged to override archaic implementations of MSXML installed by Internet Explorer.

- Installation package:
  - is at http://msdn.microsoft.com/downloads/webtechnology/xml/msxml.asp
- Package registration utility `xmlinst.exe`:

- is linked on above page for installation package.
- Latest Windows software installation utility (for .msi files):
  - is at http://www.microsoft.com/msdownload/platformsdk/instmsi.htm
  - has separate versions for NT and other systems.
- Helpful documentation (unofficial FAQ):
  - is at http://www.netcrucible.com/xslt/msxml-faq.htm

To determine the current release of an MSXML DLL module, use the Windows Explorer and examine the properties. The DLL is found in the system32 directory of the windows directory. The version tab of the properties dialogue includes an indication of the file version of the DLL.

Using the processor from within Internet Explorer.   IE5 always respects any present stylesheet association processing instruction that conforms to the W3C definition, thus viewing any XML document with such an instruction will always be automatically transformed according to the associated XSLT script or CSS property sheet. Using the processor outside the context of IE5 does *not* automatically engage any present stylesheet association processing instructions.

Note that when viewing an XML document, the IE5 standard menu function View/Source reveals the XML source and not the HTML intermediate form, as in the example in Figure D–1.

Using the processor stand-alone on a client.   MSXML can be run stand-alone in MSDOS environments. This is an invaluable tool for two useful tasks: diagnosing problems with stylesheets and creating snapshots of transformation.

Figure D–1   IE5 revealing the XML source and not the HTML intermediate information

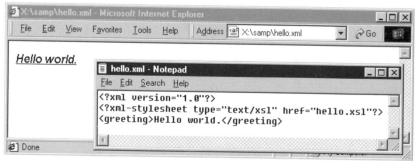

The diagnostic use allows one to bring the result of transformation into a text editor for analysis. Examining the HTML that is the content in the intermediate step between the XSLT processor and the screen rendering process reveals any nuance that may have been unanticipated by the stylesheet writer.

One can also use the stand-alone environment to make an HTML mirror of all of the XML files transformed using the file's respective stylesheets. This transformed content can then be delivered from a web server without incurring the costs of transformation (though of course incurring the costs of storage and currency of the information). By using the same XSLT processor for the static HTML snapshot as that used in the clients receiving XML source and XSLT stylesheet, consistent results are more assured.

The MSXML processor can be used from the MSDOS command line to emit transformations using the system character set.

- A command line scripting environment from Microsoft, Windows Scripting Host which executes JavaScript applications:
  - is at http://msdn.microsoft.com/scripting/windowshost/

The following is a simple script adapted from one posted to the XSL mail list. This invokes the MSXML processor after loading two Document Object Model (DOM) objects. In the following code, the processor uses the system character encoding when emitting the result tree (for example, the Latin1 character set on Western European Windows systems and the Shift-JIS character set on Japanese Windows systems).

Example D–16 Using the MSXML processor and the system character encoding

```
//File:  msxml.js - 2000-04-20 16:30
//Info:  http://www.CraneSoftwrights.com/links/msxml.htm
//Args:  input-file style-file output-file
var xml = WScript.CreateObject("Microsoft.XMLDOM");          //input
xml.validateOnParse=false;
xml.load(WScript.Arguments(0));
var xsl = WScript.CreateObject("Microsoft.XMLDOM");          //style
xsl.validateOnParse=false;
xsl.load(WScript.Arguments(1));
var out = WScript.CreateObject("Scripting.FileSystemObject");  //output
var replace = true; var unicode = false;          //output file properties
var hdl = out.CreateTextFile( WScript.Arguments(2), replace, unicode)
```

```
13  hdl.write( xml.transformNode( xsl.documentElement ));
14  //eof
```

Lines 4 through 6 load the source document into a DOM object. Lines 7 through 9 load the stylesheet document into a DOM object. Line 10 creates an external file object, preparing it to create an output file of the result.

Line 11 uses variables to contain the parameters for creating the file. This allows the parameters to be tweaked while at the same time supports self-documenting code. Line 12 actually creates the file with the command line argument supplied by the invocation.

Line 13 applies the document element of the stylesheet to the XML document, thus creating a string representing the result of transformation. This string is written to the handle created by the creation of the output file.

The following is a sample invocation batch file (the cscript program is from the Windows Scripting Host utility):

Example D–17   A simple MSXML processor invocation batch file

```
Line 1  @echo off
2  REM msxml.bat
3  REM check arguments: %1=source XML, %2=script MSXML, %3=result HTML
4  cscript //nologo ..\prog\msxml.js %1 %2 %3
5  REM post-process results
```

The following is a sample invocation:

Example D–18   A simple invocation of the MSXML processor

```
Line 1  X:\samp>..\prog\msxml hello.xml hello.xsl hello.mshtm
2  X:\samp>type hello.mshtm
3  <b><i><u>Hello world.</u></i></b>
4  X:\samp>
```

In the following code, the processor uses the UTF–8 character encoding when emitting the result tree (adapted with kind permission from Makoto Murata):

Example D–19   Using the MSXML processor and the UTF-8 character encoding

```
Line 1  //File:  msxmlu8.js - 2000-04-20 16:30
2  //Info:  http://www.CraneSoftwrights.com/links/msxml.htm
```

```
 3  //Args:  input-file style-file output-file
 4  var xml = WScript.CreateObject("Microsoft.XMLDOM");          //input
 5  xml.validateOnParse=false;
 6  xml.load(WScript.Arguments(0));
 7  var xsl = WScript.CreateObject("Microsoft.XMLDOM");          //style
 8  xsl.validateOnParse=false;
 9  xsl.load(WScript.Arguments(1));
10  var out = WScript.CreateObject("Microsoft.XMLDOM");          //output
11  out.async = false;
12  out.validateOnParse=false;
13  xml.transformNodeToObject( xsl, out );
14  out.save(WScript.Arguments(2));
15  //eof
```

Similarly to Example D–16, lines 4 through 9 load up two DOM objects with the source and stylesheet files. On line 10 the output is prepared not as a file object but as another DOM object.

Lines 11 to 13 perform the transformation, applying the DOM of the stylesheet to the DOM of the source to produce the DOM of the output.

Line 14 invokes a method of the DOM object to emit the entire instance in UTF–8 to the supplied file name.

Using the processor stand-alone on a server. MSXML can also run stand-alone on a server in order to deliver the result of XSLT transformation to an HTML client. This is appropriate for three-tiered architectures where either the client is unable to receive XML or it is decided to hide the XML source behind a server transformation firewall.

On Microsoft server platforms, Active Server Pages (ASP) running JScript can use the DOM to transform the source XML into a stream of HTML that is written to the client, as in the following example.

Example D–20   Example ASP invocation of the MSXML processor

```
Line 1  <%@ LANGUAGE = JScript %>
     2  <%
     3      // Load the XML source
     4      var xml = Server.CreateObject("Microsoft.XMLDOM");
     5      xml.async = false;
     6      xml.validateOnParse = false;
     7      xml.load(Server.MapPath("hello.xml"));
     8      // Load the stylesheet file
     9      var xsl = Server.CreateObject("Microsoft.XMLDOM");
```

```
10    xsl.async = false;
11    xsl.validateOnParse = false;
12    xsl.load(Server.MapPath("hello.xsl"));
13    // Process it
14    Response.Write(xml.transformNode(xsl));
15    %>
```

The hard-wired example above illustrates in lines 3 through 12 the loading of the XML source and XSLT stylesheet DOM objects with explicitly named resources. The final step is to write to the client the result of transforming the source with the stylesheet.

Figure D–2 illustrates the result of invoking the above ASP page on a local web server using a non-XML aware version of a browser.

Figure D–2   Accessing the example ASP from a browser

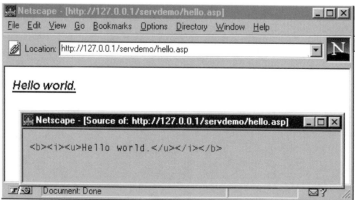

E

From XML
to press:
An XSLT
case study

From XML to press: An XSLT case study

This book has been authored, produced, and published using XML-related Recommendations. Though XML is ideal for expressing any kind of structured information in a text-based form, these three distinct stages of development in this project are described here illustrating the power of using document markup in a publishing solution. The two sections below, written by G. Ken Holman and Dmitry Kirsanov correspondingly, describe how the book's material originated and how it was brought to press.

E.1 Authoring and compilation

by G. Ken Holman

Content overview. The content of the book has been designed for quick consumption and fast learning for use in instructor-led training, run by Crane Softwrights Ltd. and its licensees around the world. This edition of the material represents over two years of content revision based on student feedback and determining the best way concepts have been understood during class. This publishing project is an edited version of the ninth edition of "Practical Transformation Using XSLT and XPath," ISBN 1–894049–06–3, `http://www.CraneSoft-wrights.com/links/trn-dxx.htm`, published only electronically by Crane Softwrights Ltd. Much of the content is reused in all training scenarios, including this book.

All content that differs in various training scenarios is authored and maintained in parallel with the shared content in a single set of XML sources, with interleaved expressions of the same teaching concepts where different language and/or form is necessary. As a result, this one set of information can be compiled for use in 45-minute, 90-minute, half-day, and full-day lectures, and with the configuration of exercises, for use in full-day, two-day, and three-day hands-on workshops. The resulting configuration for whatever length is chosen is published in HTML for classroom projection and PDF for student handouts or conference proceedings.

To accommodate this particular book, the configuration used here selects the prose version of the first two chapters and the introductory sections of each of the other chapters to help the reader with contextual information for the book itself and the major subjects in each chapter. As part of the publishing process the text throughout the book has been meticulously edited ensuring consistent language and expression.

Authoring stage. The document model for the course vocabulary evolved from an initial model needed for instructor-led training projection and handout materials. This model has been augmented over the years to support the interleaving of prose, thus accommodating different audiences with alternative portions of the content.

The XML instance is maintained as a primary file containing general entity references to external parsed general entities. These entities in turn reference other entities. In total, 48 separate XML files are edited individually and brought together during the compilation phase. These entities are not the basis of information sharing between separate Crane courses; the content is in separate entities only to ease the maintenance of the one body of information.

The content is composed to fit projected slides for use in instructor-led training. These slides correspond in the document model to panes of a frame, where only one pane is visible at a time. To ensure content used in different courses by Crane is consistent and maintained in only one place, frames from different courses are included by reference to the source XML and the frame's name. This approach avoids any problems of missing information in the parsing context of the other sources where the shared information is obtained.

These frames are authored as parts of lessons, and the lessons are authored as parts of modules. The modules of the instructor-led material are presented in this book as chapters. The lessons are presented in this book as sections. The frames are presented in this book as subsections. The individual panes within the frames are not reflected in book and the content is flowed seamlessly within the subsection.

The target use of the content that is not being shared in all presentations is flagged indirectly using attributes for specific purpose through assigned applicability, an abstract concept commonly used where many pieces of information are associated with different purposes.

Numerous parameter and general entity strings in external parameter entities express the variable information of a publication that changes with every licensee, venue, and delivery. This approach supports just-in-time branding and venue customization at publishing time. Every production takes advantage of the latest content of the constantly revised material.

Compilation stage.   The first step of compilation is the assembly of all content from all sources using XSLT. The XML processor within the XSLT processor assembles the external parsed general entities. The XSLT `document()` and `id()` functions obtain the shared frames from other courses into the assembled result. Both the stylesheets and the sources refer to the customization entities.

Copies of all licensee, venue, and delivery information are injected into the assembled instance during this part of the compilation phase. The process adds this information using elements and attributes that are reserved for the compilation process and not used during authoring. Any inadvertent or inappropriate authored content in these compilation constructs is ignored and subsequent steps can rely on these constructs having been synthesized during this initial compilation stage. A naming convention for compilation constructs determines which constructs can and cannot be used during authoring.

The resulting assembly contains all information for all possible applicability of the content. No subsequent process need visit any other source for any publishing information needed for the result. This promotes the portability of the compiled XML instance to different platforms in that no external declaration subsets or parameter or general entities are needed by any process after assembly is complete.

The assembled instance is then processed by XSLT to produce the effective instance, respecting the applicability of targeted portions of content being used only in the configured result. Inapplicable content is elided. This effective instance is also entirely self-contained, in that no additional information need be added to the instance for the target purposes.

The effective instance is processed by XSLT for each of the target projection, handout, or prose publishing compilations. For this book, only the prose publishing result was engaged, and the instance was delivered to Dmitry Kirsanov Studio for final revision and publishing.

E.2 Transformation and compositing

by Dmitry Kirsanov

Book composition — that is, going from source text and illustration sketches to the press-ready output — is one of the most complex information management tasks in existence. It involves a lot of algorithms to implement and graphic design elements to craft, as well as plenty of centuries-old traditions to admire and modern trends to get inspired by. This is a paramount example of the task for which XML and XSL were created: traversing from a complex and large but purely semantic, presentationless source to the absolutely fixed, polished, precisely laid out visual presentation.

Dmitry Kirsanov Studio (http://www.kirsanov.com) was commissioned to create the book design and write a stylesheet to implement this design. This included not only formatting the elements such as headings or itemized lists, but also defining page dimensions, laying out the running heads, page numbers, and floating illustrations, enabling all sorts of references (section references, figure references, code listing references, and so on), as well as compiling the index and the table of contents. All of these tasks were to be performed in a fully XML-based environment using XSLT and XSLFO.

Source markup. In the root of the system is an XML DTD developed by G. Ken Holman and used by him for authoring and compiling the source text for this book. This DTD defines basic markup for headings, paragraphs, code listings, and all the other semantic elements. In the ideal world, the source XML would remain unchanged during the entire stage of book composition. In reality, some bits of markup were to be added here and there, for example to mark the forced page break or figure placement in situations where a specific placement was desired. Such contamination of the source could in principle be avoided by storing the auxiliary rendition-oriented markup in separate documents to be synchronized with the source by the stylesheet generating the XSLFO code. However, this was considered not worth the trouble, because all non-semantic markup is in a separate namespace and can be easily stripped to produce the pure semantic source.

Index. Tags for building the index were also added in the source XML documents. The trivial scheme whereby entries are extracted from the source and sorted to produce the alphabetic index had to be significantly extended to produce a complex index suitable for a comprehensive technical book like this one. The two-level index tags scattered in the source were augmented by auxiliary XML documents storing cross-reference entries and all the entry expansions (for example, the index entry "head, element type (HTML)" can be simply "head" in the source text; the rest of the entry is extracted by the stylesheet from an auxiliary file).

An index is one example of source data that cannot be fully prepared without having been rendered at least once. Only the context of a compiled and sorted index allows one to review all the entries, unifying their spelling, rearranging groups of subitems, checking terminology for consistency, and performing many other cleanup tasks. Overall, developing the XSLT indexing system and creating the index turned out to be one of the most time consuming tasks of the project.

Stylesheets. The driving force of the entire system is a set of XSLT stylesheets. The main stylesheet stores all formatting parameters and generates the quite bulky and detailed XSLFO code specifying the precise fonts, sizes, and intervals of the typeset pages. A number of smaller stylesheets move the information around by compiling and processing intermediate XML documents for the index, table of contents, and cross-references. The indexing stylesheet not only compiles and sorts entries and forms page number lists, but also handles numerous special cases marked in the elements and attributes of the index source files. The intermediate documents are then fed to the main stylesheet for XSLFO generation. All stylesheets were run by the Java-based Saxon XSLT processor which proved very reliable.

Rendering XSLFO to PDF. Although both XSLFO and Adobe PDF are visually-oriented formats, they represent different levels of abstraction and therefore converting from the former to the latter is not a trivial process. The conversion software must find the optimal line and page breaks, flow the figures to their places, include the EPS illustrations stored in separate files, and last but not least, take into account and coordinate the numerous priorities and restrictions set out — both explicitly and implicitly — in the XSLFO code. The bottom line is that the quality of the printed page depends not only on the XSLFO source but also on the performance of the XSLFO renderer.

In this project, we used the XEP rendering engine by RenderX (`http://www.renderx.com`). This Java-based application is currently the most stable and complete XSLFO renderer available. I would like to take this occasion to thank Roman Kagarlitsky of RenderX for making the XEP software available for this book.

Illustrations. The only element of the book that was not XMLized in any way were the illustrations. For technical illustrations such as those in this book, one can envision a system where the author specifies all the elements of a diagram and their relations in a semantic XML-based language, later converted by a stylesheet into a visually-oriented language such as SVG to be displayed on screen or rendered as EPS for print. This would make it possible, for example, to round all the corners in all boxes, or to change alignment, font size or line width in all images by a single change in the stylesheet.

However, it is not yet clear whether a purely algorithmic approach can successfully emulate the numerous aesthetically grounded adjustments and coordinations made by a human artist in creating even the simplest and most straightforward technical diagram. This topic definitely requires further research before a workable system can be created that would produce consistently acceptable results requiring little or no manual touch-up. Therefore for this project, the illustrations were simply manually redrawn from author's sketches, saved in EPS format and included into the PDF files at the stage of XSLFO to PDF conversion.

Design of the book. This book presented unique challenges to the designer because of its non-conventional text structure. One of the most notable features of the book is its extensive use of multi-level itemized lists. A lot of effort was put into researching for the most readable, expressive, and aesthetically pleasing formatting for this element, including custom bullets that help the reader keep track of the current nesting level in long lists that break across pages.

Overall, our intent was to produce a design which is clean, consistent, well balanced and well structured, truly appealing to professionals in the field of information management. Your feedback on any aspects of the book design will be much appreciated; please write to Dmitry Kirsanov at dmitry@kirsanov.com.

Conclusion. To our knowledge, this book is the first one ever to use XSLT and XSLFO in a large-scale publishing project. In our opinion, XSLT is an almost ideal choice for projects of this kind; its laconic set of logically laid out and powerful tools, its elegance in making information equally accessible no matter where it is stored (so long as it's XML), and its flexible approaches to data processing make developing even the most complex stylesheets a pleasure. Our studio has been using XSLT for developing web sites for some time, and reusing this experience in a different subject field was very easy and very productive — here's one example of the benefits of using XML technologies for all of your information management needs.

Index